Desert Storm

Published in Cooperation with the
Center for Strategic and International Studies,
Washington, D.C.

Desert Storm

The Gulf War and What We Learned

Michael J. Mazarr,
Don M. Snider, and
James A. Blackwell, Jr.

Westview Press
BOULDER • SAN FRANCISCO • OXFORD

Copyright © 1993 by the Center for Strategic and International Studies

Published in 1993 in the United States of America by Westview Press, Inc., 5500 Central Avenue, Boulder, Colorado 80301-2877, and in the United Kingdom by Westview Press, 36 Lonsdale Road, Summertown, Oxford OX2 7EW

Library of Congress Cataloging-in-Publication Data
Mazarr, Michael J., 1965–
    Desert Storm : the Gulf War and what we learned / Michael J.
Mazarr, Don M. Snider, and James A. Blackwell, Jr.
        p.   cm.
    Includes bibliographical references (p.   ) and index.
    ISBN 0-8133-1598-0
    1. Persian Gulf War, 1991.   I. Snider, Don M., 1940–   .
II. Blackwell, James.   III. Title.
DS79.72.M384   1993
956.704'42—dc20   92-29687
                                                                                  CIP

Printed and bound in the United States of America

The paper used in this publication meets the requirements
of the American National Standard for Permanence of Paper
for Printed Library Materials Z39.48-1984.

10   9   8   7   6   5   4   3   2   1

Contents

4   The Failure of Compellence   69

5   The Air Campaign   93

6   One Hundred Hours   125

Figures

Figures

Symbols Used in Figures

◻ Armored Unit

⊠ Infantry Unit

⊠ Mechanized Unit

⊠ Airborne Unit

⊘ Armored Cavalry Unit

⊠ Marine Amphibious Unit

⊠ Air Cavalry Unit

⊠ Air Cavalry Unit

⊗ Transportation Unit

RGR Ranger Unit

SF Special Forces

▢ A roman numeral above a unit symbol

xx Division

x Brigade/Regiment

‖ Battalion

ı Company

Desert Storm

1

An Unexpected War

At 9:30 P.M. on Wednesday, January 16, 1991, the pilots and aircrew of the U.S. 48th Tactical Fighter Wing were receiving the orders that would send them to war.[1] Iraqi leader Saddam Hussein had ignored the United Nations ultimatum to leave Kuwait, and the military forces of the coalition arrayed against Iraq were preparing to push him out by force. Flying big F-111 fighter-bombers and electronic warfare planes, the 48th consisted of units based in England and Idaho, transferred to the Gulf to fight in a war no one had expected. Senior officers of the 48th briefed the squadron on its mission; across the whole front, a massive air assault on Iraqi forces and command centers was about to begin.

At 1:20 A.M. on January 17, Saudi time, the F-111s—over 70 feet long and with 60 feet of wingspan—took to the sky, their turbofan engines glowing brightly in the dark of a moonless Gulf night. On their way to attack Iraqi air bases, the fighter-bombers were accompanied by other aircraft equipped to jam and suppress enemy radar and other electronic equipment. The squadron was also supported by old F-4 fighters carrying antiradar missiles whose mission was to attack Iraqi antiaircraft and radar sites.

More than 60 F-111s crossed the Iraqi border at over 600 miles an hour, flying low—200 feet or less—to avoid being picked up on Iraqi radar. By 3 A.M., the coalition attack was well under way throughout the theater. On reaching their target, the F-111s climbed rapidly to 5,000 feet and engaged their "Pave Pack" systems—a combination laser and infrared television camera used to mark targets. Similar equipment would soon provide many of the stunning images of the war: videotapes of bombs crashing into Iraqi command posts or hitting the front doors of aircraft hangars. Weapons system operators (WSOs) sitting in the F-111s looked into their viewers and picked out targets, designating them with laser-guidance beams.

The Iraqi defenders were wide awake and aware of the attack, and soon F-111s detected the search radars of surface-to-air missiles. The F-4s swung into action, shooting high-speed antiradar missiles (HARMs) to silence the Iraqi

1

positions. Deadly streams of antiaircraft gunfire reached up to the U.S. planes. The Iraqis were trying desperately to knock them out of the sky before they delivered their ordnance—accurate laser-guided bombs, thousands of pounds of them on each aircraft. The WSOs dropped their bombs and watched as targets exploded—weapons storage bunkers, maintenance hangars, aircraft shelters.

Most of the planes were over Iraqi airspace for about forty minutes, flying 200 or more miles inside hostile territory. The sky, the pilots reported on their return, was filled with coalition aircraft. This first night over 2,000 "sorties"—individual attacks by coalition aircraft—were flown.

On the squadron's return, a reporter noticed a unique shoulder patch being worn by one of the squadron's pilots. Bearing a crude image of the F-111, it had been designed especially for the occasion. "Baghdad Bash," it read. "Let's Party."

The Uniqueness of the Gulf War

Reviewing the story of how U.S. F-111 fighter-bombers came to fly over Iraq, helping to start a conflict in January 1991, is a fascinating—and often depressing—enterprise. As recently as March or April of 1990, no one in the U.S. government would have suspected that the United States and an international coalition would be at war with Iraq just months later. U.S. defense and foreign policy had focused on the Soviet threat for forty years, viewing other conflicts as examples of a global U.S.-Soviet competition. But here was Saddam Hussein at the head of a half-million-man army, equipped with some of the world's most advanced military equipment. His scientists were speeding to build chemical, biological, and nuclear weapons, which would pose a grave threat to the world's oil supplies. Where did this crisis come from? How did the U.S. military come to be so quickly reoriented from deterring Soviet expansion in Europe to fighting a brutal dictator intent on regional hegemony?

The story of the war, of its prelude and aftermath and, most of all, of its lessons, is the focus of this book. Before we delve into the history of the conflict, though, it is important to understand the war's wider context. To understand the Gulf War one must know where it fits into U.S. foreign policy and why the Bush administration was disposed to react as it did. What business did U.S. troops have intervening in a war between Arab states thousands of miles from U.S. shores? And what is the war's place in history? Ten or fifty years from now, will the Gulf War be viewed (as many instantly proclaimed) as the prototypical conflict of the post–cold war order? Or will it be seen as an interesting but largely discrete event that can do little to inform our understanding of conflict, or to prevent it, in the modern era?

Answering these questions is difficult, in part because the Gulf War was many things to many people. For Saddam Hussein, it was an opportunity to solve his pressing economic problems and become master of 40 percent of the world's oil reserves while staking a bold claim for leadership of the entire Arab world. For George Bush, Hussein's aggression created a clear need to respond to unprovoked aggression and in so doing to begin the redefinition of the U.S. role in the world in the aftermath of the cold war—a necessary exercise for which the administration was ill-prepared. Israel's leaders undoubtedly viewed the war as a once-in-a-lifetime chance to see one of their primary nemeses crushed. For the Arab nations of the coalition, a conflict with Iraq was a necessary, if regrettable, response to Hussein's fanaticism and deception; Palestinians and Jordanians, however, welcomed a menacing blow against the rich Arab states, which they believed did not sufficiently share their oil wealth. For Iran it was a chance to condemn and achieve vicarious revenge against its former adversary. For Europe, Japan, and other non-U.S. and non-Arab members of the coalition, the war varied in importance and response from country to country.

Analysis of the Gulf War is further complicated by the fact that it was in many ways a unique conflict. Saddam Hussein's aggression was so brutal, so calculated, so clearly designed for personal and national aggrandizement that it made possible the rapid assemblage of an international consensus against him. The members of the United Nations (not blocked, crucially, by the Soviet Union and China) firmly backed a vigorous response to Iraq's invasion of Kuwait and, following the U.S. lead, granted legitimacy to the coalition's operations with a remarkable series of resolutions. U.S. public opinion was subsequently buoyed by the knowledge that although the war was largely a U.S. effort, it was not entirely so—other nations were also willing to put their soldiers in harm's way to evict Iraq from Kuwait.

The importance of Soviet cooperation cannot be overestimated. If Moscow had continued to support Iraq (as it had during the cold war), the effort to oust Hussein from Kuwait would have become a much more thorny enterprise. In all likelihood, the United Nations Security Council could not have passed any of its resolutions if Moscow had vetoed those proposals. Continued Soviet military supplies to Iraq and Soviet purchases of Iraqi oil would have undermined the economic embargo. It would have been far more difficult to keep an international coalition together on an issue that divided the United States and the Soviet Union: Moscow's few remaining friends and allies would have opposed U.S. actions, Europe may well have become more wary of a conflict, and China might have acquired a new incentive to obstruct U.S. policy. The risks of escalation to U.S.-Soviet conflict would have been present, and as in Vietnam, they might have complicated U.S. military actions. In short, Moscow's assistance in placing pressure on Iraq and its tacit agreement to the use of force played critical roles in the coalition victory.

Equally important was the cooperation of the Arab world, in some cases a quite surprising cooperation. Several Arab states, betrayed by Saddam Hussein or glad to see Iraq defeated, became members of the coalition and in many cases allowed their territories to be used for military operations against Iraq. Others adopted a wait-and-see attitude, forestalling widespread reactions on the "Arab street." Had either group of nations opposed a strong U.S. response to Iraq's aggression, they could have rendered a war far more challenging from a military as well as a political point of view.

Although the war was fought thousands of miles from the United States, it was waged largely from a country—Saudi Arabia—boasting a superb logistical base. Partly with the help of U.S. security assistance, the Saudi government had constructed an amazing complex of huge, modern military installations: King Khalid Military City, the massive air base at Dhahran, the magnificent Gulf port of Jubail, and other such facilities. The full capabilities of this infrastructure, including prestocked supplies, are classified, but it is no secret that the U.S. military enjoyed the advantage of sharing well-maintained, well-stocked bases and ports capable of supporting a large war effort. If those facilities had not existed, or if they had been seized and destroyed by Saddam Hussein's army, the coalition would have faced crippling logistical problems. The buildup of U.S. and coalition military forces would have taken far longer, and the prosecution of the war would have been far more difficult.

Once the coalition began sending thousands of ships, tanks, and planes into Saudi Arabia, Saddam Hussein did little to impede its effort to prepare for war. It is almost unprecedented that one nation would begin a conflict, then sit back and wait, trusting that its potential opponents would not have the political will to respond. Hitler followed a similar strategy for a time—invading Poland and other states, then delaying war with the West in the famous sitzkrieg. But even Hitler, once he recognized that war was inevitable, struck first, sending his armies slashing into France in May 1940. In retrospect Hussein was obviously but inexplicably confident he could absorb the first blow. This provided the coalition with a big edge—but this will certainly not hold true for every adversary the United States will face.

Nor will U.S. forces always operate in terrain that so magnifies their advantages. The flat, featureless desert—with its wide temperature swings between day and night—made even dug-in Iraqi tanks superb targets for U.S. target acquisition and precision weapons systems. Once the coalition gained control of the sky—and there was never much doubt that it would do so quickly— Iraq's forces were immobilized because to move in the open desert was to invite destruction. In other wars, adversaries might be able to hide their forces better in forests, jungles, or cities, and finding and engaging them will be a more difficult enterprise, one less suited to the application of smart weapons.

Finally, the nature of the war also played to the strengths of the United States and its allies. This was a conventional war with battles fought out in the open desert between tanks, planes, and artillery. We knew where the Iraqis were, we knew by and large how many personnel they had, and the front lines were relatively easy to distinguish. This picture contrasts sharply with the conflict in Vietnam, where U.S. and Allied forces fought a hidden, secretive enemy, dispersed within the jungle, seldom emerging in large numbers to fight set-piece battles, relying on hit-and-run raids and the crushing effect of a decade-long war to achieve its victory. President George Bush declared that he would not fight a piecemeal war, as the United States did in Vietnam. Fortunately, he did not have to—Iraq's army was ready and willing to give the coalition a conventional desert war.

Many things that could have gone wrong for the United States and the coalition therefore did not. But any of them could have, and we must not be sanguine about U.S. power and influence because of one unique war. Others can be expected to be very different. It was not so long ago that a collection of ill-equipped, ill-fed, but superbly motivated jungle fighters held the United States at bay for ten years. As Anthony Cordesman and Abraham Wagner concluded after looking at the Arab-Israeli wars: "One must be careful about generalizing too much from the lessons of the Arab-Israeli conflicts. . . . [T]he lessons of one war are not necessarily the lessons of the next. Further, modern war is simply too complex to reduce it to a short list of simple lessons."[2]

In a way the Vietnam and Gulf wars form two extremes, examples of the worst and best U.S. leaders can hope for in war. Our concern is to draw lessons from the Gulf War for the more likely cases in between. And although the distinctiveness of the Gulf War obviously circumscribes our ability to draw from it broadly applicable lessons, it does nevertheless offer confirmation of earlier lessons as well as qualifications of still others that had become conventional wisdom. The war in the Middle East is not a perfect subject for study, but no war will be.

The Gulf War and U.S. Policy Changes

The Gulf War, unique as it was, held a broader meaning and carried wider implications than those relating only to military questions or weapons systems: It was both symbol and substance of the sea change in U.S. foreign policy that has taken place since the mid-1980s. It is now almost difficult to believe that Ronald Reagan was elected to the presidency just over a decade ago partly on a promise to confront and roll back the imminent threat of Soviet expansion. The cold war images of Reagan's first term, terrifying enough at the time to rejuvenate worldwide peace movements, now resonate only faintly. NATO's deployment of U.S. cruise and Pershing missiles, the announcement of the Space Defense Initiative (SDI) program, the massive U.S. military buildup to match perceived Soviet advantages—today these events read like ancient history. Almost in a single stroke—the assumption of power in Moscow by Mikhail Gorbachev—U.S.-Soviet hostility began to fade; by the end of his second term, even Ronald Reagan was pronouncing Gorbachev a legitimate advocate of peace. The cold war had begun to thaw.

Describing this new era in dry political and economic terms might not do justice to the dramatic nature of the changes. It is perhaps best to think of the global security environment in a series of images, each representing one aspect of the new context for U.S. national security planning.

January-June 1989. Squat, menacing Soviet tanks sat on railcars, waiting to be removed from Poland and East Germany. In the wake of Soviet president Mikhail Gorbachev's dramatic December 1988 United Nations speech, the Soviet armed forces began withdrawing from Eastern Europe. After forty-five years of occupation, over a half-million military personnel would return to Russia and other former Soviet republics. A year later, the Warsaw Pact suffered a death blow because of rebellions or changes of government in all East European states except Albania; later, pact members would officially disband. By the mid-1990s, the equipment and personnel limits of the Conventional Forces in Europe (CFE) Treaty and the confidence-building measures of the Conference on Security and Cooperation in Europe (CSCE) will limit the size and the provocative nature of the Soviet military deployed west of the Ural Mountains.

In short, the threat of premeditated Soviet conventional aggression in Europe, for forty years the bedrock of U.S. and Allied defense planning and the rationale for much of our defense establishment, has disappeared, at least temporarily. Preoccupied with internal political struggles and economic needs, the fractious Commonwealth of Independent States has for the foreseeable future abandoned any notion of territorial expansion or worldwide empire-building. Reforms that Gorbachev unleashed—the radical political and economic change in Eastern Europe and the democratization and fragmentation of the Soviet Union itself—have destroyed almost completely the Commonwealth's formerly monolithic military power.

August 1989. Filipino protesters demonstrated outside U.S. bases, hurling anti-U.S. slogans and demanding the removal of the facilities. During the 1990s, the U.S. military will be hard-pressed to maintain its international network of bases. NATO ally Spain had already set the precedent for such nationalistic base closures in the late 1980s when it asked Washington to leave air bases there. U.S. defense budget cuts will demand that many U.S. bases be closed, and powerful members of Congress will demand in turn that most closures be abroad. Nationalism within Europe and in the third world will undermine local political support for the facilities. And the decline of the Soviet threat will increasingly render unnecessary such a global system of forward deployments.

August 1990. Iraqi armored units blitzed through Kuwait in a lightning campaign and stood poised at the Saudi border, ready to invade and gain control of 40 percent of the world's daily oil production. Saddam Hussein's bold gamble immediately demonstrated at least two salient facts: The free world still relies on the Middle East for the bulk of its petroleum products, and the United States must continue to plan for a war in the Middle East as perhaps the most likely scene for the employment of U.S. military forces in the 1990s. Saddam's army, a half million men strong and boasting over 5,000 tanks, also exemplifies the new type of third world threat to U.S. interests—a huge, modern, mechanized force capable of extensive and rapid military operations.

June-July 1990. West Germany—soon to be a single, reunited Germany—took the lead in reshaping the European map, just as Japan began to assert itself more seriously in Asian diplomatic and economic circles. The vocal and influential role played by Germany, Japan, and other major powers during 1990 and 1991 demonstrated beyond doubt that the long-predicted emergence of a multipolar world had arrived. Washington is no longer—if it ever was—in a position to dictate outcomes in Europe or elsewhere. For forty-five years the two superpowers presided over their respective alliances in a world bifurcated firmly along east-west lines; already today at least four or five major democratic powers are jostling for position at the apex of the world community.

The Gulf War, led so clearly by the United States, interrupted this trend. It appeared to confirm the impression of a unipolar world in which the United States is the world's only true superpower. But the impression was misleading: Although the United States does possess the world's most advanced military force, it is dependent upon other nations for political legitimacy, logistical support, and economic backing. The unipolar moment is likely to be a brief one, particularly as the emphasis on military power, so obvious during the Gulf War, is increasingly replaced by a measurement of national strength in economic and political terms.

June 1990. Reports from London that North Korea was "six months away" from a nuclear capability were followed by U.S. intelligence information that the North was testing an indigenously produced, intermediate-range missile. Within the developing world, the most salient feature of the emerging security context is the extensive proliferation of weapons of mass destruction. More than twenty nations across the globe possess or are in the process of acquiring chemical, biological, and nuclear weapons, and long-range missiles and aircraft to deliver them. Very high technology conventional weapons, including advanced aircraft and electronic warfare devices, have also found their way into the eager hands of third world militaries.

July 1990. At the executive-legislative budget summit, President Bush was forced to abandon his pledge not to raise taxes amid reports that the savings and loan crisis would eventually cost the government $500 billion or more. There will be very little money left for defense. The initial Bush-Cheney plan, calling for a 25 percent cut in force structure but only a 10 percent cut in spending over the next five years, will probably not survive intact. Many weapons systems will have to be cut along with forces. The need for a wise defense investment strategy is more apparent than ever.

January-February 1991. Coalition military forces smashed Iraq's military with a devastating six-week air campaign and a lightning ground operation. The nature of major warfare is changing. The lethality of modern conventional weapons is such that traditional large-scale military operations, particularly Soviet-style armored thrusts, are becoming an anachronism. The advent of long-range smart weapons, low force-to-space ratios (induced by arms control and budget cuts), and advanced reconnaissance and command-and-control technologies will produce nonlinear battlefields populated by smaller (perhaps brigade-sized), independent mobile units.

June-July 1991. Yugoslavia stood at the brink of civil war, with rebellious republics declaring independence and marshaling their civil defense forces against the central government. In the newly democratized regions, the forces of fragmentation may be stronger than the forces of integration in society. The threats to peace that remain in Europe will issue not from Soviet intimidation but from resurgent ethnonationalism and other divisive forces. Tensions between Serbs and Croats, Romanians and Hungarians, Greeks and Turks, Azerbaijanis and Armenians, and other groups could lead to civil wars within nations or conflicts between states. Regular U.S. military forces probably cannot play a significant role in responding to these unconventional dangers. Multilateral institutions, especially under CSCE auspices, will be required to keep the peace.

September 1991. Speaking from the Oval Office, President Bush announced the most dramatic steps ever to reverse the nuclear arms race: All U.S. ground-based tactical nuclear weapons would be destroyed, and all tactical weapons at sea would be withdrawn. For the first time since the beginning of the nuclear age, the United States would not have strategic bombers on alert. In the future, the nuclear components of U.S. military and deterrent strategies will fade into the background. Increasingly, advanced conventional munitions will assume many of the deterrent and warfighting roles previously assigned to nuclear weapons.

December 1991. The Soviet Union collapsed and was replaced by a looser, increasingly democratic and capitalist Commonwealth of Independent States led by Russia. The post–cold war era had arrived in force.

The New World Order

The international situation—the context for U.S. foreign and defense policy—has therefore changed dramatically in the past five years. During the Gulf War, the Bush administration coined a new phrase for this new era: the new world order. It is worth examining this notion in some detail to see what lessons it holds about U.S. foreign policy at a time of historic change.

On April 13, 1991, President Bush gave a major speech billed as a primer on his concept of the new world order. As yet poorly defined, this notion formed the backbone of many U.S. justifications for opposing the Iraqi seizure of Kuwait. First mentioned by the president in February 1990 and introduced in the context of Iraq's invasion of Kuwait the following August, the notion had been the intellectual backbone of U.S. Gulf War rhetoric. In his April 1991 speech, President Bush was to explain just what the new world order was. As it turned out, much of the analysis was of little help in distinguishing the new world order from past notions of U.S. foreign policy. The president said that the phrase referred "to new ways of working with other nations to deter aggression and to achieve stability and, above all, to achieve peace," phrases that might have been uttered in 1950 about U.S. containment policy. In the post–cold war era, he continued, with the predictability of a bipolar standoff gone, the challenge was "to keep the dangers of disorder at bay," and the growing international cooperation of the new world order was meant to help.

There is little doubt that the concept of a new world order was never intended to be a rigorous one, nor was it supposed to define U.S. foreign policy goals in fundamentally new ways. According to a May 1991 report in the *Washington Post*, President Bush and National Security Adviser Brent Scowcroft came up with the phrase while fishing in August 1990. Since the April 13 speech, administration officials have used the phrase less often and have done little to draw attention to it. The same *Post* report noted Scowcroft's frustration with the public attention garnered by the issue; recently, Scowcroft "complained that it was just a 'catch phrase' that had become endowed with grandiose meanings beyond anything he or Bush originally conceived."[3]

We should therefore not expect the idea of a new world order to explain or prescribe much, and indeed it does not. Instead, the concept mirrors long-standing notions about U.S. foreign policy. Compare its phraseology with that of Henry Kissinger, circa 1968: "In the years ahead," Kissinger wrote, "the most profound challenge to American policy will be philosophical: to develop some concept of order in a world which is bipolar militarily but multipolar politically." Kissinger concluded: "We will never be able to contribute to building a stable and creative world order unless we first form some conception of it."[4]

Alexander George and Richard Smoke, two of the most perceptive contemporary observers of U.S. foreign policy, came to similar conclusions in 1974. "The challenge to U.S. foreign policy remains, therefore, one of finding a longer-term image of a desirable world order—a genuine international community—which will be acceptable domestically and which can enlist cooperation among the nations."[5] President Bush's new world order merely faces up once again to this same challenge. It does not yet define the goals or conduct of U.S. foreign policy in any profoundly new ways.

What the concept does do, however—and in this regard it has significance beyond what the Bush administration originally intended, or even might concur with—is recognize changes in the international community, changes that do raise the prospect of a fundamentally new era in international politics. President Bush did make one brief remark that pointed to the true significance of the new world order. "This order gains its mission and shape," he said on April 13, from both "shared interests and shared ideals." The notion of a new world order points to a key fact of modern international politics: The world is becoming an increasingly open, interdependent, and cooperative place, and many nations of the world have recognized that this is to their advantage; indeed, on some issues cooperation is indispensable for their survival. Those nations, even when embarked in past centuries on anarchic, balance-of-power stratagems, have always shared some interests in common. The hopeful argument of world order theories is that the *scope of shared interests* may be expanding. Whereas in the past the subjects of cooperation, especially in U.S.-Soviet relations, were limited to such unavoidable issues as nuclear arms control and crisis management, now the list of areas requiring and benefiting from international accord appears to be expanding, if slowly. The dissolution of the cold war's bipolar confrontation has been especially critical in this revival of long-dormant progress toward global accord on several issues.

The trend toward internationalism perhaps manifests most powerfully in a worldwide consensus—if temporary and incomplete—against military adventurism. Russia, to many the world's beacon of expansionist dogma, has for the time being abandoned the practice. Deprived of Moscow's transport ships and ideological backing, Cuba has seen its global reach contract as well. Now regional aggressors such as Iraq, North Korea, and Libya face stiff international penalties, up to and including United Nations–sponsored military force, if they choose to invade their neighbors. Opposing adventurism has become a clear priority of all the world's major powers, a shared global interest, a fact reflected in the United Nations deliberations of early 1992 aimed at abolishing the causes and rewards of aggression.

Another shared interest, and a corollary of the decline of adventurism, has arisen in the area of arms control. Once again Soviet reform set the tone for progress. In his December 1988 announcement of unilateral Soviet force reductions and his subsequent agreement to disproportionate cuts in Warsaw Pact armed forces as part of the CFE treaty, Mikhail Gorbachev breathed new life into a process nearly dead after over a decade of stagnation. His notion of "defensive sufficiency," though still ambiguously defined even within the former Soviet Union, has nonetheless established a rough minimalist benchmark for measuring military force levels. Confidence-building measures have attained new prominence with the CSCE. Similar arms-reduction and confidence-building packages are being proposed for other tension-ridden flashpoints—the Middle East, the Korean Peninsula, and elsewhere. The global consensus is becoming more and more robust: If there is to be no adventurism, then levels of arms can be reduced to those necessary for defense.

Another area of progress is in the spread of free societies. Again Soviet reform lies at the core of the trend: Moscow's more spare view of its own security requirements has directly set free Eastern Europe and indirectly set in motion partially democratic transitions in a host of socialist developing states including Nicaragua, Angola, Vietnam, and perhaps eventually Cuba and North Korea as well. Partly as the result of natural political progress, and partly because the end of the cold war has allowed Washington to cast free or place greater pressure on some of its own distasteful allies, countries frozen in right-wing authoritarianism by the cold war are now emerging and inching toward democracy in Latin America, Asia, and Africa. In many cases the move toward political freedom has entailed growing economic liberties as well.

The rise of environmental issues has also encouraged, indeed demanded, growing international cooperation. Environmental threats often transcend international boundaries, and addressing them has become a shared interest of dozens of nations.

By helping to ratify and encourage these various shared interests, international organizations have acquired new strength and importance. Today the United Nations is supervising electoral processes in Angola and Western Sahara, implementing peace plans in Afghanistan and Cambodia, and conducting nine other peacekeeping operations, while actively promoting environmental cooperation and disarmament. Smaller regional organizations have become involved in peacekeeping as well—such as the Economic Community of West African States, which has helped end a civil war in Liberia.

There are of course very real limitations to the progress that has been made in each of these areas. Small-scale adventurism is often ignored, and there are some states that might still benefit from large-scale aggression. The political will for arms control has not yet reached the Middle East or Korea. Big gaps exist in the worldwide fabric of democracy; China, North Korea, Cuba, certain areas of Africa, and other states are potential problem areas. International organizations may have little autonomous power and may be primarily useful to implement and monitor binational or multinational agreements once in place. Religious fundamentalism and ethnonationalism continue to drive civil wars, insurgencies, and interstate quarrels. The principle of free trade is not fully accepted by such nations as Japan and South Korea, and the future of GATT (General Agreements on Tariffs and Trade) is clouded.

Another major limitation is imposed by the nature of U.S. interests. As the chief spokespersons for the "new order," the U.S. leaders will play a key role in defining the limits to collectivism. U.S. leaders will not want to be restrained by their own internationalist rhetoric; they may want to draw a distinct line between unilateral acts based on the national interest (for example, the U.S. intervention in Panama) and multilateral operations like the Gulf

War. In pressing for arms control in the Middle East, President Bush is already grappling with the question of how much internationalism is acceptable in U.S. policy: Selling U.S. arms for the "legitimate defensive needs of U.S. friends in the region," as U.S. officials often say, obviously conflicts with the simultaneous request for a "multilateral suppliers' cartel" to control arms shipments to this volatile region.

We now have a reasonably sound idea what sort of international order we want, as Henry Kissinger recommended almost a quarter-century ago: non-aggressive, democratic, committed to reasonably free trade, stable and governed by the rule of law, and increasingly cooperative on concerns of global stature. The challenge for U.S. foreign policy is therefore no longer to make that judgment; nor is it really to encourage movement toward that goal, because such movement, as documented previously, is already well under way. The true challenge will be reconciling U.S. interests and the U.S. ability to act unilaterally on issues of national importance in an increasingly independent and multilateral international framework.

The Future of U.S. Foreign Policy

Such overwhelming changes in the threats and concerns faced by U.S. policy-makers could not help but shake U.S. foreign and defense policy to the core, and so they have done. It was an unusual coincidence—but a telling one—that on August 2, even as Iraqi tanks rolled through Kuwait, President Bush was giving a speech on foreign and defense policy that heralded the end of the cold war, the onset of a new world order, and the need for a new U.S. military strategy focused on "regional contingencies." By 1990 it was plainly apparent that the international challenge facing U.S. policy had changed dramatically since 1985, change that required nothing less than a fundamental reassessment of U.S. foreign policy. Such an analysis is beyond the scope of this book, which is about one war and its lessons. As an example of post–cold war foreign and defense policy, however, the Gulf War does speak to broader notions of U.S. diplomacy. And to put the war's lessons in some sort of perspective, we must have an understanding of the imperatives that will guide U.S. policy in the years ahead.

During the cold war, U.S. interests and the regions in which the truly vital ones resided were relatively clear, if sometimes magnified by the zero-sum rhetoric of the period. Containment was the goal; economic and military aid around the Soviet (and, for a time, Chinese) periphery and—as we shall see—the concept of deterrence provided the means to achieve it. After 1945 U.S. foreign policy retained the European focus it had reaffirmed during the war, and protecting Western Europe against Communist aggression was the linch-pin of containment.

Now that the Soviet threat has declined, nothing is clear for the makers of U.S. foreign policy, least of all the scope of our vital interests. Defense planners have turned to a strategy of regional contingencies, but the strategy has not come complete with a new articulation of the interests and objectives at stake in these regional wars. In fact, now that the Gulf oil-producing states are reasonably safe—at least temporarily—it is difficult to imagine what regional instabilities would demand U.S. intervention other than a possible U.S. commitment to defend South Korea against the North. The Gulf War has obscured this fact because it took place in the single region outside Europe where U.S. and world interests were clearly at stake. It is possible that Operation Desert Storm will rank as the first—and last—major example of the contingencies strategy. If this analysis is valid, the question becomes this: What happens to foreign policy in the absence of a major global threat?

Primarily—and this is a well-publicized point—foreign policy assumes a more economic and less military focus. Without a global military confrontation, the attention of world leaders will shift more and more to economic matters. Even now that the cold war is over, the truly vital U.S. national interests (apart from the security of our borders) still lie in Europe and Northeast Asia. Taken together, Europe, Japan, South Korea, and Canada (a NATO member), account for the vast majority of U.S. trade and foreign investment. U.S. cultural, historical, and political ties with those regions, particularly with the European nations, are far more robust than those with other regions. The Middle East will remain significant to the United States as long as it holds oil and Israel. Bush administration officials have recognized these facts (although they have not made this recognition very public) and have focused foreign policy attention on developments in Europe, Northeast Asia, and the Middle East. In short, the evaporation of the Soviet threat has not altered the fundamental orientation of U.S. interests; it has only redirected them to economic as opposed to military concerns.

The most important task for U.S. diplomacy today is therefore maintaining warm and cooperative economic and political relations with and promoting stability in Europe, the Middle East, and among the economic powers in Asia and our own hemisphere.[6] The challenge will be to compete economically yet do so within bounds that facilitate the cooperation necessary for the pursuit of mutual global interests, including security interests. This challenge is especially acute today given the long-term U.S. tendency to isolationism and the strong tradition of a defense based on "minutemen," citizen-soldiers rather than a large standing army. With the major exception of the cold war, throughout our nation's history U.S. administrations and congresses have repeatedly disarmed in the wake of major conflicts, eschewing the opportunity to maintain a ready force capable of projecting power at all times. Yet this is precisely the sort of military demanded by the Bush administration's strategy of responding to regional contingencies. The question arises again: In a world in which economic considerations are paramount and threats to U.S. security unlikely, what role is there for U.S. military force?[7] And more broadly, what U.S. role in the world should this force support? The Gulf War emphasized once again the salience of this last question, without providing a conclusive answer.

Foreign Policy Alternatives

We will not attempt to resolve this debate here. Indeed, as in any period of strategic interregnum, it is likely that the U.S. answer to the question of role will be several years in coming. What we can do is sketch out the parameters of the choices to be made and discuss several of the alternatives.

Most popular among foreign policy practitioners and analysts schooled in cold-war thinking is the notion of an *interventionist* U.S. foreign and defense policy aimed at world leadership. U.S. influence, such observers claim, is useful to promote certain U.S. goals around the world. Usually broad and philosophical, these goals include regional stability, the spread of democracy and free trade, the growth of multilateral economic and political institutions, and human rights and national self-determination. Without the capability to support these goals with force when necessary, the United States would lose an important tool in its campaign to promote them.

U.S. foreign policy, some contend, has long been concerned with more than the mere security of U.S. borders; since its founding, the United States has been a nation with a mission, its leaders and people determined to serve as a beacon—and sometimes an imposer—of democracy, free trade, peace, and prosperity. During the cold war, the pursuit of such goals on a global scale was justified as an element of containment: Although the security of a South Korea or a South Vietnam was largely irrelevent to the United States, in a zero-sum competition such states assumed great importance and came to be viewed as symbols of U.S. resolve. Vietnam was hardly important on its own, it was said, but abandoning it would encourage a wave of Communist expansion that would one day threaten truly vital U.S. interests in Europe and, eventually, at home.

Outside the cold war context, these regional concerns are of slight concern to U.S. leaders.[8] Although the neoisolationist argument that a global foreign policy will somehow "bankrupt" the United States is vastly exaggerated, the critics do have a point: Why spend money on causes that do not directly affect vital U.S. interests? If the military threat to U.S. friends and allies has receded, why maintain a worldwide military presence at all?

The Gulf War, interventionists agree, suggests two good reasons. First, an ambitious foreign policy can help promote favorable aspects of the new world order. As most architects of U.S. foreign policy have long recognized, a stable, prosperous world order works to the benefit of U.S. interests. As a fundamentally nonaggressive trading nation, the United States gains by peaceful relations and trade and generally loses when instability, war, or protectionism arise to threaten nations or regions around the world. Although the U.S. government can dedicate only limited funds to the enterprise, making the world over in our image—that is, promoting the development of free and open democracies—is indeed in the U.S. national interest.

In response to suggestions that the only goal of U.S. foreign and defense policy ought to be the protection of national borders, to erect a defensive wall around ourselves in a "fortress America" and await any aggressors, interventionists point out that sitting in a fort and awaiting attack is usually not the best strategy. In the long term, the best means of making our borders truly secure is to reach out and reform those who might attack us, to encourage changes in potential aggressors. Even to achieve basic security-related goals, an ambitious policy makes more sense than an isolationist one—a conclusion reinforced by the Gulf War: Without U.S. leadership in opposition, Iraq's power would have grown unchecked until it someday posed a direct threat to U.S. security, either through control of oil supplies or by the development of nuclear weapons capable of supporting Hussein's ambition for regional dominance.

In contrast, *neoisolationist* critics have long charged that the pursuit of such secondary interests is unnecessary and fiscally irresponsible. Many recent "declinist" writings have discussed the implications of a gap between material capabilities and commitments. The most powerful enunciation of the limits to U.S. power in recent years was Paul Kennedy's *The Rise and Fall of Great Powers*. Kennedy argued that a sweeping U.S. foreign policy risks military and political overextension, an "imperial overstretch" that threatens economic security. As applied to the United States, this analysis suggests that "in 1945 the United States commanded a 40 percent share of the world economy; today its share is half that, and yet our military commitments have grown dramatically. This imbalance, which conforms to a classic historical pattern, threatens our security, both military and economic."[9]

Other neoisolationists agree. Alan Tonelson has argued that the attempt to commit U.S. power to all corners of the globe and "the failure to debate priorities"—to distinguish between vital and merely important national interests and reserve true commitments for the former—will lead simultaneously to foreign policy insolvency and a loss of respect by allies and adversaries alike.[10] Even Eliot Cohen, far from isolationist in his views and a supporter of the Gulf War, contends that the "core American commitments" remained in force while the relative U.S. economic power underlying them declined. "In sum," Cohen concludes, "the United States today is an overextended power."[11]

Now that the cold war is over, however, a rejection of isolationism does not imply that the United States must become a world police power, enforcing its own laws and interests. The choice simply is not so stark as between complete interventionism and world leadership and isolationism. Rather, the United States can promote peace through a third strategy—a *balancer* policy of somewhat more detached military presence, which helps dampen regional instabilities and reduces the incentive for arms races and war. The Gulf War provides an example of how this strategy can work: Washington did not intervene actively in the Gulf region, overturning governments and pursuing gunboat diplomacy; its presence, and eventual assistance to Kuwait and Saudi Arabia, merely served to counterbalance Iraqi power. In the case of Iraq, this balancing effort was not made clear enough in advance—largely because the United States was not sure how far it was willing to go—and Saddam Hussein was able to convince himself that the United States would not attempt it. But in other contexts where the U.S. commitment is clearer, the U.S. presence may not only defeat aggressors but prevent them from resorting to military force at all.

Zbigniew Brzezinski writes similarly that the United States should pursue a policy of "selective global commitment." As Europe moves toward economic and political union while attempting to restrain its explosive national and ethnic tensions; as the Soviet Union inches toward economic reform and an evolution into a looser confederation of republics; as the nations of the Far East attempt to accommodate growing Chinese power and established Japanese influence; and as the Middle East struggles toward peace, the U.S. role, Brzezinski writes, "will be centrally important." No other nation "currently possesses the attributes needed for effective global leverage: military reach, political clout, economic impact as well as social and cultural appeal."

Brzezinski recognizes that the concerns animating U.S. political leaders are increasingly domestic in nature and that if the United States wishes to lead abroad it needs to reinvigorate itself at home. These facts demand "a more subtle American contribution to sustaining global security," he admits, than during the cold war. Nonetheless, he rejects isolationism along with calls for a Pax Americana. Brzezinski's preferred vision for a future world order is "an incipient global security structure, derived from widening and increasingly self-reliant regional cooperation, backed by selective and proportionate American commitments." In performing such a role, which closely parallels a balancing strategy, the United States "will remain the principal source of nuclear deterrence and the ultimate guarantor of the proposition that any disrupter of security will be faced by a dominant coalition."[12]

Others have outlined a similar framework for U.S. involvement in the world, hanging on it various specific tasks or emphases. Paul Nitze notes that because of its breadth of political, cultural, economic, and military strengths and because it boasts no ideological or territorial ambitions, the United States can play a "unique role in bringing its powers to the support of order and diversity among the world's diffuse and varied groups." Like Brzezinski he emphasizes that the United States, with more elaborate domestic concerns than in the past, must play a more restrained role, and in fact he foreshadows Brzezinski's later article by calling for a "carefully selective" U.S. global commitment. Nitze sounds the same themes about worldwide instability—in Europe and the Middle East—and the need for a balancer in the Pacific. "In a world of growing interdependence," he concludes, "where even the problems of distant neighbors are increasingly our own, it is not now the time for the United States to retreat from the world stage."[13]

A balancer strategy reflects in part the worldwide application of what has long been the U.S. role in Asia.[14] Although Soviet military power in Asia was significant during the cold war, it never approached the overwhelming conventional superiority Moscow enjoyed in Europe. Much of the Soviet Union's strength in the East was focused in any case on China and did not pose an overwhelming threat to U.S. friends or allies. The U.S. strategy in Asia has always therefore consisted of more than containment, even though containment's two great "police actions" were fought there. In Asia the United States has been as concerned with regional instabilities—the face-off on the Korean Peninsula, tensions between China and both Taiwan and Vietnam, and a dozen other reservoirs of malevolence. Asian states had sought the United States, viewed as a less aggressive imperialist than its European contemporaries, as a balancer since the turn of the century, and the United States began to fulfill that role in earnest after 1945. In the wake of the cold war, such a role will be appropriate for U.S. policy around the globe.

Proponents of a balancing strategy argue that the Gulf War pointed to another, more immediate reason for playing such a role: It provided the United States with leverage in its primary areas of interest—political and economic relations with the other two economic power centers, Europe and Northeast Asia. Many nations besides the United States have an interest in stability and peace but do not possess the military forces or political will to help guard those interests alone, or at all. Although it would be wrong for the United States explicitly to assume the mantle of world police power, it is true that security forces of whatever type draw a salary; for its international troubles, the United States can expect payment in the form of political and economic influence vis-à-vis its major trading partners. The resulting leverage can be used in political bargaining, trade talks, and other bilateral and multilateral negotiations.

Indeed, were the United States to forfeit its world role, it might pay a stiff economic price—a fact that turns Kennedy's argument on its head. The near-term economic advantage of smaller defense budgets "might be more than overwhelmed by the long-term costs resulting from unwarranted retrenchment," costs including lost economic influence and, potentially, expensive wars, writes Richard Haas.[15] Though Haas does not mention the example of Korea, it is a fitting one: A slightly more expansive definition of U.S. vital interests in 1950 might have discouraged the North from attacking and saved billions of dollars and tens of thousands of lives. Joseph Nye concurs, arguing that curtailing defense spending and abrogating commitments "likely would exacerbate" the United States' geopolitical problems because such actions would reduce U.S. economic leverage and could endanger the security of economically critical areas like the Gulf. Emasculating the United States' role would also foster regional instability, terrorism, and nuclear proliferation, all of which would negatively effect U.S. economic interests abroad.[16]

Fourth and finally, there is the alternative of *multilateralism,* or collective security. This would not be completely distinct from any of the other strategies as there would be an element of multilateralism in all of them. But the emphasis is different. Rather than attempting to impose a U.S. vision on issues of international security, as both an interventionist and, to a lesser extent, a balancing strategy would do, a collective approach would have the United States work almost entirely through international organizations and ad hoc coalitions. It would require much more compromise in U.S. policy than other strategies and would demand that the United States cede important elements of its position as leader of the free world to nations such as Germany and Japan. Yet it would remain an active, engaged foreign policy, very distinct from isolationism.

The distinctions between these four schools may become more apparent if we consider their approach to a single security issue—avoiding conflict and promoting a lasting peace in the Middle East. An interventionist foreign policy might see the United States extending security guarantees to Israel in order to reassure Tel Aviv about its security and allow it to make security-related concessions; in order to sell arms to Arab states to obtain their cooperation; in order to serve as the sole sponsor of all negotiations and discussions in the region; and in order to underwrite a permanent settlement with economic and military aid and additional security commitments. Isolationists would argue that the United States has no business meddling in disputes so far from its shores and would have it play virtually no role whatsoever.

A balancing policy would have the United States pursue a circumscribed version of interventionism, in all likelihood without the security guarantees, without the economic and military aid, and without some of the arms sales. U.S. diplomats would help establish negotiations and support the process, but they would not impose a settlement. Finally, multilateralism would see the United States working through the United Nations to establish international talks; to cooperate with global arms embargoes in order to halt and reverse the regional arms race; and to cooperate with multinational attempts to halt the spread of weapons of mass destruction in the Middle East.

As these last examples make clear, the United States already seems to have evolved toward a combination of balancing and maintaining collective security: It steps in and guides events when others are unwilling or unable to do so while working through international organizations whenever possible.[17]

Post–cold war U.S. geostrategy could settle comfortably into policies along these lines, or it could lurch toward isolationism. It seems clear that an interventionist strategy is a thing of the past; yet U.S. policy during the Gulf War may have demonstrated interventionism as much as maintenance of a balancing strategy or collective security,[18] and it may take only the emergence of a new regional threat for the United States to once again become assertive.

The spectrum of choice for the architects of a U.S. world role is therefore broad. What choice the United States makes will determine the nature of its relationships with former adversaries and current allies, with the nations of the developing world, and with potential regional aggressors and hegemons. As we will see in Chapter 7, the nature of U.S. military strategy will also evolve in service of its world role.

It is indeed ironic that the Gulf War emerged when it did at the conjunction of two geostrategic eras. The cold war was in rapid decline, and in the Gulf War the United States and the Soviet Union would be de facto allies. A new, as yet undefined period—variously known as the new world order, the post–cold war era, a time of geoeconomics rather than geopolitics, or by other names—had begun, and the Gulf War was quickly seen as an example of the sort of security threat offered by this new era.

But as we have seen, there are reasons to doubt to what degree the Gulf War is representative of post–cold war security threats. For many reasons, the conflict was unique. And yet there is much we can learn from it: the textured history of its events, a few key nuggets of military or political information that suggest the need for change, a handful of specific policy recommendations based on U.S. shortcomings in the war. In the following chapters we will examine all these areas. This book's aim is twofold: to provide a brief, accurate history of the buildup to war, the combat itself, and the war's aftermath; and to isolate those military and political lessons we learned from the war.

"War," wrote Thomas Mann, "is only a cowardly escape from the problems of peace." And so it was for Saddam Hussein, an attempt to solve his economic and political problems with one bold, brutal stroke. In a broader sense, however, the Gulf War was only a momentary escape from the problems of peace for all its participants. In early 1992, the Arab nations and Israel were circling warily around each other in less than successful peace negotiations; the Soviet Union had collapsed and the United States was debating not how much to spend to deter or undermine Russia but how much economic aid to send Moscow; and the civil war in Yugoslavia had given clear evidence of yet another challenge of the post–cold war era. For policymakers around the world, the Gulf War must seem a decade old already. Yet it ended less than two years ago, and its legacy is powerful. We hope this book provides a useful early survey of that legacy and its implications for the future of U.S. foreign and defense policy.

2

The Failure of Deterrence

One of the first lessons drawn by some during the recent Gulf crisis was that the United States had bungled deterrence in classic fashion. Both a historical analogy and a villain came easily to hand. The analogy was Korea 1950, when a U.S. unwillingness to name South Korea explicitly as part of its Asian "security perimeter" supposedly tempted the North (and the Soviet Union) to attack. The villain was U.S. ambassador to Iraq April Glaspie: Had she been firmer on July 25, it is said, Saddam might have held his armies in check. If the United States had only made a clear deterrent threat, Kuwait could have been spared invasion.

Thus we find Leslie Gelb arguing in the *New York Times* of August 1991 about President Bush's "fateful blunder." Not only did April Glaspie fail to convey U.S. seriousness on July 25 but three days later, President Bush sent a weak message to Saddam Hussein that "lacked even the hints of steel" suggested by the State Department. "Why never once in this period," Gelb asks, "did a senior Administration official deliver a tough warning?" If one had, he implies, "war might have been prevented."[1] Senator David Boren agrees: "If we had had six months of warning," he suggested in July 1991, "the war might have been avoided." The United States could have gone to King Fahd of Saudi Arabia, Boren argued, and taken some joint action to deter Saddam's aggression.[2]

In fact Iraq's occupation of Kuwait may well suggest nothing of the sort.[3] What has gone unnoticed is the degree to which the call for a "deterrent threat" rests on traditional deterrence theory—the notion that wars are the result of rational but expansionist countries whose leaders can be deterred if the United States makes a clear commitment to the defense of threatened nations. That theory has come under severe criticism since the mid-1970s by a group of scholars concerned that any portrait of rational leaders in full command of policy and able to communicate clearly with their adversaries did not capture reality. Critics of deterrence would argue that the 1990–1991 war over Kuwait is further proof of their contention that deterrence as a national security strategy is risky. The truth about U.S. policy toward Iraq before and during the crisis, however, is extraordinarily complex.

Deterrence Theory

First we must decide what deterrence is. "To deter" is defined in *Webster's* as "to keep a person from doing something through fear, anxiety, etc.; [to] discourage."[4] To deter someone is to influence their behavior, to discourage them from doing something they wish to do—and something that presumably would run counter to the deterring nations' interests. In the present example, the United States would have liked to deter Iraq from invading Kuwait.

It is important to distinguish between two kinds of deterrence.[5] Central nuclear deterrence is the familiar practice by which nations with sizable nuclear arsenals keep others with such weapons from attacking them, usually by threatening a prompt and devastating response (mutually assured destruction). Extended deterrence is different and is the focus of this chapter. It is the process by which nations attempt to protect friends or allies with deterrent threats and promises. Hence the United States threatens a military response, including the use of nuclear weapons, if the Soviet Union attacks Europe or Japan, or if North Korea invades the South. Extended deterrence is a trickier thing than its central cousin: It is easier for a state to argue that it would defend itself than it is to suggest it would go to war on someone else's behalf.

In both cases, however, the basic elements of what might be called "classical deterrence theory" are the same. Janice Gross Stein outlines the basis of that theory.

> Elaborated largely through deductive reasoning, [formal theories of deterrence] build on the central proposition that, when a challenger considers that the likely benefits of military action will outweigh its probable costs, deterrence is likely to fail. If, on the other hand, leaders estimate that the probable costs of a use of force are greater than its putative benefits, deterrence succeeds. Crucial to these estimates of a challenger is the credibility of a defender's commitment, either to punish or to deny.

At base, Stein concludes, "the concept of deterrence assumes that a rational challenger weighs all elements of the deterrence equation equally and pays attention to probability, cost, and benefit in choosing whether or not to use force."[6]

Deterrence theory thus posits an aggressor intent on changing the status quo, in many cases by challenging U.S. interests; in the past this challenger was the Soviet Union (or one of its proxies), though in 1990 it was Iraq, and in 1992 or 1995 it might be North Korea, or Libya, or Syria. This aggressor will be deterred if it calculates that the costs and risks of military action outweigh the potential gains, and a real chance that the United States will respond militarily to such aggression would add much to the "risk and cost" side of the equation. Generating the belief that the United States will respond, then—"or more exactly, raising this estimated probability—is therefore the object of U.S. deterrence policy," and the requirements for generating this belief are that potential aggressors "perceive a U.S. 'signal' of intent to defend and find the signal 'credible.'" The United States must therefore communicate that signal and do so in a way in which it "appears to become *committed* to carrying out its intention to defend the attacked nation."[7]

The seminal explication of this strategy can be found in Thomas Schelling's *Arms and Influence*. In Chapter 2, "The Art of Commitment," Schelling, for many years a Harvard University professor and the father of modern deterrence theory, lays out all the central elements of deterrence theory. "It hardly seems necessary," writes Schelling (confirming the distinction between central and extended deterrence),

> to tell the Russians that we should fight them if they attack *us*. But we go to great lengths to tell the Russians that they will have America to contend with if they or their satellites attack countries associated with us. Saying so, unfortunately, does not make it true; and if it is true, saying so does not always make it believed. We evidently do not want war and would only fight if we had to. The problem is to demonstrate that we would have to.[8]

In other words, we must become bound so firmly to the nation in question that we have virtually no choice but to defend it, thus creating a "credible" commitment. "What we have to do," Schelling argues, "is to get ourselves in a position where we cannot fail to react as we said we would—where we just cannot help it—or where we would be obliged by some overwhelming cost of not reacting in the manner we had declared."[9]

Schelling proposes a number of ways to do this. One is to act irrational and hot-headed, counting on our impetuosity to persuade an aggressor not to test our pledges. Another is to "relinquish the initiative," placing oneself in a position where the other side holds the power to begin a war. The most common tool for achieving that end is the well-known "tripwire" force, placing Americans in harm's way to inform an aggressor that an attack on a U.S. ally would spill U.S. blood and thus inevitably draw the United States in. The deterring nation can also make a strong political commitment to the subject of an aggressor's interest, thus staking its national honor on responding to any aggression that does occur.[10]

The Absence of Prewar Deterrence

The United States did not do any of this with regard to Kuwait, even though the threat of Iraqi expansion had been growing for some time. Saddam Hussein was a brutal dictator, unpredictable and potentially dangerous, but ten years earlier in 1980, Washington was obsessed with Iran as the chief threat to the stability of the region. Even though it was Iraq that attacked Iran to begin their eight-year war, the emotional reaction in Washington to the revolutionary regime in Teheran tilted U.S. policy firmly toward Baghdad. The result was a nearly ten-year U.S. effort to build closer ties to Iraq, which included economic incentives and military assistance. The Reagan and Bush administrations protected Kuwaiti tankers and thus indirectly Iraqi oil and economic support, shared intelligence information about Iranian troop movements, and fought attempts by the U.S. Congress to place sanctions on Iraq in response to its use of poison gas. During this period, as *Wall Street Journal* writer Paul Gigot has explained, "the United States, in effect, became Iraq's silent ally."[11]

U.S. officials were convinced that their policy of moderating Iraq was working. To be fair, Hussein did take a number of steps that encouraged this perception: After the United States and Iraq formally reestablished diplomatic relations in 1984, Iraqi officials down to the level of customs agents discovered a newfound sympathy for Americans, and Iraq toned down its anti-U.S. rhetoric. Hussein even sent a gift of cookies to a 1984 party for U.S. citizens in Baghdad.[12] Iraq expelled many known terrorist groups and moved closer to the positions of the moderate Arab states on issues related to Israel. By 1990, even after Iraq's use of chemical weapons against its own people and against the Iranians, and despite Hussein's brutal rule at home, many viewed Iraq as a mature member of the international community. U.S. business and Middle Eastern specialist journals discussed the economic opportunities in Iraq, and U.S. officials continued to trumpet Washington's desire for cordial relations.

As Hussein's military power and ambition grew, Washington did consider a tougher policy toward Baghdad. In 1985, Howard Teicher, a Defense Department official, and Graham Fuller of the CIA wrote a policy memo warning that Hussein's behavior within Iraq could presage his external behavior. They argued that Iran was a critical state in the region and that any hope of reaching an accommodation with Teheran was being undermined by the distinct U.S. tilt toward Baghdad. Three years later, Zalmay Khalilzad, a Columbia University professor advising the State Department, argued similarly that Iraq, by virtue of its victory in the Iran-Iraq war, posed a real threat to U.S. interests. Khalilzad predicted that Hussein's desire for regional hegemony would eventually lead him to demand a reduction of U.S. presence in the Middle East and recommended a strategy of "containing" Iraq. These studies failed to cause a shift in U.S. policy, primarily because of the Iran-contra scandal: Any view that appeared to counsel rapprochement with Iran was rejected.[13]

So the U.S. attempt to engage Iraq persisted. The relationship was manifest in a February 12, 1990, meeting between Hussein and John Kelly, the

U.S. assistant secretary of state for Near East and South Asian Affairs. Kelly, following a well-established U.S. pattern, expressed in general terms the U.S. hope that Saddam might help stabilize the volitile region. The Bush administration continued to desire improved relations with Iraq, Kelly said. Hussein was apparently impressed enough to telephone the news to King Hussein of Jordan.[14]

Yet Iraq also faced perilous economic and political challenges that may have led Saddam Hussein to believe his rule was in some jeopardy, and in fact Iraq's growing economic problems were Hussein's real motivation for seeking closer ties with the United States, the friend of its enemy, Israel. Iraq labored under a massive foreign debt of roughly $100 billion, and the falling prices of world oil held out little hope of large near-term cash infusions. Other Arab nations were contributing to Iraq's woes: On the very day after the Iran-Iraq war ended in August 1988, Kuwait began violating its OPEC production quotas, increasing the supply of oil and lowering its price. Baghdad claimed its oil revenues fell to $7 billion annually—precisely the amount it owed in debt servicing. By the end of that year Iraq began defaulting on loans owed the West; Western banks refused further loans, and France stopped providing arms. Hussein refused to pay off the principal, seeking new loans and refinancing old ones. Between 1988 and August 1990, his debt increased by $10 billion.

Over the coming months, Saddam Hussein would place increasing pressure on other Arab states to help rescue Iraq from its economic difficulties. In February 1990 he would demand forgiveness of his $30 billion war debt to Saudi Arabia and Kuwait as well as $30 billion in new aid. Gradually his anger against the richer Gulf states would grow: They were partly to blame for his problems because of their oil overproduction, he argued, and they should share in the cost. Gradually Hussein stopped requesting aid and started demanding it.

The Iraqi government had trouble demobilizing its troops after the war with Iran because there were no jobs for them. By the end of 1989, Iraqi resentment was being directed at the foreign workers who had flooded in to take vacant civilian jobs during the war, and violent clashes erupted between Iraqi veterans and Egyptian workers. As *New York Times* reporter Elaine Sciolino noted, "By the end of 1989, Saddam needed to do something drastic to occupy the Army he had built so assiduously."[15]

Politically, Hussein had other worries. His people had just fought an exhausting eight-year war against Iran and had emerged with little to show for their leader's aggression. Hussein betrayed a constant fear of assassination. The Iraqi leader may have believed he needed, at minimum, a new scapegoat, or, more ambitiously, a new military campaign to galvanize his people.

Either out of genuine belief in U.S. malevolence or in an attempt to deflect criticism, Saddam Hussein began complaining that the United States was behind a plot to destroy his regime. His concern was evident by 1989. In a meeting with Secretary of State James Baker on October 6, Tariq Aziz charged that U.S. intelligence agencies were attempting to destabilize Iraq. Baker denied the accusation. To demonstrate its good faith, the Bush administration extended a further $500 million in credit guarantees that November, and the following January, to head off congressional sanctions, the United States declared that trade with Iraq was in the national interest.[16]

Nonetheless, shortly afterward Hussein's growing paranoia sparked the first serious flare-ups in U.S.-Iraqi relations since 1984. At the time they appeared to be simple misunderstandings, not signs of things to come. But Hussein's overreaction was nevertheless perplexing. On February 15, 1990, a Voice of America (VOA) broadcast celebrated the advent of democracy in such former dictatorships as Romania; it mentioned Iraq on a list of countries where "[t]he secret police are still widely present." Hussein was furious, and his deputy foreign minister complained to U.S. ambassador Glaspie that the editorial was a "flagrant interference in the internal affairs of Iraq."

"Our guess," Glaspie cabled the State Department, "is that the President [Hussein] himself heard it on February 15." She quickly apologized in a letter to the Iraqi foreign ministry: "It is absolutely not United States policy to question the legitimacy of the Government of Iraq nor to interfere in any way in the domestic concerns of the Iraqi people and government." After that, VOA editorials on Iraq reportedly received much closer scrutiny from State before clearance—on July 25, a VOA piece noting that "the U.S. would take very seriously any threat that put U.S. interests or friends [in the Gulf] at risk" was canceled by State for fear of angering Hussein.[17] (State's own annual report on human rights had emerged on February 21 complete with twelve pages of damning accusations against Hussein's government.)

Rather than accepting the U.S. apologies or seeking a clarification of U.S. policy, Hussein retaliated. On February 24, at an Arab Cooperation Council meeting in Amman, he warned other Arab states that the post–cold war era would see a rebirth of U.S. imperialism in the Middle East and called on them to join Iraq in resisting what he on other occasions termed the "imperialist-Zionist conspiracy." (Fearing assassination, he had arrived at the meeting secretly in an unmarked jet.)[18] "We believe," he warned on February 24, "that the United States will continue to depart from the restrictions that govern the rest of the world" and will pursue "undisciplined and irresponsible behavior." This threat would be focused through Israel: "The Arabs must take into account that there is a real possibility that Israel might embark on new stupidities" within the next five years "as a result of direct or tacit U.S. encouragement. . . . If the Gulf people, along with all Arabs, are not careful," Hussein warned, "the Arab Gulf region will be governed by the U.S. will."[19] Zalmay Khalilzad's prediction was coming true: Hussein was seeking to oust the United States from the Middle East.

The more moderate Arab states were angered by this rhetoric, partly because it appeared to be directed against them and their relationships with the United States.[20] King Hussein of Jordan arranged a meeting on the evening of February 24 between Egyptian president Hosni Mubarak and Saddam Hussein to encourage the two men to patch up their differences. But diplomacy was not the order of the day. If the Gulf states did not provide an additional $30 billion in assistance, Saddam bellowed, "I shall take steps to retaliate." The meeting reportedly ended on a distinctly unfriendly note.

Just what Saddam's steps might be had been outlined by a prominent Middle Eastern banker in late February 1990, according to U.S. journalists. In a confidential report on the state of the Iraqi economy, the banker argued that Iraq's debt was essentially unmanageable and would crush its economic progress. Saddam's incompetent economic policies would push the country only further into ruin. Hussein recognized this, the report concluded, and knew that he had few options. "But there is always Kuwait, situated just a few miles from where [Saddam's] idle army is massed."[21]

Prewar Diplomacy

In late February and early March 1990, Jordan's King Hussein undertook what would become one of many attempts at shuttle diplomacy. Flying between the Gulf states, he sounded out their leaders on the possibility of a compromise with Iraq. The results were disappointing: On March 3, he met with Saddam Hussein and informed him that the Gulf states appeared intransigent. Diplomatic correspondents Pierre Salinger and Eric Laurent reported that it was at this time that Saddam ordered his generals to begin a buildup of military force on the Kuwaiti border;[22] whether or not this charge is correct, it must have been about this time that Iraq began preparations for its assault on the post–cold war complacency in the West.

Meanwhile Hussein became even more outspoken on the question of Israel. On April 2, he spoke before a group of Iraqi military officers. His rhetoric against the supposed U.S.-Israeli conspiracy had heated up. "This is the biggest conspiracy in modern history," he railed. "We have a duty to defend Iraq. . . . A foreigner must not attack the Arab homeland." Hussein warned that he would use chemical weapons against Israel if attacked. "By God," he raged, "we will make the fire eat up half of Israel, if it tried [anything] against Iraq!"[23]

In threatening Israel so blatantly, Hussein had finally aroused some serious concern in the United States. The *Washington Post* and the *New York Times* both reported Hussein's remarks on their front pages. State Department spokeswoman Margaret Tutweiler called Saddam's remarks "inflammatory, outrageous, and irresponsible." The *Post* later editorialized that "that was a particularly crude threat President Saddam Hussein made. . . . There was a contemptuous and defiant quality" to it; such outrages "keep supplying fresh reminders of the dangers that loom in diplomatic neglect."[24] An official White House release termed the speech "particularly deplorable and irresponsible." President Bush reacted personally. "This is no time to be talking about chemical or biological weapons," he said on April 3. "This is no time to be escalating tensions in the Middle East."[25]

Within the Bush administration, Assistant Secretary John Kelly and Dennis Ross of the Policy Planning Staff now outlined possible economic sanctions against Iraq in retaliation for its new belligerence. These included an elimination of both credits for wheat purchases and exports to Iraq of military or dual-use technologies or equipment. Proposals for sanctions were presented at an April 16 deputies meeting between high-ranking officials of U.S. cabinet departments. The Department of Commerce, concerned as always with the impact on U.S. business, and the National Security Council opposed sanctions. The Bush administration had in any case been objecting strenuously to congressional attempts to place sanctions on Iraq and would continue to do so through July 31; a reversal of policy might be politically embarrassing. The sanctions idea was dropped.[26]

Even without a knowledge of that debate, Saddam Hussein must have suspected that his threats had been excessive. He telephoned King Fahd of Saudi Arabia and requested a visit from a Saudi diplomat familiar with the United States. Fahd sent his nephew, Prince Bandar bin Sultan, the Saudi ambassador to the United States, to meet with Hussein in Baghdad in early April.[27] As reported in Bob Woodward's *The Commanders*, the interview was a strange one, full of deception and vague hints about what Saddam had in mind. Hussein began by insisting that his remarks had been blown out of proportion; he only threatened to retaliate against Israel, he told Bandar, not to strike first. He asked Bandar to convey this message to Bush and King Fahd—and through them, to Israel. Bandar agreed.

But Saddam's discussion with Bandar also revealed his growing paranoia. His concern about another attack by Israel—something like their 1981 raid on his Osirak nuclear plant, or even larger—was real, he claimed. Saddam had just executed an Iranian-born British journalist because of alleged ties to Israel. The Iraqi leader also expressed concern for his political future within the country: "If I am attacked by Israel now," he fretted, "I would not last six hours." Saddam also worried about "imperialist-Zionist forces" who were "pushing the theory that I have designs over my neighbors," meaning the smaller Gulf states to his south. "I don't have designs over my neighbors." Bandar assured him that his Arab brothers knew this.

Yet Saddam's final remarks left an ambivalent air over the discussion. He had to threaten Israel the way he did, Saddam insisted. His people were becoming soft. "I must whip them into a sort of frenzy or emotional mobilization," he told Bandar, "so they will be ready for whatever may happen."

A New Warning

On April 24, about three weeks after Saddam Hussein's threat against Israel and three months before his invasion of Kuwait, noted terrorism expert and Center for Strategic and International Studies scholar Robert Kupperman wrote an article for the *Christian Science Monitor* warning anew of Iraq's intentions. "Iraq's leader has an agenda of domination," Kupperman wrote, "and he is determined to carry it out." Yet despite his use of poison gas against his own people and the threat of its use against Israel, "the only reaction from the Bush administration . . . has been verbal criticism."

Top officials in the Bush administration had to know, Kupperman pointed out, "that Saddam Hussein poses an unpredictable but increasing threat to U.S. and allied lives and interests. They must also understand that left alone, Iraq is quite capable of unleashing weapons of mass destruction." Yet, he suggested, those officials were using "psychological denial and wishful thinking" to delude themselves into continuing a policy of benign neglect. Kupperman himself suggested several stronger alternatives, including open or covert military strikes against Iraq's chemical and nuclear weapons plants, or possibly a U.S.-Soviet effort to coordinate "the total economic and diplomatic isolation of Iraq."

"There are no easy options," Kupperman admitted, "only very hard and costly choices with little time."[28]

Barriers to Deterrence

By the summer of 1990, then, the Iraqi government had become increasingly strident and belligerent. Hussein's regime had already proved its brutality—invading Iran in 1980, using poison gas to massacre its own people—and by June 1990 it had begun casting about for a more ambitious regional role. The risk of instability seemed clear. The United States had considered a change in policy toward Iraq but had rejected it. Why did the United States not react at this point? What held it back?

Some of the reasons can be found in the multifaceted critique of deterrence theory. The elements of this critique will unfold further on. Most pertinent here is one of the fundamental flaws in deterrence: It is not always possible to send a deterrent signal when one is required. Barriers to making deterrent threats come in a number of forms, perhaps the most common of which are domestic political barriers. A national leader often cannot pledge an unequivocal response to aggression if it is not clear that the population will support it. In the Falkland Islands case, for example, the Thatcher government, already viewed with suspicion by moderate Britons, had no desire to appear anxious for war.[29] When only 44 percent of the American people believed Washington should use U.S. troops to defend an East European nation against the Soviet

Union, it would have been difficult for a president to guarantee the use of force if the Soviets intervened.[30] This is not an insurmountable hurdle—only about half of all Americans favor defending South Korea against the North, yet Washington signed a mutual defense treaty in 1954 and U.S. troops stand on the demilitarized zone ready to trigger an intervention—but it does immensely complicate deterrence.

Other political barriers are more insidious than public opinion. In the case of Iraq, domestic lobbies hoping to maintain and promote U.S. trade with Iraq opposed any efforts at punitive sanctions. In 1988, sanctions cosponsored by an unlikely team of senators, liberal Claiborne Pell of Delaware and archconservative Jesse Helms of North Carolina, swept through the Senate but were stalled in the House, in part by powerful agricultural interests. Within the executive branch, the Commerce Department acted as the voice of U.S. business and opposed the sanctions proposed by State in April 1990.

A final political consideration was provided by the legacy of the Iran-contra affair. After the U.S. arms sales to Iran were exposed, Reagan and Bush administration officials apparently feared that any policies appearing to tilt toward Iran might raise new charges that the residue of Iran-contra was alive and well. Proposals for a reversal of U.S. policy toward Iran thus fell on unsympathetic ears attuned closely to political considerations.

A second barrier to deterrent signaling might be a lack of military capability. A nation concerned with deterrence cannot threaten a military action if it does not possess the capability to carry it out. When considering military responses to a potential Iraqi invasion of Kuwait, for example, Bush administration officials had few military forces in the region in July 1990 for deterrence purposes.

Third, other nations can create barriers to a deterrer's signaling—sometimes in contravention of their own interests. For political, economic, or cultural reasons of their own, they may oppose the enunciation of a clear deterrent policy. Without the expectation of Allied backing, U.S. officials may have felt constrained in their policy options before August.

Fourth and finally, another powerful roadblock to making unequivocal deterrent threats is the risk that they might backfire—the threat-versus-reassurance dilemma. As useful as it may be at times, pursuing deterrence is immensely complicated by the fact that sometimes what is required is not a deterrent threat but a reassuring promise. Threats can provoke an aggressor as easily as they can restrain one.[31] If a potential challenger is motivated by fears and not ambition, as when it expects a negative shift in a regional balance of power or has concerns about its domestic stability, then measures designed to enhance its security can help avoid war. The problem is especially acute because it is so difficult to tell the difference. National leaders—and intelligence services—are notoriously bad at predicting when restraint will avoid war and when active threats are necessary.

History provides numerous examples of times when leaders' calculations proved wrong. In the 1930s, Britain and its European allies attempted to appease Hitler and paid the price in the form of a six-year war. In 1973 Israel, convinced that it had started a war prematurely in 1967 when the Arab states were defensively oriented, believed that a new war would be the product not of Egyptian or other Arab aggression but of "a spiral of fear and misunderstanding"; therefore, "as late as a day before Egypt attacked, Israel thought that the source of tension was the Arabs' expectation that they were about to be attacked, and the last-minute efforts of Israel and the United States were to reassure the Arabs that this was not the case."[32] In the early 1980s, Britain, having resolved earlier disputes with Argentina over the Falklands in 1977, believed that "caution was likely to reap a handsome dividend. Not surprisingly, therefore, the consensus in both the Foreign Office and the Cabinet Office in March 1982 was for the need to avoid any public display of British resolve." Lord Carrington argued in Parliament that strong deterrent signals would merely spark a violent Argentine response and that in fact "nothing would have been more likely to turn the Argentines away from the path of negotiations and towards that of military force."[33]

Similar thinking apparently guided the U.S. reaction to Saddam Hussein's bullying of Kuwait. As we shall see, when on the eve of war the United States provided two aerial refueling planes to the United Arab Emirates, UAE officials were furious when the United States publicized the assistance, fearing that the information would anger Saddam. Kuwaiti and Saudi leaders were equally unwilling to provoke Saddam Hussein by calling in U.S. military forces in the days and weeks before the invasion. Even the Kuwaiti government itself took this approach. "On the recommendation of Arab leaders who advised against provoking Saddam and who hoped against mounting odds that appeasement could still work," writes Elaine Sciolino, "Kuwait did not position troops at the Iraqi border" in late July 1990. "Instead, it took its sentries off alert status."[34] "Even if the United States had correctly analyzed the intelligence reports on Iraq's military buildup," Sciolino continues, "it could have done little except threaten Saddam with military action, a strategy that was anathema to the Saudis, the Kuwaitis, and the Egyptians, who pleaded for silence and discouraged any American military response."[35]

Columbia University political scientist and eminent theorist of deterrence Robert Jervis has outlined a useful theoretical framework for these two strategies. He distinguishes between deterrence and "spiral" models of conflict. The former identify the threat to peace in the premeditated, rational actions of aggressors; the latter posit that wars often begin through an accelerating process of threat and response, alert and counteralert, mobilization and countermobilization. Two handy symbols for the models can be found in this century's two world wars: the First World War's escalation of interlocking mobilizations, the "Sarajevo scenario," represents the spiral model; Hitler's calculated aggressions in Europe beginning in the 1930s, the "Munich scenario," represent a deterrence model of conflict.[36] Yet as Jervis is the first to point out, neither of these models is universal, and the proper means of avoiding conflict will vary depending upon which process is under way. The problem becomes divining an aggressor's beliefs and intentions—a dangerous guessing game, with the difference between peace and war often hanging in the balance.

These four barriers to deterrence suggest that except for a very few contingencies that would involve vital interests, deterring nations often cannot be certain in advance what they would do. In some cases, when deterrence fails, the rationale for a response becomes suddenly much clearer than it had been before. Historian of diplomacy Ernest May has made this point with regard to the Korean War, noting that before the conflict U.S. policymakers pursued a "calculated policy," carefully weighing ends, means, risks, and benefits and deciding that they were not ready to guarantee intervention. Once the war began, May explains, the president and his advisers rethought; "their minds flew to an axiom—that any armed aggression anywhere constituted a threat to all nations everywhere."[37] As Robert Jervis notes about Korea, "In the actual moment of attack, the costs of not responding loomed much larger than they had previously," perhaps because "people do not ordinarily examine their basic beliefs unless they are confronted with shocks and unpleasant choices."[38] One suspects that exactly the same process was at work in the Bush administration before and after Iraq's invasion of Kuwait.

Korea is an example where the United States intervened when it thought it might not. There are other cases where U.S. leaders did not intervene where their rhetoric had suggested they might—in China during the civil war, in Cuba during the Bay of Pigs invasion (when the United States refused to follow up the Cuban exile invasion with U.S. troops), and elsewhere. One result of this unpredictability is that aggressors may not believe marginal commitments. Jervis continues: "Because decision-makers do not always know how they will act, others will disregard statements of intent if they believe that their predictions of how the decision-maker will act are more accurate than those the decision-maker himself can make."[39] The only solution is to follow Schelling's central elements of deterrence theory and create a situation in which it is impossible for the United States not to respond. But that will be an option in only a precious few cases.

In the 1990 Gulf crisis, Washington therefore took no military action, and the effect on Saddam Hussein's thinking seems understandable in retrospect. Pierre Salinger and Eric Laurent make the connection. "One thing that must have been obvious to Saddam Hussein from the exchanges of views he had had with [U.S.] officials," as well as "from the contradictory positions adopted by Washington [was that] the American leadership was irresolute and inclined more toward compromise than confrontation."[40] The implications of that belief would soon become clear.

The Soft Line Continues

Just over a week after Saddam Hussein's inflammatory threats against Israel, a U.S. congressional delegation was in Baghdad to discuss Iraq's acquisition of advanced weapons. Senator Bob Dole led the delegation, which delivered a stern letter warning that better relations with the United States hinged in part on Saddam abandoning his drive for chemical and biological weapons.[41] In private conversation, however, the senators gave little impression of toughness—at least according to transcripts the Iraqis released later. "After listening to you for about an hour," said Senator Howard Metzenbaum according to the Iraqi transcript, "I realize you are a strong and intelligent man, and that you want peace." Dole reportedly assured Saddam that President Bush and many members of Congress would fight sanctions against Iraq. Saddam repeated his claims about a Western media campaign against him; Dole told him (based on incorrect information from the U.S. Embassy) that the Voice of America writer responsible for the February 15 broadcast had been fired. Senator Alan Simpson went further: "The press is spoiled and conceited," he told Saddam. "All the journalists consider themselves brilliant political scientists. They do not want to see anything succeeding or achieving its objectives. My advice is that you allow those bastards to come here and see for themselves."[42]

At about the time the senators went to Baghdad, Prince Bandar returned from his visit to Baghdad and spoke with President Bush.[43] The Saudi ambassador reportedly explained that Saddam remained paranoid, that he feared attack from Israel backed by the United States. Bush, well aware that there was no "imperialist-Zionist conspiracy," doubted Saddam's honesty and remained skeptical of the Iraqi leader's true intentions. He put Bandar off, but two days later the Saudi was back, pleading for assurances that Israel was not going to attack Iraq. Bush finally gave in: White House officials spoke with Israeli diplomats, who agreed they had no intention of attacking Iraq if they were not attacked first. This was passed back through Bandar to the Iraqis.

As far as Bush and other U.S. officials could tell, the small crisis over Saddam Hussein's threats against Israel had passed. The United States had made its complaints, the Saudis had vouched for Saddam, and Saddam had been reassured of Israeli intentions. It may never be known whether Saddam sought this explanation because he was worried—or because he was planning military action of his own.

At the beginning of May, according to Pierre Salinger and Eric Laurent, both the CIA and a visiting group of Israeli defense and political experts passed warnings of a possible Iraqi attack on Kuwait to high-ranking U.S. officials.[44] These would not have contained conclusive evidence that an invasion was imminent but would have represented additional hints of Iraqi intent. They were apparently dismissed.

The month of May saw increasingly strident Iraqi rhetoric about overproduction of oil in OPEC. Later Iraq would claim it lost $1 billion in revenues every time the price of oil fell by one dollar. At the Arab summit on May 30, Saddam claimed that Kuwait and other quota-busters were "virtually waging an economic war against my country. . . . War doesn't mean just tanks, artillery, or ships," Saddam complained. "It could take subtler and more insidious forms, such as the overproduction of oil, economic damage, and pressure to enslave a nation." Lest anyone doubt his seriousness, Saddam issued a direct threat. "One day," he said earlier in the speech, "the reckoning will come."

According to participants at the meeting, the Kuwaiti response was one of contempt.[45]

Another Warning Ignored

In the middle of June, the summer issue of *Foreign Affairs* hit the newsstands. The issue contained an article about the Middle East by Barry Rubin, a senior fellow at Washington's Institute for Near East Policy. After a summary of the region, Rubin assessed U.S. policy.

The Middle East remained critical to U.S. interests, Rubin pointed out, and not just in the form of the Arab-Israeli conflict. There were other considerations as well: "There is the problem," Rubin emphasized, "of ambitious, aggressive, radical states that could try to dominate the region, subvert an Arab-Israeli peace settlement, oppose U.S. interests, sponsor terrorism, and overthrow U.S. allies. The most important of these is Iraq, with its victory over Iran, huge oil resources, large army and ruthless leadership." The United States, Rubin argued, "must deter and counter threatening and destabilizing actions by these states."[46]

This task would be eased, Rubin suggested, by the " 'paradox of perception.' In the Third World in general and the Middle East in particular, U.S. omnipotence and omnipresence are firmly rooted in the belief systems of leaders and populace alike. . . . History has shown that even relatively modest displays of U.S. fortitude can have remarkably salutary effects." This was not to argue that the United States should press for military bases in the region or meddle in its internal politics. But "the simple reality is that if the United States does not take a decisive stand to discourage aggressive radical states and prevent the flourishing of new weapons systems—including open threats to use them against U.S. allies—the danger will grow."

To support his case for a more engaged U.S. policy toward expansionist regimes, Rubin cited a prominent Middle Eastern government official. "Aggressors thrive on appeasement. The world learned that at tremendous cost from the Munich agreement of 1938," the official was quoted as warning.

"How could the German generals oppose Hitler once he had proven himself successful? Indeed aggressors are usually clever at putting their demands in a way that seems reasonable." That official was Iraq's Deputy Foreign Minister Nizar Hamdoon.

Edging Toward War

By mid-July, tensions among the Arab states had reached fever pitch. The week of July 16 was in many ways the turning point. At the outset of that week, Iraq made detailed, specific charges against Kuwait and the UAE, presented to the Arab League in a lengthy memorandum. Saddam Hussein made another flaming speech in which he charged that Kuwait and the UAE were part of a "Zionist plot aided by the imperialists against the Arab nation." As ABC journalist John Cooley has written, Arab League Secretary General Chedli Klibi "felt that the memorandum and the speech were an Iraqi declaration of war against Kuwait."[47]

A key signal was a July 17 speech by Saddam Hussein, later broadcast on Iraqi radio. Low oil prices, he charged, were a "poisoned dagger" pointed at Iraq. He reiterated his indictment of the Gulf states: They were robbing Iraq of its economic lifeblood, and they would have to pay. But this speech was a special occasion: For the first time in public, Hussein made a clear threat of some form of punitive action. "If words fail to protect us," he said, "we will have no choice other than to go into action to reestablish the correct state of affairs and restore our rights."[48]

It quickly became clear that Saddam Hussein's threat was not an idle one. U.S. satellites orbiting high above the Middle East began to detect units of Iraq's elite Republican Guard divisions deploying in southern Iraq in the desert opposite Kuwait.[49] U.S. intelligence services watched the growing evidence intently, and by the second day the satellites disclosed a stunning fact: One full Republican Guard division, the Hammurabi, had moved just north of Kuwait, its 300 tanks and 10,000 soldiers poised to strike south. It was already being joined by a sister division, the Medina; by the next day, a third division was streaming into the area. Yet the evidence was not conclusive that Iraq intended to invade. For one thing, the supply and support units accompanying the divisions were reportedly believed by some in the U.S. government to be inadequate to sustain a major offensive. Besides, in the Iran-Iraq war, Baghdad had always rehearsed its offensives meticulously before launching them. No such practices had been observed taking place above Kuwait.

A consensus quickly emerged that the deployments were meant to intimidate Kuwait into concessions. Colin Powell, chairman of the Joint Chiefs of Staff; his operations chief on the Joint Staff, Lieutenant General Thomas Kelly; and most of the intelligence services concurred in this judgment. Many would continue to believe it until the invasion actually occurred. *Wall Street*

Journal writer Paul Gigot quotes one "ranking source" as saying that "the theory was that everything Saddam was doing was to coerce" Kuwait. Saddam "wanted the money, or maybe the two islands" in the Gulf, "but not Kuwait. So what was the problem?"[50]

This opinion was much in evidence at a remarkable seminar hosted in Washington by the RAND Corporation on July 18 and 19. Involving many of the U.S. government's top intelligence, defense, and diplomatic officials concerned with the Middle East, the seminar was originally designed to focus on a number of different contingencies. As reports began rolling in of Iraq's troop deployments, however, attention shifted very quickly to the Iraq-Kuwait dispute. There was no consensus at all that Iraq actually intended to invade—many still thought it was a bluff. Some even continued to oppose sanctions on the ground that better ties between Washington and Baghdad would serve to moderate Saddam Hussein. As for U.S. policy goals, the group argued in part that the United States should deter Hussein—definitely from attacking Saudi Arabia, perhaps from moving into Kuwait as well. But the idea of a U.S.-led war to retake Kuwait was still considered extreme; some of those present even flatly opposed the idea.[51]

Still, neither Kuwait nor the United States were taking any chances. On July 18, the Kuwaiti cabinet called for a meeting of the Gulf Cooperation Council and put its tiny military—barely 20,000 troops with a couple of hundred tanks—on alert, though as we have seen, it would not deploy them to the border and would eventually take them off alert. Perhaps hopefully, the emir of Kuwait termed the crisis a "summer cloud," but everyone recognized that if Iraq decided to move, the Kuwaitis would be able to do little in response. King Hussein of Jordan and Yasir Arafat of the Palestine Liberation Organization (PLO) spoke repeatedly with both sides in an attempt to defuse the crisis. On July 19, Secretary of Defense Dick Cheney told reporters that "We would, in fact, take seriously any threat to U.S. interests or U.S. friends in the region." Chairman Powell met with Norman Schwarzkopf, the commander in chief of the U.S. Central Command, at about this time and asked that he prepare contingency plans in case Iraq invaded Kuwait and some response was called for.[52]

Leaders of the United Arab Emirates, a tiny collection of sheikhdoms along the Gulf, requested military assistance of sorts from the United States in the form of two KC-135 aerial refueling tankers. After some opposition from the State Department, the mission, later termed Ivory Justice, was approved the night of July 21. Washington announced a sudden naval exercise with the UAE, and on July 24 Pentagon spokesman Pete Williams noted that the naval exercise and tanker support were meant as a signal of U.S. support for its friends in the Gulf. UAE officials were stunned—they had intended the operations to be secret and had no desire to provoke Saddam.

At the same moment, Arab leaders were receiving what they believed to be reassurances from Hussein. Egyptian president Hosni Mubarak traveled to Baghdad hoping to add his voice to those calling for moderation and compromise. Given the bad blood between Mubarak and the Iraqi president, there was reason to distrust any message Hussein delivered. Nonetheless Hussein made an unequivocal pledge: He would not invade Kuwait, he said, *as long as negotiations were under way.* While there was still a possibility for a negotiated solution, he would hold his armies in check.

Mubarak promptly flew to Kuwait and told the Kuwaitis, and eventually the Bush administration as well, what Hussein had said. But Mubarak left out a very important qualification: He told the Arab and U.S. leaders that Hussein had promised he would not use force, period. He said nothing about the telling condition that would free Saddam Hussein to attack as soon as the talks faltered.[53]

Warning Failures

As Iraq prepared to invade, the U.S. intelligence community remained silent. The consensus that Iraq's belligerence was merely a bluff remained strong, and apparently no intelligence services clearly predicted that Hussein would invade. This fact highlights another problem with deterrence: In some cases it relies on warning of aggression, and that warning may not come. Strategic warning can fail for two basic reasons. First, a government can commit what is commonly known as an "intelligence failure": Professional intelligence services do not warn of an impending attack, thus preventing officials from bolstering deterrence with new rhetoric or actions. A common example of such a failure is Pearl Harbor, where the evidence of a Japanese attack was plentiful yet no specific warning was transmitted to the highest political authorities.[54]

As many critics of deterrence theory recognize, it would be wrong to expect much more of intelligence than it usually provides. We should be uncomfortable with the phrase "intelligence failure" because it suggests that there is objective evidence that makes clear that intelligence services should have known an attack was coming. In fact, in most cases evidence is extremely ambiguous, and there are many signals indicating that no attack will be forthcoming. Merely because history proves certain analysts wrong does not mean they should have known better; people are right in such things as often as not by accident, or because of previous biases.[55] There were very good reasons for believing that the Japanese would not attack Pearl Harbor or that Buenos Aires would never invade the Falkland Islands.[56]

In the case of Iraq, few specialists thought Hussein would resort to force. Indeed, there was very good evidence for the case that Hussein was bluffing. Most Arab leaders insistently argued that this was the case. If Hussein intended to invade, many analysts asked, why would he conduct his buildup in such a blatant fashion? Moreover, the risks of attacking a "brother" Arab state were—as we have seen—legion. In retrospect, given the way the war went, those who were arguing that Iraq would not invade had a point—Hussein obviously should not have done so; the risks were too great.

A second, and probably more common, type of warning failure occurs when a nation has a warning but does not make use of it. Leaders may ignore warnings for a number of reasons. Some of the practical barriers to making bold deterrent threats were noted previously; these would inhibit any response to a warning. In a case such as Kuwait, where no formal security commitment had yet been made, the problem was especially acute. Deterrence theorists Alexander George and Richard Smoke have written of the Berlin crisis in 1948 that

> seizing upon the available warning to "reinforce" deterrence would not have meant the reaffirmation of an existing commitment, since a commitment to West Berlin did not yet exist. Rather, a new decision would have had to be made whether to make such a firm commitment and to accept significant costs and risks in upholding it. Officials within the [Truman] administration were badly divided over the wisdom of trying to defend the Western outpost that lay deep in Soviet-occupied East Germany.[57]

Once the intelligence services did predict an Iraqi invasion, Bush administration officials undoubtedly went through similar pains in 1990.

Faced with strong evidence of an impending challenge to deterrence yet unwilling or unable to respond to it, government officials can respond with a psychological strategy known as cognitive dissonance. Seeking to justify their preconceptions and shore up their hope for peace, officials will gradually discount or eliminate in their own minds evidence to the contrary. Preexisting biases and beliefs obviously play a strong role in this process, which Robert Jervis terms "protecting an established belief"[58]—something British leaders certainly did in discounting the risks of an Argentine invasion.[59] One danger of this tactic is that it distracts attention from a search for means of bolstering deterrence or plans for responding to deterrence failure; faced with a crushing dilemma over Berlin, for example, it was easier for Truman administration officials "to believe that the Soviets would not undertake serious action against West Berlin than to decide beforehand what the American response would be to such an eventuality."[60]

There is some evidence that this process was at work within the Bush administration in the months before the Iraqi invasion of Kuwait. U.S. officials had pressed for better relations with Iraq since 1980, attempting to counter Iran's growing fundamentalist influence. The Reagan and Bush administrations maintained close contacts with Baghdad, approved vast credits and high-technology exports, and fought hard against congressional attempts to sanction Iraq for its abysmal record on human rights.[61] This long history created a strong predisposition for U.S. officials to reject the notion that they had created a political and military monster in a region of vital U.S. interests—to reject, that is, the idea that Iraq would resort to force of arms in its dispute with Kuwait.

The Fateful Meeting

It was in this context that U.S. ambassador April Glaspie met with Saddam Hussein on July 25. Glaspie had been trying to see him for a week, ever since his July 17 threats; she had met with other Iraqi officials and conveyed the U.S. concern over the escalating tensions and Iraq's bullying of its Arab neighbors. Now she was summoned at short notice to see Hussein himself. Perhaps, she would later say, the U.S. exercise with the UAE had caught his attention. She had no time to confer with the State Department in Washington, but there seemed little need to do so; U.S. policy toward Iraq was well established, if confused. Washington continued to desire better relations with Baghdad; the Bush administration was concerned about inflammatory Iraqi rhetoric, both toward Israel and Kuwait, but the United States was unwilling—and perhaps unable—to make anything but unemotional statements of support for Iraq's Arab neighbors.

This was the flavor of Glaspie's message to Saddam—a perfectly understandable reiteration of U.S. policy. Glaspie says she explained that the United States "would not countenance violence or in fact threat of intimidation," that "we would defend our vital interests, we would support our friends in the Gulf, we would defend their sovereignty and integrity." Yet at the same time Glaspie admitted that the United States had "no opinion on the Arab-Arab conflicts, like your border disagreement with Kuwait." Later she would claim that this point was made in a different context, that she was pointing out that the United States could not help Iraq press its claim on Kuwait. Glaspie also joined the bandwagon of U.S. officials hammering the Western media for their portrayals of Hussein and his regime, calling a recent ABC news story "cheap and unjust." She reiterated the U.S. desire for better relations with Iraq.[62]

In later testimony before the U.S. Congress, Glaspie defended her actions, portraying her warnings to Hussein as stern and her conciliatory tone as unimportant. But a group of secret State Department cables released several months after her testimony suggests that she did little to convey U.S. seriousness about Iraq's threats against Kuwait. The cables, sent by Glaspie after her meeting and on other occasions, reportedly indicate that she repeatedly expressed to Hussein the Bush administration's desire for better relations and opposed confronting the Iraqi leader. "I believe we would now be well-advised," she wrote, "to ease off on public criticism of Iraq until we see how the negotiations develop."[63]

In her congressional testimony, Glaspie claimed she told Hussein directly that the United States considered Kuwait a vital security interest. According to reporters who have had access to them, the cables contain no reference to such a statement. They also apparently indicate that Glaspie's admission that the United States took "no position on" Arab border disputes may have occurred in a broader context than she suggested to Congress. The questions she posed about Iraq's buildup opposite Kuwait, she wrote, were asked "in the spirit of friendship, not confrontation."

At the end of the meeting, satisfied that Saddam would continue to engage in negotiations with Kuwait and sensing that the crisis might be on its way to resolution, Glaspie decided to leave Baghdad the following Monday for the United States. Saddam Hussein's "emphasis that he wants peaceful settlement," she cabled the State Department, "is surely sincere."

Perhaps reflecting that the tone of her cables was more conciliatory than previously admitted, other U.S. diplomats were not so sanguine about Hussein's intentions. Before she left Baghdad, Glaspie sent an account of her discussion to the U.S. Embassy in Kuwait. One report even suggests that U.S. ambassador W. Nathaniel Howell and chargé d'affaires Barbara Bodine were worried about Saddam's language; they found it bellicose and threatening. They may also have feared the consequences of Glaspie's overly polite rebukes. The two diplomats drafted a long cable for the Department of State, predicting that Saddam might take out his frustration on the Gulf states by seizing parts of Kuwait.[64]

On Friday, July 27, the growing impression that Saddam was bluffing seemed to be confirmed.[65] Prince Bandar met with Chairman Powell and said all his contacts in the Middle East—in Iraq and elsewhere—agreed that Iraq would not invade. King Hussein of Jordan had added his voice to that of Mubarak in saying that he had received a promise from Saddam Hussein that the troop movements were only "exercises." That same day, Under Secretary of State for Political Affairs Robert Kimmitt chaired a deputies meeting on the Iraq-Kuwait situation. Most of those present had been put at ease by the repeated reassurances from other Arab leaders about Saddam, and in any case there were still strong reasons to believe Iraq would not tempt fate by attacking another Arab nation. The meeting approved a mild note calling on Iraq to reciprocate the U.S. desire for improved relations; this was apparently sent on July 28.[66] Proposals by Assistant Secretary of Defense Paul Wolfowitz for stronger signals were rejected, first by the deputies committee and later by Colin Powell.

A Call for Action

Again, a prescient warning emerged outside the government. On July 29, Center for Strategic and International Studies Middle East expert Shireen

Hunter warned in the *Los Angeles Times* that Hussein's policies might not be all bluff after all. "The West is once more in danger of misreading the nature of Iraq's president, Saddam Hussein, and his ambitions for his country," she began. "Unless there is a clear-sighted view of his intentions and an effective response to them, Western interests in the Persian Gulf will be in deep jeopardy."

Hunter went on to argue that Hussein had proved his expansionist bent with his attack on Iran and that his muted rhetoric in recent years was purely a tactical device. His policy had succeeded in garnering massive Western support despite Iraq's vast abuses of human rights. Now, Hussein's threats against Kuwait were being viewed "as pure posturing" by Western analysts who "cautioned against antagonizing Hussein."

"This analysis is seriously in error," Hunter warned. "There can be no doubt that Iraq wants to become the dominant power in the Persian Gulf, which its own 30 miles of coastline does not merit. Thus, it must control the Iranian shoreline or that of Kuwait."

Hunter did not predict a full Iraqi invasion, but neither did she rule it out. At the least she expected the Iraqi president to extort oil fields or oil-rich islands from Kuwait. Hunter recommended economic sanctions on Iraq; if cutting credits was not enough, "an economic boycott, including Iraq's oil, may be necessary."

In general, Hunter urged that the United States and its allies "see Hussein for what he really is and stop entertaining false hopes." Some signal had to be sent that Iraqi expansionism would not be tolerated. "The West must act," she pleaded, "before it is too late."[67]

The Final Chance for a Warning

Meanwhile, new warning bells were again going off in the government as well, but even at this late date, they would have little effect. On July 31, the *Washington Post* published a CIA estimate that there were now 100,000 Iraqis on the border.[68] That same day, Pat Lang, the Defense Intelligence Agency's warning officer for the region, reportedly wrote his first direct warning that the Iraqis would invade and do so quickly.[69] Lang was ordered to relay the most recent information about Iraqi movements to the Kuwaiti ambassador. Yet even this new analysis failed to change the widespread perception within the U.S. government that Saddam was merely bluffing. If Bob Woodward's recent book is to be believed, up until the last minute virtually everyone but Lang discounted the chance of an invasion.

On July 31, therefore, the administration continued about its business of vague promises of support to "friends in the Gulf" and statements of a desire for closer ties with Iraq. Assistant Secretary for Near East and South Asian Affairs John Kelly testified that day before a subcommittee of the House Foreign

Affairs Committee. Even this close to the invasion, the focus of the hearing was surprisingly diffuse: Of Kelly's spoken statement, one-half page deals with Iraq and two-and-a-half pages with Israel, the peace process, Lebanon, and other topics; only a page and a half of his ten-page written statement focuses on Iraq; and just over fourteen of thirty-six question-and-answer pages of transcript deal with Iraq. Even at this late date, Kelly brushed off congressional demands for sanctions on Iraq, arguing that the administration needed flexibility in dealing even with problem nations.

The U.S. government was worried by Iraq's belligerence, Kelly testified, and intended "to do all we can to support our friends when they are threatened and to preserve stability." The administration had indeed responded to Hussein's buildup on the Kuwaiti border, Kelly argued—"by speaking out publicly against these Iraqi tactics" and supporting Arab efforts at mediation. "Iraq is a major power in the region," Kelly concluded. "This power carries responsibility with it. We would hope that Iraq could act in a manner that demonstrates it appreciates this point." And although the United States had taken no position on regional border disputes, it had "taken a strong position in support of the sovereignty of all states in the area."[70]

But just how far, the Congress wanted to know, did this "position" extend? Congressman Lee Hamilton pressed the point. "What is precisely the nature of our commitment to supporting our friends in the Gulf?" Hamilton said he had read a press report that seemed to indicate Defense Secretary Cheney had committed U.S. troops in case Kuwait was attacked.

"I am not familiar with the quotation that you just referred to," Kelly replied, "but I am confident in the administration's position on the issue. We have no defense treaty relationship with any Gulf country. That is clear." Washington did support "the security and independence of friendly states in the region" and the "peaceful resolution of any differences." But it had no binding treaty obligations.

After another brief exchange in which Kelly repeated that "we have no defense treaty relationships with any of the countries," Hamilton posed a hypothetical question. "If Iraq, for example, charged across the border into Kuwait, for whatever reason, what would be our position with regard to the use of U.S. forces?"

Kelly did not like the question. "That, Mr. Chairman, is a hypothetical or a contingency, the kind of which I can't get into. Suffice it to say we would be extremely concerned, but I cannot get into the realm of 'what if' answers."

Hamilton was undeterred. "In that circumstance, it is correct to say, however, that we do not have a treaty commitment which would obligate us to engage U.S. forces?"

"That is correct," replied Kelly.

For emphasis, Hamilton asked again. "That is correct, is it not?"

"That is correct, sir."

The BBC World Service carried a report of Kelly's testimony around the globe—including to Baghdad. Kelly was merely stating fact: The United States had no security treaties with Arab states. But to the rest of the world, especially to top leaders in Baghdad undoubtedly trying to reassure themselves about their imminent, monumental gamble, the testimony must have sounded strikingly like a write-off.

The same day, at a meeting among top Defense Department officials including Secretary Cheney, "the consensus was that [Saddam] would not invade."[71]

The Challenge of Deterrence

Although it had not yet fully accepted the imminent reality of an Iraqi invasion, the Bush administration did at the last moment attempt to send deterrent signals to convince Baghdad that the United States would not tolerate aggression. As is often the case, however, these signals failed. The Gulf crisis and war demonstrated once again that it is enormously difficult to calibrate signals with the degree of exactness demanded by classical deterrence theory. In the case of the Falklands conflict, for example, the Thatcher government sent a few signals, but none were public or clear enough to convince the Argentine leaders, already enmeshed in cognitive dissonance, that Britain would fight. In particular, signals can be missed if they are not sufficiently different from the norm—mere rhetoric about commitments or general policy may not be enough.

In part the signals failed because the Iraqi government was not about to be deterred. In earlier sections of this chapter we examined deterrence problems that issue from the deterring nation, but critics of classical deterrence theory have also pointed to shortcomings related to the nature of the aggressor states that are the targets of deterrence. Of most interest is the attitude and thought process of the aggressor. The way in which expansionist nations conceive of their own interests, and those of potential adversaries, modify the degree to which they are subject to deterrent threats.

For one thing, aggressor nations may have a starkly different view of their interests than outside observers can conceive of.[72] Many nations and national leaders feel far more intensely about certain issues than can be detected by others. Partly due to an accelerating and unstable internal political dynamic, for example, Argentina's leaders wanted the Falkland Islands back more strongly than London imagined at the time. Similarly, Saddam Hussein must have possessed regional ambitions, resentment of the Kuwaitis, and fear of domestic opposition of a nature Westerners were not able to appreciate. The targets of deterrence can have many reasons for desiring hostilities—such as an expectation of a shift in a regional balance of power, a tottering political system, and the weakness of individual political leaders.[73] An aggressor's calculation of its own interests is not entirely predictable, making the sort of risk-and-cost calculations of classical deterrence a very difficult—and risky—business.

In part this unpredictable thought pattern is a result of the inward focus of most developing world leaders. If a potential aggressor does not understand a nation that is attempting to deter it, it may make unwarranted conclusions about the deterrer's ability or willingness to fulfill its commitments. As in Korea in 1950 and in many other cases, Iraq in 1990 was ruled by a man who fundamentally miscalculated the U.S. response to his aggression; like Kim Il Sung before him, Saddam Hussein had little knowledge of the Western world.[74]

An aggressor's calculation of costs and benefits, then, can be irrational or at least subjective. In this sense aggressors suffer from the same sort of cognitive dissonance that plagues deterring states—once determined to challenge deterrence, they will reject evidence or views that do not accord with their presumptions. "Once a state is committed to a belligerent policy," Jervis notes, "it will downgrade the risks involved and come to believe, in the face of massive evidence to the contrary, that the other side will not dare to go to war."[75] Argentine leaders did this before they invaded the Falklands; it is likely that Iraqi officials did the same thing in 1990.

Arab Negotiations Fail

Negotiations among the Arab states were coming to a head. The Saudis had managed to put together a last-minute meeting in Jeddah with the Kuwaitis and the Iraqis.[76] The meeting opened on a poor note when the Kuwaiti emir spurned the session, sending the crown prince instead. Hussein retaliated by refusing to attend and sending some of his top aides in his stead.

Once the conference officially began, on the evening of July 31 Saudi time, things did not go much better. The Iraqis made lengthy accusations against Kuwait, which denied all of them. The Iraqis demanded $10 billion in cash, either as aid or as a loan; the Kuwaiti crown prince offered $9 billion but was rebuffed. Later the Saudis would offer to make up the difference with a billion of their own. But the crown prince then issued a demand: The border dispute between Iraq and Kuwait would have to be resolved before the issue of aid or loans could be discussed. It was now the Iraqi turn to refuse and to issue thinly veiled threats of what might happen to Kuwait if the various issues were not settled to Iraq's satisfaction.

The meeting broke up the next day, August 1, having settled nothing. Flying back to Kuwait City, the crown prince confided to other Kuwaiti officials. "I have a premonition," he said, "of disaster."[77]

3

The Failure of Diplomacy

On August 2, 1990, it became painfully clear that the United States had failed to deter Saddam Hussein from seizing Kuwait. Even on August 1, however, the signals of Hussein's intentions remained mixed. There was certainly reason to believe an invasion was imminent. U.S. satellite photos then showed the Iraqi units north of Kuwait deployed in battle line, ready to move onto a four-lane highway running into Kuwait City. Support and supply troops—with ammunition, food, water, and gasoline—were deployed as well. All was ready for an invasion. Pat Lang at the Defense Intelligence Agency (DIA) sent out a flash warning: The invasion was imminent. Even the CIA, cautious to this point, now concluded that an invasion was probable.[1]

Still, many continued to believe that these elaborate preparations were merely designed to firmly convince the Kuwaitis that Iraq was about to invade. After all, a bluff will not work if it does not look like the real thing. Reportedly, at a top-level briefing by General Schwarzkopf that afternoon, neither the Central Command chief nor Secretary of Defense Cheney predicted an invasion.[2] That same day, King Hussein called Bush from Jordan, arguing that Saddam was not going to invade.[3] The State Department called in the Iraqi ambassador at 3 o'clock that afternoon—as it turned out, roughly one hour before the Iraqi invasion began—and sternly warned him that the United States would insist on peaceful settlement of disputes. The ambassador assured U.S. officials of his government's peaceful intent, and many U.S. officials continued to believe that the warning had been heeded. In fact, the Iraqi ambassador was probably still sitting at State chatting with U.S. officials when Saddam's tanks began moving south.

The Iraqi Invasion

On August 2, at roughly 0100 hours Kuwait time, Saddam Hussein's army rolled into Kuwait (see Figure 3.1). The Kuwaitis, helped by a new surveillance radar attached to a balloon, received a few hours' warning of the attack, and the emir, the ruling Al Sabah family, and certain elements of the Kuwaiti military were able to flee.[4] The Kuwaiti people were not so lucky; within a number of hours, the whole of tiny Kuwait was in Iraqi hands. The apparent speed and efficiency of the operation impressed U.S. military officials watching the terrible spectacle through the precise eyes of orbiting intelligence satellites. The voluminous Department of Defense report on the war summarized the assault this way:

> At 0100 (Kuwait time), 2 August, three Iraqi Republican Guard Forces Command (RGFC) divisions attacked across the Kuwaiti frontier. A mechanized infantry division and an armored division conducted the main attack south into Kuwait along the Safwan-'Abdally axis, driving for the Al-Jahra pass. Another armored division conducted a supporting attack farther west. Almost simultaneously, at 0130, a special operations force conducted the first attack on Kuwait City—a heliborne assault against key government facilities. Meanwhile, commando teams made amphibious assaults against the Amir's palace and other key facilities. The Amir was able to escape into Saudi Arabia, but his brother was killed in the Iraqi assault on the Dasman Palace.
>
> The three attacking armored and mechanized formations, supported by combat aircraft, linked up at Al-Jahra. The two divisions conducting the main attack continued east to Kuwait City, where they joined the special operations forces by 0530. By 1900, Iraqi forces had secured the city. Concurrently, the supporting armored division moved south from Al-Jahra to establish blocking positions on the main avenues of approach from the Saudi border. By the evening of 2 August, Iraqi tanks were moving south of the capital along the coast to occupy Kuwait's ports.[5]

The reaction of the United States, and indeed the world, was swift. Within a day both President Bush and the United Nations had condemned the invasion and demanded an unconditional Iraqi withdrawal. Bush and his aides held series after series of sober, sometimes tense, meetings; everyone agreed that providing guarantees for the security of other Gulf states would constitute the minimum U.S. reaction. As early as August 4, however, Bush committed himself to something far more ambitious: "This will not stand," he said on the White House lawn, "this aggression against Kuwait."

Other pieces of the world response were falling into place. On August 5, the United Nations voted an economic embargo against Iraq; on the twenty-fourth, it would authorize the use of force to implement that embargo. In Saudi Arabia on August 6, King Fahd gave Defense Secretary Cheney Saudi approval for a massive U.S. military buildup in the kingdom. Reached by Cheney after the meeting, Bush authorized the Department of Defense to implement its Operations Plan 1002, providing for the defense of Saudi Arabia.

That Saddam Hussein did not take seriously the risks inherent in his new course became apparent on August 6. On that day, Saddam met with Joseph Wilson, the chargé d'affaires at the U.S. Embassy in Baghdad. The Iraqi

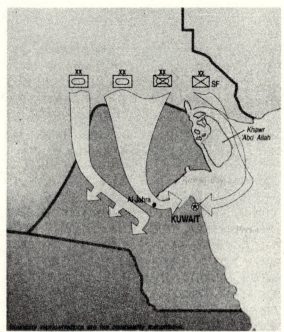

FIGURE 3.1 Iraqi Assault Operations, August 2, 1990. *Source:* Department of Defense, "The Conduct of the Persian Gulf War," Final Report to Congress, April 1992, p. 2.

leader appeared to believe that relations with the United States could quickly return to normal. Hussein pledged that he would not invade Saudi Arabia and hinted that a powerful Iraq could become a major U.S. ally in the Middle East. His megalomania was in high gear; he warned the United States against a war it would lose. According to *New York Times* reporter Elaine Sciolino, Saddam concluded the interview with childish braggadocio. "By the way," he said as Wilson was leaving, "say hello to President Bush. And tell him that Jaber and his clique are finished; they're history. The Sabah family are has-beens."[6]

President Bush intended otherwise. Bush seems to have decided almost immediately on a vigorous response to Hussein's aggression, one that would guarantee Iraq's total withdrawal from Kuwait. That such a course would mean war only became apparent later, although the prospect did not deter Bush. The violation of international law and the threat to the world's oil life-line were so clear that appeasement would be a disaster. Given Saddam's stubbornness, war may have been inevitable after August 4.

Meanwhile, the huge military buildup that Bush had authorized began creaking into motion. The first members of what would become an army half a million strong—a single brigade of the 82nd Airborne Division and a handful of U.S. F-15 fighters—arrived in Saudi Arabia on August 8. There were U.S. Navy vessels in the region as well—most notably the carriers *Independence* and *Eisenhower*—but on the whole, even when combined with Saudi Arabia's 70,000-man army, the U.S. forces on the ground probably would not have been able to stand up to an Iraqi attack. U.S. officials knew this—the question was whether the Iraqis did.

"It is idle to speculate," wrote Middle East expert Fouad Ajami, "what Saddam's intentions were once his forces had amassed on the Saudi-Kuwaiti border." Whatever Saddam's plans, Ajami wrote after the war, "Saudi leaders hold no illusions about what would have come to pass had Saddam's army swept across the border: Iraqis could have reached the capital city of Riyadh in three days. Saddam could have decapitated the regime and shattered the ethos of its Nadji heartland, based as it is on conquest and chivalry and the memory of a warring past. The entire social contract of the Saudi state could have collapsed. Saddam could have severed the eastern province of the kingdom with its oil reserves from the rest of the Saudi realm. The state bequeathed to the House of Saud by Ibn Saud would have been up for grabs."[7] From the perspective of the U.S. government, an Iraqi push into Saudi Arabia would leave Saddam Hussein's armies astride 40 percent of the world's oil reserves, with his fist firmly clenched around the world's economic neck.

Postinvasion Deterrence

By August 3, Iraqi armies stood poised to take northeastern Saudi Arabia and become masters of almost half the world's oil. The economies of the developed world lay vulnerable to Saddam's whim, and the U.S. and Allied task quickly shifted to deterring an invasion of Saudi Arabia. The previous chapter outlined potential flaws in deterrence theory, but it would be wrong to write off the theory completely. The basics of deterrence theory—that if the United States is strongly committed to the defense of an ally, attacks on that ally will be discouraged—make a great deal of sense. And not a single nation boasting a strong U.S. political commitment and the presence of a U.S. "tripwire" force has been attacked since 1945. It is only when U.S. leaders have been unable to implement fully the strategies of the deterrence theorists that problems have arisen. But the theory should be regarded as merely one additional arrow in the U.S. diplomatic and military quiver, to be employed selectively and where vital interests are clearly at stake.

Saddam Hussein's bold gamble allows us to place the debate over classical deterrence theory in a new light. Part of the criticism of that theory has clearly been validated: Because rational deterrence does not always work, the United States will not always be able to prevent other countries from threatening its interests, and once they have begun to do so, the United States will not always be able to make them stop. But those shortcomings are a product not of the bankruptcy of deterrence theory itself but of the inability of the United States to implement that theory on all occasions. In the present example, deploying a tripwire force of soldiers to Kuwait was not a political option in July 1990. If it *had* been, however—and this recognition is what demands some reform of the antideterrence case—it is possible that deterrence would have worked.

A recent study of extended deterrence indeed suggests that it often does work. Scholar Paul Huth subjected numerous cases of deterrence success and failure to statistical analysis, and his conclusions were somewhat surprising: Indices of classical deterrence, including reputation for strength, tough retaliatory policies, and "firm but flexible" diplomatic strategies, significantly increased the chance of deterrence success. Huth writes:

> One important conclusion of this book . . . is that short-term military and diplomatic actions do have a strong impact on crisis outcomes. . . . The adoption by the defender of both a firm-but-flexible position in negotiations and a policy of tit for tat in military escalation contributed substantially to the success of deterrence, whereas alternate diplomatic and military strategies were less effective, if not counterproductive.[8]

Indeed, once Hussein had taken Kuwait, U.S. policy advanced to a second deterrent goal: preventing an Iraqi attack on Saudi Arabia. Iraq had thrown into Kuwait tens of thousands more troops than it actually required to capture the tiny nation, and U.S. officials were concerned that the extra forces spoke to a desire to keep rolling south. In the hours and days after August 2, U.S. intelligence agencies watched the growing Iraqi force in Kuwait with great concern. A quick Iraqi push into the Saudi oil fields probably could not be stopped.

The First Phase of the Coalition Military Buildup

The Iraqi attack did not come, but U.S. and coalition soldiers did, by the hundreds of thousands. The first phase of the conflict involved a more rapid buildup of military power than in Vietnam or Korea—Operation Desert Shield. Beginning in early August and extending through February, dozens of military units converged on Saudi Arabia from all over the world. In the beginning, President Bush said that the mission of these troops was wholly defensive, to protect the Saudi kingdom.

The first major combat unit to arrive was the U.S. 82nd Airborne Division; quickly following were the 101st Air Assault and the 24th Mechanized divisions, the other major units in the U.S. rapid deployment force. The 24th Division in particular had an impressive deployment schedule:[9] On August 13, the first of seven 55,000-ton fast sealift ships, as well as three slower transport ships, left the U.S. Gulf coast with the division's equipment. Meanwhile other equipment and many of the division's personnel began flying to Saudi Arabia in almost 60 aircraft, mostly civilian airliners. The fast sealift ships averaged a fourteen-day transit to the Gulf, the slower ships twenty-six days; the first heavy equipment, the division's M1A1 tanks and Bradley armored fighting vehicles, began arriving at the end of August, and the last ship arrived on September 20.

The 24th Division arrived in Saudi Arabia through the port of Damman on the eastern or Gulf coast after having traveled over 10,000 miles from the port of Savannah, Georgia, on the U.S. Atlantic coast. Once ashore, the division moved 160 miles into the country and set up a defensive position over about 4,500 square miles of territory near the town of As Sarrar. When fully deployed and in place, the division consisted of 18,000 men and women—a small city transplanted from continent to continent—1,574 armored vehicles, 3,500 wheeled vehicles, and 90 helicopters.[10]

On August 15, the first marine units were in place. The marines traveled differently than the army: Marine divisions use maritime prepositioning, prestocked equipment stores loaded aboard ships and placed at strategic locations throughout the world. Marine units therefore did not need to bring all of their equipment from the United States. Many marine units fly only their soldiers to the trouble spot, where the troops meet their maritime prepositioning ships (MPSs) and receive their equipment. This economizes transportation assets: A Marine Expeditionary Brigade (or MEB), about 17,000 strong, can deploy in just 250 C-141 transport flights, rather than the 3,000 it would take if all the equipment had to be flown in.

The marine corps deploys three MPS "squadrons"—one in the Atlantic, one in the Pacific, and one at Diego Garcia. Each consists of about four MPSs, which together hold a vast amount of equipment and supplies: some 50 tanks, 100 amphibious vehicles, 30 armored cars, 40 artillery pieces, 300 trucks, and over a million meal packets. *Each* ship carries roughly 12,000 tons (over $5 billion worth) of equipment and supplies, enough to keep the 17,000 men of an MEB supplied for a month. Using such equipment, major elements of the 1st Marine Expeditionary Force—the equivalent of a division, containing three MEBs—were in place by the end of August.

Coalition members besides the United States also committed major ground units. On August 10, the Arab League voted to support Saudi Arabia militarily, and by the end of the month Egypt alone had dispatched over 5,000 troops. Later they would be joined by units from Syria, Morocco, Pakistan, and other Arab states as well as the Gulf Cooperation Council. In September both Britain and France pledged major combat units, each sending a brigade at first and later expanding those forces to a full division in anticipation of ground operations. By February the British 1st Armored Division was in place with 180 tanks and nearly 90 artillery pieces to support the coalition's center punch into Iraq and Kuwait; the French 6th Light Armored Division (LAD) was deployed to the west, screening the coalition's left flank. A host of other nations eventually contributed military forces, medical personnel, or support units or ships: Afghanistan, Argentina, Australia, Bangladesh, Belgium, Canada, Czechoslovakia, Denmark, Germany, Greece, Hungary, Italy, the Netherlands, Niger, Norway, New Zealand, Poland, Portugal, the Republic of Korea, Senegal, tiny Sierra Leone, Singapore, Spain, Sweden, and Turkey.

U.S. tactical air units flew into Saudi Arabia, Turkey, and other regional states through November. By about the end of October, the U.S Air Force already had hundreds of aircraft in place—150 F-15 and F-16 attack aircraft, 70 A-10 ground-support planes, 22 stealth fighters, and dozens of other planes. By the beginning of the ground war in February, there were nearly 2,000 U.S. aircraft in the region, including naval planes on carriers. Twelve air force tactical fighter wings were deployed to the Gulf, as well as two wings of B-52s and selected other support and reconnaissance aircraft.

The U.S. and coalition naval presence also expanded rapidly during this period. The initial core of two U.S. aircraft carriers and several support ships would grow by January to 6 carrier battle groups, 2 battleships, and an amphibious task force—more than 100 U.S. ships in the region. Naval units from a host of other coalition countries participated in the embargo and other noncombat operations—countries including Argentina, Australia, Belgium, Canada, Denmark, France, Greece, Italy, the Netherlands, Norway, Spain, and the United Kingdom. The French carrier *Clemenceau* was deployed to the region, and the British carrier *Ark Royal* steamed into the Mediterranean to replace U.S. carriers sent to the Middle East.[11]

The Role of U.S. Reserve Units

During the early phases of the coalition military buildup, the United States began to recall tens of thousands of military reservists. Leaving home, family, and job, these dedicated individuals responded to the call and set off, in many cases to put their lives on the line. Army, air force, and marine reserve and National Guard units—combat as well as support—were recalled for the war and in general performed very well, providing critical support to coalition operations throughout the theater. This was one of the most positive aspects of the U.S. contribution to the war effort.

The reserve call-up did not take place without controversy, however, and some key lessons of the war relate to the organization and purpose of the U.S. National Guard and reserve. Within the army, a controversy arose over the status of the "roundout" brigades—National Guard combat brigades assigned to incomplete active-duty divisions to bring them up to full three-brigade strength. The Department of Defense chose not to recall these units until November, and because of the requirement for predeployment training, none of them made it to the Gulf before the war ended. From this experience, many observers suggest that "the guard wasn't ready"—a damning conclusion given that the Defense Department had spent $100 billion over the previous decade on National Guard equipment and training.

Writing off the readiness of the guard would be premature. To be sure, there are real limits on what can be expected of guard and reserve forces—and what is most important, some of these limitations have particular relevance for the U.S. shift to a regional contingencies strategy. Guard and reserve forces cannot be expected to be as deployable as active-duty forces, and including them as part of rapid-deployment forces is a mistake. If a unit is expected to be on the way to battle inside of a week, it will have little time to prepare, and the guard and reserve needed more time.

Certain guard and reserve units can be ready very quickly. Support and supply units, which need little predeployment training, deployed rapidly during Operation Desert Shield, as did particular kinds of combat forces. Units organized around a single weapon or function, which require fewer large-unit, combined-arms exercises than combat brigades, deployed effectively. Reserve artillery units assigned to U.S. VII Corps, for example, performed well in the Gulf War according to the corps commander. Finally, smaller combat units (companies or battalions) can be given predeployment training and made ready to fight far earlier than bigger units like brigades and divisions, which have to master the intricate integration of large-unit, combined-arms operations, logistics, and so on. Indeed, this is the way the marines used their reserves, at the company and battalion level, to fill out their divisions.

Moreover, the guard probably *could have* played a larger role in the Gulf War. Secretary of Defense Cheney authorized the first reserve call-ups on August 24 but specifically prohibited recall of the roundout brigades. He later explained that because of the six-month limit on presidential call-up authority, he was advised that the brigades might not be available long enough to make a recall worthwhile. Only in November, after the Congress authorized call-up authority for a full year, were the three roundout brigades—the 48th, 155th, and 256th—activated. This shift in time schedules necessitated a revamping of the brigades' postmobilization training, which caused much of the subsequent controversy.

Given the need to create a total army force structure more applicable to the post–cold war era, the relevant issues are for what missions and in what time frames should guard units be organized, staffed, and equipped. Larger guard units are not and will never be as prepared for war in peacetime as active-duty forces, but they are capable enough to be ready for an appropriately designed mission within weeks of being activated. Political considerations also suggest that it would be unwise to abandon the total force concept entirely, and the army would undoubtedly not favor such a step. The policy was begun in 1973 near the close of the Vietnam War by an army determined to not be committed piecemeal again to an unpopular war. So the army shifted many of its support and supply units to the guard and reserve, expecting that the need to call major portions of civilians to battle would both deter unpopular wars and solidify public support behind just ones. In this respect the total force policy can be said to have been a complete success: Polls showed that President Bush's decision to call up the reserves, though done incrementally, indeed was an important element in galvanizing public opinion.

Two reforms appear necessary. First, the army and the guard must reexamine the issue of what kind of guard and reserve units are to be included in its contingency forces. The army and the guard would not want to eliminate reserve forces entirely from the mix—eliminating reserve elements would undermine not only military capabilities but also the public support value of callups—but they might wish to limit the units more rigidly to supply, support, and single-weapon or single-function units, which would counsel against roundout combat brigades in contingency forces.

Second and more broadly, the army and the guard must rethink the larger issue of the appropriate size and structure of the post–cold war National Guard. With the decline of the Soviet threat, there is little apparent value in keeping the same number of major reserve combat elements, particularly if they are not needed in contingency operations. The concepts of fill-out and cadre force structures should also carefully be considered as the new post–cold war force structure is sized and organized.

Assembling an International Consensus

Through August and much of September 1990, the Bush administration labored to assemble an international consensus on the need to reverse Iraq's aggression. Providing backbone to the coalition were a series of United Nations resolutions, the most important of which—save one—were in place by the end of August. Resolution 660, adopted on August 2, condemned the Iraqi invasion and demanded an immediate and unconditional withdrawal. Four days later, Resolution 661 imposed the trade and financial embargo; Resolution 622, passed August 9, declared Iraq's attempted annexation of Kuwait null and void. On August 25, the United States secured permission, in Resolution 665, for member states enforcing the embargo to halt and inspect ships. During this period U.S. officials traveled the globe promoting opposition to the Iraqi invasion and building a case for the use of force.

By the end of September, the risk of war was palpable. If it was strangled by the embargo, Baghdad warned on the twenty-second, it would lash out at Saudi Arabia and Israel. Three days later, Soviet foreign minister Eduard Shevardnadze spoke before the United Nations (UN) General Assembly and suggested that Moscow would support UN-sanctioned military action against Iraq. That same day the Security Council voted to expand the embargo against Iraq to include aircraft, raising the potential of a midair confrontation.

During September, both Iraq and the United States began making unequivocal statements and demands, closing off options and dimming the potential for a negotiated settlement. On September 21, the Iraqi Revolutionary Command Council denounced the coalition deployment and promised that there was no possibility of a retreat from Kuwait. "There is not a single chance for any retreat," the announcement warned. "Let everybody understand that this battle is going to become the mother of all battles."[12]

One week later, President Bush met with the emir of Kuwait in the Oval Office. Bush was moved by the exiled leader's plea for help, although neither reportedly discussed the possibility of offensive action by the coalition to drive Iraqi forces from Kuwait. But Bush's conviction to secure the freedom of Kuwait and its people may well have been strengthened.

Regardless, the efforts to promote a negotiated solution continued. French president François Mitterrand suggested on September 24 that Iraq withdraw and the Kuwaiti people make a "democratic expression of choice" about their government. Mitterrand's proposal did not require the return to power of the Sabah family in Kuwait and thus ran counter to the U.S. and UN positions. In early October, Soviet envoy Evgeny Primakov went to Baghdad and urged an immediate Iraqi withdrawal, implying that Hussein might be able to keep the Rumaylah oil field and Bubiyan and Warba islands. By the middle of the month, Soviet news agencies were reporting that Hussein might just accept such a bargain.

Later in October, however, and into early November, the positions of both sides hardened as each apparently prepared for war. Tariq Aziz had spoken uncompromisingly before the General Assembly on October 5, leaving little hope for agreement. On the sixteenth, Secretary of State James Baker rejected the notion of territorial concessions, refusing to accept the transfer of any oil fields or islands as a reward for Iraq's aggression. By early November, Baker was jetting around the world garnering support for a military option; on November 6 the Chinese said they would not veto a UN resolution authorizing force. Polls of U.S. public opinion were beginning to show support for a military option. On November 6, British prime minister Margaret Thatcher vowed to push Iraq from Kuwait by force if necessary; the following day, Soviet foreign minister Shevardnadze admitted that Iraq's intransigence might necessitate war.

In fact, U.S. officials began discussing the offensive war option in detail as early as October 10.[13] That day Chief of Staff Major General Robert Johnston of the U.S. Central Command (CENTCOM) presented draft war plans to top U.S. military leaders in the Pentagon. (See Figure 3.2.) CENTCOM was con-

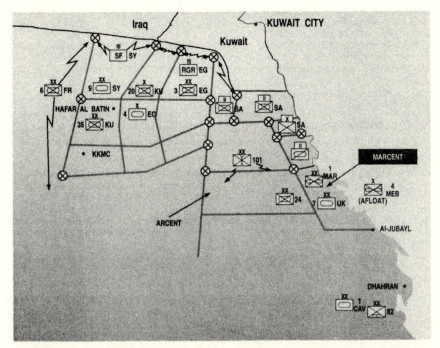

FIGURE 3.2   Coalition Defense, October 1990. *Source:* Department of Defense, "The Conduct of the Persian Gulf War," Final Report to Congress, April 1992, p. 52.

sidering a four-phase operation with three phases of air attack followed by the coup de grace on the ground. The three air stages mirrored very closely the plan that eventually guided U.S. forces. But this early version of the script for war sent the U.S. ground attack directly north into Kuwait City against the most heavily defended Iraqi positions. Powell, Army Chief of Staff Carl Vuono, and Cheney all worried that a direct blow was risky, especially because Iraqi forces still outnumbered U.S. ones. Johnston replied that CENTCOM knew the plan wasn't very good—in fact it believed U.S. forces were not ready for a ground attack and would need an additional armored corps to make one work well.

The next day, Johnston gave the same briefing to President Bush. Again the subject of the ground attack was raised. What would you need, Bush asked, for a full offensive? He was told a specific list of forces would be prepared. Bush promised to make his own decision soon about whether to go over to the offensive.

At the very end of October, in another series of meetings among top officials, Bush made the decision he would announce a week later to the U.S.

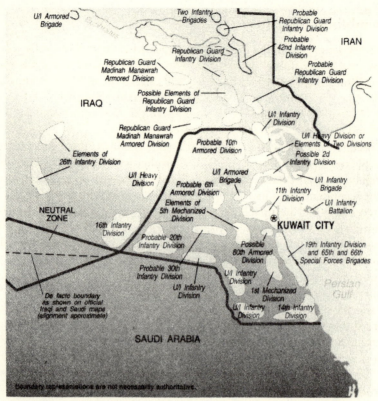

FIGURE 3.3   Iraqi Forces' Disposition as of October 23. *Source:* Department of Defense, "The Conduct of the Persian Gulf War," Final Report to
Congress, April 1992, p. 86.

public. He would prepare for the operation he had been ready to undertake
since August: offensive military operations against Iraq. He gave his military
commanders the go-ahead: He told them to deploy what they needed to prepare to go to war.[14]

In Baghdad, Saddam Hussein had apparently recognized that war might
be inevitable. Just before the Pentagon began discussing CENTCOM's offensive plan, in one of his meetings with Soviet envoy Primakov, Saddam discussed the possibility of war. (See Figure 3.3.) If you do not withdraw,
Primakov warned him, the United States will attack, and Moscow would not
try to prevent it. Saddam said he knew this.

According to Pierre Salinger and Eric Laurent, Primakov replied bluntly.
"But you'll lose," he told Saddam.

The Iraqi leader thought for some time. "Perhaps," he finally replied.[15]

Assembling a Coalition

While Saddam delayed, the Bush administration was methodically assembling a powerful international coalition of nations. Some, like the Arab states, France, and Britain, were major players, key allies in the military buildup; others, like the Soviet Union and China, were important because they did not oppose U.S. policy. Together the coalition gave the U.S. effort political legitimacy and economic, military, and logistical support.

This international assistance was not merely useful; it was absolutely indispensable to the U.S. effort in the Gulf. Another lesson that this war demonstrated beyond any doubt is that the U.S. military is both politically and logistically dependent upon its friends and allies for operations of this scale. The United States will be unable to perform any major contingency operation without a substantial degree of assistance from other nations. The option of going it alone simply does not exist, and all foreign and defense policy decisions must be made with this realization.

In many ways, of course, this war confirmed the general impression of a "unipolar" world in which U.S. power and influence is preeminent. The crisis and war provide yet another example of the sort of threat to U.S. and global interests that appeared to demand a predominantly U.S. response—U.S. leadership, U.S. commitment, and, when the time came, U.S. troops. Without an opposing Soviet-led bloc of Communist nations, the United States appears to have been left as the world's sole remaining superpower, the only nation with overriding political and economic as well as military power. Thus, as noted earlier, Washington led the response to Saddam Hussein's aggression.

It is easy to exaggerate, however, the degree of robustness of the U.S. leadership role in this "unipolar" era. U.S. leaders must execute this role mindful of the expanding roles of multilateral institutions. In the future, as more and more developed and developing states gain a firm stake in the maintenance of the world economic and political order, responses to crises and aggressors will assume an increasingly multilateral dimension.

This multilateralism has already taken the form of explicit U.S. dependence on friends and allies, a dependence that became clearly apparent even during the early buildup of Operation Desert Shield. U.S. leaders must recognize the very real limitations on their freedom of unilateral action. U.S. dependence is threefold: political, logistical, and industrial. These areas are particularly important for the coming era in which facets of national power besides the military—including political and economic power—are of growing importance relative to brute force. This war confirmed that the United States is the world's preeminent military power; politically and economically, however, it remains dependent on allies for legitimacy and assistance.

Politically, the Bush administration depended upon its friends and allies, particularly the Arab members of the coalition, for both international and domestic legitimacy. Internationally, it was support from the United Nations that granted the coalition military operations almost unprecedented legitimacy; participation of major Arab states in the coalition may have been the unique precondition for such world support. U.S. public support for President Bush's policies benefited greatly from the creation of an international coalition and the knowledge that if blood were ultimately to be spilled, it would not be Americans' alone. Such international support helped make the early U.S. deployment both robust and symbolic.

The economic contributions of allies—which had not yet been obtained by August but which would become a prominent element of the war effort—also had very significant political effects. In the strictest sense, the United States could have conducted its military operations without foreign economic support, but justifying those operations to a skeptical U.S. public would have been much more difficult if Washington alone were footing the entire bill. This lesson has not been lost on either the U.S. Congress or the public. In the future, growing constraints on U.S. defense resources will make this sort of multilateral burden-sharing effort even more necessary for the granting of U.S. public support.

Of greatest import to an analysis of Operation Desert Shield, U.S. dependence also has an important logistical aspect. In both the deployment and operational phases, U.S. military forces were dependent on coalition logistical support to a degree that is not widely appreciated. For example, the movement of U.S. VII Corps from central Germany to Saudi Arabia required dozens of European trains, barges, and ships. This logistical operation was orchestrated primarily by four NATO nations using both military and civilian agencies, in essence reversing well-rehearsed NATO plans for the reinforcement of Europe. This intertheater movement would have been beyond the capability of U.S. transportation assets, at the time already overwhelmed with movements from the continental United States.

This issue of military dependence is a pressing one and not restricted to intertheater operations. Without Arab oil, Saudi trucks, and heavy tank transporters from Germany and East European countries and without the coalition's effort to deny Iraq its requirements with the economic embargo, the U.S. military campaign would have been a vastly more difficult proposition. Within the theater, the Saudis alone provided 800 transport trucks for general use, 5,000 tankers and trucks for distribution of 20.4 million barrels of Saudi fuel, water, additional spare parts, communication facilities, and other crucial logistical elements.

Besides being logistically dependent, the United States is also industrially dependent upon friends and allies, even in the defense sector. The near-universal nature of the coalition mitigated the effect of industrial dependence in the Gulf War, but next time U.S. planners might not benefit from such robust international partnerships. During this war U.S. officials were reminded to their discomfort that many badly needed microchips and other electronic equipment in deployed U.S. equipment are now made only in Japan; if Japan decides to sit out the next war, this could become a real problem. Our own defense industrial capacities proved to have previously unrecognized limitations, which may well be best resolved through partnerships with our allies.

Nor was U.S. dependency limited to the prewar and wartime phases of operations. In the aftermath of the war, U.S. forces continued to depend upon allies—for political legitimacy in continued military and refugee operations, for financial and relief support, and for a host of efforts related to clearing away the political and military residue of the war. A good example of the latter was the postwar coalition minesweeping operation in the Gulf: U.S. mine-clearing capabilities, which proved inadequate during the war, were augmented with two-dozen minesweeping ships from nine nations to clear over 1,000 mines from the waters off Kuwait. Even Japan sent four minesweepers—the first time it had sent military forces abroad since 1945.

The lesson is clear: The United States was dependent on allies before, during, and after this war, and there is almost no prospect of being less dependent in any major future war. The implication is that joint planning and training with our allies during peacetime, in bilateral or multilateral forums, is more important than ever. Peacetime agreements, plans, and exercises lay the critical foundations on which effective wartime deployments and campaigns are built.

From Deterrence to Compellence

On November 8, President Bush made his famous decision to double U.S. troop strength in the region. "I have today directed the Secretary of Defense to increase the size of U.S. forces committed to Desert Shield to insure that the coalition has an adequate offensive military option, should that be necessary to achieve our common goals," Bush said. Early estimates suggested that 150,000–200,000 additional troops would be sent, bringing the U.S. total to 380,000 by early 1991.[16]

President Bush was switching strategies in midcourse. No longer would the units deployed to the Gulf have a strictly defensive mission; by doubling their troop strength, Bush was giving CENTCOM additional offensive firepower, making it absolutely clear that the coalition had the wherewithal to drive Hussein's armies from Kuwait. In the language of this analysis, Bush was moving from deterrence to compellence, from preventing an Iraqi drive into Saudi Arabia to compelling an Iraqi withdrawal from Kuwait.

This second phase of the buildup involved major ground units from around the globe. The core of the new forces was the Europe-based U.S. VII

Corps, including the 1st and 3rd armored divisions and the 2nd Armored Cavalry Regiment from Germany. The 1st Mechanized Infantry Division would be sent from the United States, and a second Marine Expeditionary Force would be deployed in the Gulf.

By the outset of the ground war on February 24, the coalition had a truly massive military force deployed opposite Kuwait and on ships in the region, a force of three-quarters of a million—some 540,000 from the United States and 205,000 Europeans, Arabs, and others. The coalition possessed 3,300 tanks (2,000 U.S.), 3,350 armored combat vehicles (again 2,000 of them U.S.), 1,450 artillery pieces (1,000 U.S.), over 2,000 combat aircraft (some 1,800 of them U.S.), and 1,850 helicopters (1,700 of them belonging to U.S. units).

All of this movement required a massive amount of transportation.[17] At the peak of airlift, for example, nearly 10 planes per hour were arriving in Saudi Arabia. U.S. military and civilian aircraft averaged about 600 flights every ten days; the peak was reached in late December at almost 1,000 flights in ten days; during that week and a half, airlift brought roughly 50,000 personnel and over 30,000 tons of people, equipment, and supplies to the Gulf. Transportation duties were split between the mainstays of the U.S. airlift fleet—the C-141 (flying over half the total missions), the massive C-5 (about a quarter of the flights), and commercial aircraft called into service as part of the Civil Reserve Air Fleet (CRAF) program (some 20 percent of flights).

The story of equipment brought by sea was equally impressive. The tiny U.S. fleet of 8 fast sealift ships worked overtime rushing heavy divisions to the Gulf. Some 76 ships of the Ready Reserve Fleet (RRF) were activated, though the limitations of this poorly maintained fleet quickly became apparent: During the month of August, only about 20 percent of RRF ships were delivered on time; some 60 percent were up to a week and a half late; and almost 20 percent arrived more than ten days after schedule. From September to January, the picture improved somewhat, 65 percent of the requested RRF ships arriving within five days of schedule. A full 25 percent, however, were still over ten days late.

In addition to RRF ships, 152 chartered vessels and about two-dozen prepositioning ships were used by U.S. transportation chiefs. All played an important role in delivering massive amounts of equipment and supplies to the Gulf. The core of the U.S. sealift fleet, the fast sealift ships, RRF, and prepositioned units, accounted for roughly two-thirds of the total deliveries; chartered and other vessels made up the balance. By December 5, this fleet had delivered about 1.5 million tons of dry cargo; by February 18, a week from the ground war, the total was up to 3.5 million tons.

By the end of Operation Desert Shield, U.S. transportation units had moved more than a half-million people and 13 *billion* pounds of equipment and supplies. "No nation in history," said U.S. Transportation and Military

Airlift Command head General Hansford Johnson afterward, "has ever moved so much, so fast, so far."[18]

Strategic Mobility

Each day, day after day, thousands of troops and tons of equipment poured into Saudi airfields and ports. It was perhaps the most rapid assembly of military forces since World War II. And it brings out another lesson of the war, having to do with strategic mobility—the ability to transport U.S. military units rapidly around the globe. Simply put, the United States does not have enough transport capability. It did not have enough in the cold war, but the shortfall was somewhat camouflaged by the presence of 300,000 U.S. troops in Europe. In the post–cold war era, however, when the United States is relying on a strategy of contingency response, its inability to transport military force around the globe will become immediately evident, as it did in the Gulf War.

This shortfall did not cause a disaster in this war, because Saddam Hussein inexplicably allowed the coalition to build up forces in Saudi Arabia for five months, constrained only by the number of available ships and planes. If, however, Iraq had struck Saudi Arabia in August and challenged the United States to perform a more rapid buildup, the U.S. response might not have been adequate to halt the Iraqi advance. The first full heavy division, the 24th Mechanized Infantry, was not in place until over a month and a half after the deployment decision was made on August 7. The complete, sustainable U.S. land force embodying an offensive capability took almost seven months to get into position, in large measure because of transport limitations.

Of particular concern is the U.S. inability to transport robust forces around the globe. Modern regional armies like Iraq's possess hundreds or thousands of tanks, infantry-fighting vehicles, and artillery pieces. To stand up to such heavy forces, rapid deployment units must have a strong antitank capability. Existing U.S. assets for strategic mobility are inadequate to deploy anything but very light units with any speed. Tactical air units will provide critical firepower to U.S. expeditionary forces, in part because they can fly to the scene of action very quickly, albeit with limited sustainment. But to transport ground forces and the massive amounts of equipment, personnel, and supplies that will be necessary, U.S. contingency responses will require more strategic mobility.

One solution is obvious, but expensive: Purchase more ships and aircraft designed for rapid, strategic lift. This recommendation points to two specific systems—more fast sealift ships (of which the United States now has only 8, enough to transport only a single heavy division) and more intertheater transport aircraft. The air force has estimated that its planned fleet of 120 new C-17 transports would have allowed the United States to deploy its forces to the

Gulf almost a third faster than it did. The C-17 is also designed to operate from shorter runways (just 3,000 feet, compared to 5,000–6,000 feet for current U.S. aircraft).

The key challenge for the U.S. military will be to decide how much and what kind of strategic lift is most efficient when combined with increased prepositioning and available Allied capabilities. This demands completion of the careful ongoing assessment within the Department of Defense of likely contingencies and the force requirements to respond to them. For example, in this war we could have made more efficient use of the sealift assets at hand: The inadequate utilization of our merchant transport during the early phases of the buildup suggests a strong need for procedural reform. Additional sealift is clearly required. One decision has already been announced: the first installment toward reducing the sealift shortfall will be made up of standard 25-knot diesel transport ships—not 30-knot "fast" sealiftships—in sufficient quantities to move two heavy divisions with sustainment anywhere in the world in thirty days or less.

Another part of the solution is offered by increased prepositioning. This technique, used extensively by the army and marines, provides preset packages of equipment and supplies housed on land at key sites or stored on ships that can be moved rapidly to trouble spots. Troops are then flown in to meet the equipment. Because only soldiers and a little equipment need be taken by air, and heavy equipment like tanks, artillery, and logistical base structures are prepositioned, this tactic can slash lift requirements. An MEB, for example, uses four prepositioned ships to carry its equipment; the troops can deploy in just 250 transport flights rather than the *3,000* it would take to transport the unit and its equipment. Using prepositioning, two full MEBs were in place, complete with tanks, helicopters, and fixed-wing aircraft, by August 27— fewer than three weeks after President Bush announced his decision to deploy forces.

Additional resources should be devoted to expanding the U.S. stock of prepositioned equipment. Planned cuts in the size of the U.S. military can help in this regard: As units are deactivated, their equipment could be used for prepositioning. Given the increasing political sensitivity to U.S. bases in many countries and the fact that static equipment might not be placed in the right location, continued attention should be given to seaborne prepositioning such as the marines use today. It must be recognized that prepositioning can in some cases be more difficult, vulnerable to preemptive attack or sabotage, expensive (because of maintenance requirements), and perhaps a less effective option than lifting equipment from the continental United States. Some consideration of an effective balance between airlift, fast sealift, and prepositioning is what is required, and this is well under way within the Pentagon.

A third solution to the problem of strategic mobility may reside in a redesign of forces to make them inherently more transportable. Such reforms would be most pertinent to land forces, of course. They might involve increased use of air-transportable weapons with tactical mobility and antitank punch.

In short, this war once again demonstrates that the most advanced military equipment is useless if its owner cannot get it to the scene of trouble in a timely manner. We were lucky in this war to have extensive help from our coalition allies, and as noted, U.S. dependency on friends and allies appears to be a fact of life. Even in the context of multilateral operations, however, the United States needs to be able to move its forces around the world more readily than it can today. This is a clear shortcoming that needs to be addressed. Obtaining funds for lumbering transport aircraft or ships has never been easy; Defense Department money usually finds its way to more exciting equipment such as fighter aircraft or tanks. But in the aftermath of this war, and in particular to support the new U.S. strategy of regional contingencies, there are few more urgent priorities than the acquisition of better transport.

The Economic Embargo

While the buildup was taking place, coalition naval and air forces were denying Iraq any supplies at all through the economic embargo. On August 17, U.S. Central Command headquarters ordered U.S. and coalition vessels to intercept oil or supply ships heading for Iraq. Focused for forty years on the possibility of a global conflagration with the Soviet Union, the U.S. military suddenly became very interested in the movements of dozens of obscure tankers and cargo ships in the Middle East. A U.S. frigate, the USS *John L. Hall*, made the first interception on the seventeenth in the Red Sea of an empty Iraqi oil tanker, the *Al Fao*. Because it was carrying no cargo, the tanker was allowed to continue on its way. That night, in the Gulf, the cruiser USS *England* challenged two small Iraqi vessels and let them pass again because they were empty.[19]

Very quickly a routine of challenge and response emerged. Coalition ships would reach ships headed for Iraq or Kuwait, or Iraqi cargo ships moving about the region, by ship-to-ship radio. Coalition naval officers would demand an account of the ship's cargo and destination. In most cases, ships were allowed to pass when they were bound for any of a number of Middle Eastern countries besides Iraq or occupied Kuwait, were empty, or had some other explanation that confirmed they were not violating the embargo. Most challenges occurred without incident.

Not all embargo operations went smoothly, however. In a number of cases coalition boarding teams had to seize ships and physically redirect them when their crews refused to do so. On September 4, for example, crew members of the USS *Goldsborough* boarded the Iraqi ship *Zanoobia*, carrying 1,000 tons of tea. The *Zanoobia's* crew stubbornly refused to divert its course from Iraq, but after a few tense moments, the *Zanoobia*'s crew turned over control of the ship. U.S. sailors brought it to a port outside Iraq. Recognizing that the Navy crew was not trained for such operations, U.S. ships took aboard various teams of specialists—Coast Guard Law Enforcement Detachments (LeDets), marine special operation teams, and small groups of navy SEALs (SEa Air Land navy commandos). Iraqi ships reacted to reports of boardings by soaking their decks with water to play havoc with the footing of coalition boarding teams; some Iraqi captains refused to comply with the order of these teams by trying to block searches.

U.S. boarding crews were put to use on a number of occasions, but perhaps none as exciting as the seizure of the *Amuriyah* on October 28.[20] The massive oil tanker, 157,000 tons in displacement and almost 900 feet long—twice the weight of and similar in length to a U.S. Nimitz-class aircraft carrier—had steamed from the port of Aden in Yemen, at the southern tip of the Arabian Peninsula. On the twenty-eighth the *Amuriyah* was racing through the North Arabian Sea on its way to the Gulf and Iraq. It looked like a prime candidate to violate the embargo.

Once the Iraqi tanker was sighted, three coalition vessels quickly rushed to meet it: the Australian frigate *Darwin*, its British counterpart *Brazen*, and the U.S. frigate *Reasoner*. Also present was the USS *Ogden*, a 570-foot amphibious assault vessel capable of carrying some 900 troops, 4 landing craft, and 6 helicopters. Normally used as part of seaborne invasions, in this case the *Ogden* would stand by to provide troops if things turned nasty and the *Amuriyah* had to be seized by force.

The captain of the *Reasoner*, an older Knox-class frigate built in 1971, took charge of the little coalition flotilla and ordered the Iraqi tanker to prepare to be boarded and searched. There was no response. The *Amuriyah* continued on, plowing ever closer to the Gulf. Over and over the *Reasoner* hailed the Iraqi vessel, and finally it responded. The Iraqi captain asked for two or three hours to get in touch with the shipping line in order to obtain permission for coalition troops to board.

The captains of the coalition ships had seen this tactic before; Iraqi ships commonly attempted to delay a search in this manner until they were closer to their home port. The captain of the *Reasoner* was having none of it: "Stop in 15 minutes," he ordered the Iraqis, "or risk being fired upon." Fifteen minutes passed, and the stubborn Iraqis had not even slowed down.

The *Darwin* drew the unenviable task of maneuvering in front of the huge Iraqi ship. The frigate was a modern ship, a version of the U.S. Perry class built in 1984 and sold to Australia; it was armed with modern Harpoon antiship missiles, an advanced 76mm gun, torpedoes, and a host of other weaponry. Standing ten to forty miles from the *Amuriyah*, the *Darwin* could have hammered it with missiles and torpedoes, but coalition vessels were intent on avoiding force when possible. So the skipper of the *Darwin* maneuvered his little 3,600-ton vessel into the path of a ship fifty times its size. Again the Iraqi captain refused to stop, and the *Darwin* had to speed out of its way to avoid a collision.

The captain of the *Reasoner* decided that more drastic actions were called for. He had the *Darwin* fire a machine gun across the *Amuriyah*'s bow; when that failed, his own ship fired a much bigger cannon. Neither impressed the Iraqi captain, perhaps confident that coalition vessels would never actually sink his ship. U.S. carrier-based aircraft, F-14 fighters and FA-18 fighter-bombers, buzzed the *Amuriyah*, again to no avail.

Finally there was no alternative but to seize the Iraqi ship. Two helicopters left the *Ogden*—one a heavily armed helicopter gunship, the other carrying a detachment of marines. They approached the Iraqi tanker warily, not knowing if its captain intended to put up a fight. The gunship hovered nearby while the transport helicopter delivered its marines to the *Amuriyah*'s deck. Once there, the marines split up and rapidly controlled the key parts of the ship—its bridge and engine room. The ship was stopped and boarded by Australian and U.S. sailors as well as law enforcement officers. Amazingly, after making such a determined effort to avoid search, the *Amuriyah* was clean—not carrying anything (especially oil) that would have violated the embargo. The coalition vessels packed up and went home, having conducted another important mission in enforcing the embargo—and having narrowly avoided firing on an Iraqi ship. (Figure 3.4 illustrates maritime interceptions operations.)

The Ultimatum

Throughout November, the political and diplomatic maneuvering continued. Despite Baghdad's intransigence, many observers continued to believe that a settlement was inevitable. Saddam Hussein could hardly accept a war against the entire world. President Bush had decided to risk a more direct confrontation with the U.S. Congress by his November 8 decision to double U.S. troop strength in the Gulf, but his consultations with Capitol Hill continued. On November 14 he met with congressional leaders who were concerned that his policy was leading inevitably toward war. Once all those U.S. troops were in the Gulf, some congressional leaders worried, they would not be able to stay long; U.S. and Arab public opinion would guarantee that. For many, Bush's November 8 decision made war inevitable. For his part, the president would only promise consultation in the event force became necessary. Unsatisfied with this pledge, five days later over forty congressmen sought an injunction restricting Bush's ability to begin a war without congressional assent.

On November 21, President Bush arrived in the Middle East to meet with a host of Arab leaders. Following in the footsteps of his secretary of state, Bush was laying the final groundwork for a United Nations resolution authorizing the use of force. During the next three days Bush would meet with

66

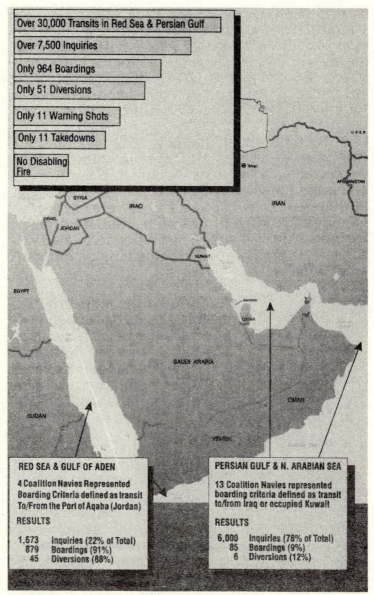

FIGURE 3.4 Summary of Maritime Interception Operations. *Source:* Department of Defense, "The Conduct of the Persian Gulf War," Final Report to Congress, April 1992, p. 78.

King Fahd of Saudi Arabia, President Mubarak of Egypt, and President Hassan Asad of Syria. By the twenty-third Bush announced that final agreement on a UN resolution was "very near"; three days later Baghdad replied that it would never succumb to the pressure of the United Nations.

Hussein soon would have no choice. On November 29, after weeks of Bush administration prodding and persuasion, the UN Security Council voted 12 to 2 (with Cuba and Yemen opposed and China abstaining) to authorize member states cooperating with Kuwait "to use all means necessary" to bring about an immediate and unconditional Iraqi withdrawal. The resolution also set a deadline, a specific challenge: Iraq must withdraw by January 15, 1991.

In Baghdad, Saddam Hussein announced that he was prepared for war. On the same day that the United Nations laid down its gauntlet, Hussein spoke to an Arab youth group in Iraq. He brushed off the threat of conflict: Iraq is "neither shaken nor panicked," he boasted, "by the air and sea fleets of America and its aides." Hussein made repeated reference to the Palestinian question, trying to link his cause to theirs. He talked of the greatness of the Iraqi nation and urged his followers to remain steadfast.

Toward the end of his speech, Hussein sought to emphasize the danger of war for the United States, and in particular for George Bush. In truly Orwellian fashion, Hussein had come to define his seizure of Kuwait as a "peaceful" enterprise designed to benefit the entire "Arab nation." This twisting of fact allowed him to direct some advice at George Bush that Hussein himself would have been well advised to heed four months earlier. "He who seeks war," the Iraqi president raged, "will by himself bear the responsibility for its consequences before God and his people."[21]

It would be less than two months before the consequences of Hussein's aggression became clear.

4

The Failure of Compellence

By late November the hope for peace began to fade. Four months had passed since Iraq's invasion of Kuwait, and there was no sign that Saddam Hussein intended to withdraw. Iraq continued to ignore the series of United Nations resolutions and seemed unruffled even by the November 29 resolution authorizing force. Meanwhile the coalition's determination to reverse Hussein's aggression remained firm, and its military capability in the Gulf was growing by the day. As documented in previous chapters, U.S. and Allied forces built up in Saudi Arabia and elsewhere in the region at an astonishing pace. The machinery of war was nearly ready, and though diplomatic efforts to end the crisis would continue until the very eve of war, conflict—a huge military clash between modern armies totaling over a million people—seemed all but inevitable.

Letters from the Troops

While the diplomatic dance continued, hundreds of thousands of U.S. and coalition fighting men and women remained in the Gulf, awaiting war and the risk of death it would bring. In late November, *Newsweek* magazine featured an article about letters from U.S. troops to friends and relatives back home. One particularly melancholy letter was written by Tyrone Brooks, a young sailor from the tough city of Detroit. Just 19, Brooks was engaged to his girlfriend, Juanita Smith, who was pregnant with their child. Earlier in the fall, Brooks had written to his fiancée from his ship, the USS *Iwo Jima*.

"I am just fine," he reassured her. "I miss you and the baby a lot. I wish I could be there to hold both you and her or him. Did I tell you we have gone halfway around the world? I talked to my division officer the other day, and he said if we are back before you have the baby he will make sure I am home for the birth of our child. . . . Well, I have to go now but remember I love you and the baby."[1]

Tyrone Brooks would not make it home. On October 30, he died in a boiler fire aboard the *Iwo Jima*. Though he did not die in combat, many Americans feared that his fate would be shared by thousands of others when the war began. The uneasy waiting continued, both in the Gulf and at home.

Defense Reorganization Initiatives

Even in early U.S. military operations, the process of decision-making within the Department of Defense and the executive branch as a whole was generally smooth and effective. It would continue to be so during the war, and this points to another major lesson of the conflict: the wisdom of recent defense reorganization initiatives. In 1986, the U.S. Congress passed the Goldwater-Nichols Defense Reorganization Act. This legislation was designed to strengthen civilian authority within the Department of Defense, improve the military advice given to the president, solidify the authority of the specified and unified commanders (especially the regional commanders in chief, known as CINCs), promote "jointness" among the services, and generally improve the efficiency of military planning and operations in peace and war.

The Gulf War strongly suggests that the defense reorganization laws did in fact measurably promote these goals. Civilian authority, in the person of the secretary of defense as well as his assistants, was clearly paramount. By all accounts, advice on military matters was of high quality—timely, thorough, carefully considered, and largely followed. As planned, this advice was channeled through a single voice—the chairman of the Joint Chiefs of Staff, who benefited from the day-to-day management assistance of a new vice chief, also mandated by Goldwater-Nichols. Most important, the role of the CINCs— their new authority under Goldwater-Nichols, their accountability for mission accomplishment—indicate the soundness of Goldwater-Nichols reforms in this area. In particular, the chiefs of the U.S. Central and Transportation Commands, CINCCENT and CINCTRANS, exercised new authority over military units, civilian agencies, defense contractors, and Allied forces that allowed them to meld their forces into coherent, integrated organizations that performed superbly throughout the crisis and war. The war also documented improvements in the formulation of strategy and contingency planning, such as the early 1990 planning guidance that encouraged a CENTCOM shift in focus away from Soviet intervention into the region as the primary threat. Finally, the spirit of jointness promoted in the legislation was widely evident in the war, with the services working together by and large in a harmonious fashion, at least until the war ended and the budget battles started again.

Thanks in part to recent legislation—though it must be admitted that much of the credit for the smooth operations must go to Bush administration policymakers—the U.S. military is now organized at the top levels to promote efficient combat operations and effective intragovernmental coordination. This organization, and the newly recommended changes to it, should serve the military well in the post–cold war era. More broadly, however, several elements of U.S. defense policy need reexamination in the context of the new regional contingencies strategy.

The Debate over War

Meanwhile the world economic embargo against Iraq continued. By March 1991, coalition ships enforcing the embargo had compiled an impressive resume. Well over 9,000 transport ships in the waters near Iraq had been challenged—and such challenges would continue well into 1991, past the end of the war, because the embargo was officially still in place. Of the ships challenged, roughly 1,100 were boarded—600 by personnel from U.S. ships, 500 by coalition personnel, and some by joint teams; ten of the sixteen NATO nations, for example, provided ships to enforce the embargo. Only about 60 ships actually had to be diverted from their intended destination.

The embargo's impact on Iraq was crippling. At a single stroke it eliminated about 90 percent of Iraq's imports and 97 percent of its exports—the latter consisting mostly of oil. Before the war, Iraq imported some 70 percent of its food; the embargo blocked 90 percent of those food imports. Oil production fell from 3.4 million barrels per day in July 1990 to 400,000 barrels by March, and only about 60,000 barrels were finding their way out of Iraq into neighboring Jordan. These cuts in oil production cost Baghdad over $1.5 billion every month. Before the war, Iraq was a major industrial power in the Middle East; by January 1991 its foreign trade was reduced to some desultory smuggling across a few inhospitable borders. Tens of thousands of foreign workers had fled, dozens of industries were shutting down for lack of spare parts or supplies, civilian production plummeted by almost half, and the price of food soared.

These figures, and the general impression that sanctions were crippling Iraq, led many observers to argue that war had become unnecessary. In a remarkable set of hearings in November and December 1990, the Senate and House Armed Services Committees heard from a variety of witnesses who urged that the Bush administration slow its march to war. Less than a month before, in early November, Bush had made his fateful decision to double U.S. troop strength in the Gulf, creating what many viewed as a pressing need to answer Iraq's aggression with force.

Zbigniew Brzezinski testified before the Senate on December 5 that war was unnecessary. Sanctions are working, he said; "Iraq has been deterred, ostracized, and punished." Brzezinski granted that sanctions would take some time to force Iraq from Kuwait, but he feared that the administration was "impatient" for a war that held deadly risks for U.S. interests in the Middle East. The threat posed by Iraq was far from catastrophic. "Therefore, in my view," Brzezinski concluded, "neither an American war to liberate Kuwait nor a preventive war to destroy Iraq's power is urgently required, be it in terms of the American national interest or of the imperatives of world order. . . . By any rational calculus, the trade-offs between the discomforts of patience and the costs of war favor patience. Both time and power are in our favor—and we do not need to be driven by artificial deadlines, deceptive arguments, or irrational emotion into an unnecessary war."[2]

Admiral William Crowe, former chairman of the Joint Chiefs of Staff, agreed. "I firmly believe that Saddam Hussein must leave Kuwait," he testified. "At the same time given the larger context I judge it highly desirable to achieve this goal in a peaceful fashion, if possible. In other words, we should give sanctions a fair chance before we discard them. . . . The trade-off of avoiding war with its attendant sacrifices and uncertainties would, in my view, be more than worth it."

Former secretary of defense James Schlesinger argued on November 27 that "to allow our political rhetoric to obscure the severe punishment that has already been meted out or to suggest that our current policy is in some way unsuccessful and that Saddam's position is now or is potentially enviable strikes me as misconceived." His special concern was the potential impact of a war. "The Middle East," he worried, "would never be the same. It is a fragile, inflammable, and unpredictable region. The sight of the United States inflicting a devastating defeat on an Arab country from the soil of an Arab neighbor may result in an enmity directed at the United States for an extended period. . . . Moreover, the United States will be obliged to involve itself deeply in the reconstruction of the region in the aftermath of a shattering war."

Some were unwilling to endorse a war but recognized that only the threat of war might dislodge Saddam Hussein. Brzezinski, Crowe, and Schlesinger all admitted the value of bluffing war. Dr. Phebe Marr of the National Defense University, testifying before the House Armed Services Committee, thought that sanctions alone would not force Saddam out of Kuwait; creating the impression of a war was necessary, but war itself would not be "if [the policy was] handled carefully." The key was holding up a risk of the war that Saddam "is so clearly trying to avoid."[3]

There were those who argued that, if war came, it would be justified and would entail acceptable risks. Eliot Cohen of Johns Hopkins contended that the apocalyptic premonitions of a war were mistaken, that the cost would be worth the risk. His primary hope was that "if it comes to war . . . that we will fight not only well, but wisely."[4] Former United Nations ambassador Jeanne Kirkpatrick argued that there was a reason besides those residing in the UN resolutions to punish Saddam Hussein more firmly: "to deter future aggressors from similar violence and make the world safer for all."[5]

By far the strongest voice defending the option of war was that of Henry Kissinger. He warned repeatedly of the danger of coddling Saddam, suggesting that if Iraq's aggression went unchecked, Saudi Arabia and other Gulf oil producers would have little option but to accommodate Hussein's wishes—including higher oil prices. U.S. power and authority in the region would be undermined, and a signal would go out to other would-be hegemons that their adventurism would be unopposed. "Without doubt," Kissinger concluded in one editorial, "the military option would prove painful and difficult. But these dangers must be weighed against the risks of an even larger conflict later on if a demonstration of American impotence leads to a collapse of moderate governments, to escalating crises and the disintegration of all order."[6] Kissinger gave similar testimony before the Congress.

Even beyond that, Kissinger argued against any negotiated settlements. Negotiations, he contended, imply that each side has a legitimate claim; Iraq had no such claim to any part of Kuwait. "In these circumstances, saving Iraq's face is the exact opposite of what is needed. For it would enable Saddam Hussein to claim some gain from his aggression, while the goal of gulf strategy must be to demonstrate its failure."[7] Kissinger favored an unequivocal defeat for the Iraqi leader—if necessary, by war.

Perhaps the most perceptive observers, however, were those who recognized that the debate over a war option was truly moot. Having committed to deploy half a million soldiers, sailors, and aircrew to the Middle East, the United States did not enjoy the option of waiting a year or more for sanctions to work. It simply could not keep such a huge force—including thousands of reservists pulled from home, job, and family—deployed indefinitely. To pull troops out would provide Saddam Hussein with a huge victory. Edward Luttwak, strategist and historian at the Center for Strategic and International Studies (CSIS), testified on November 29 that "the option of protracted sanctions is now closed. To wait with 200,000 troops or so would have been feasible perhaps. To wait with 400,000 and more is quite impossible. . . . War may thus be unavoidable unless Saddam Hussein capitulates."

And no one was betting on such a capitulation. "It will be an easy decision," pointed out James Akins, the former U.S. ambassador to Saudi Arabia, if Saddam were "given the choice between glorious martyrdom and humiliation."

Planning the Final Diplomacy Effort

Despite such analysis, it seemed to many at the time that the November 29 UN resolution authorizing force might have had some effect, for on December 1 Iraq accepted Bush's invitation to hold direct talks. It was not at first clear what there was to discuss, as both sides had declared inflexible and utterly incompatible positions. But given that war appeared to be in no one's interests, especially Iraq's, many hoped that the talks would provide a forum for the last-minute concessions people began to expect Iraq to make. Perhaps as a gesture of goodwill, Iraq through the second week of December released most of the foreign hostages it had been holding.

The rest of December and early January involved maneuvering over the dates and substance of the U.S.-Iraqi meetings. The European Community quickly got itself out of the way; by December 18, the EC had decided not to meet with Tariq Aziz until the U.S.-Iraqi sessions were complete to avoid the impression of a split in the coalition. Iraq attempted to delay the meeting with Baker as long as possible, perhaps hoping to create a glimmer of hope just before the UN deadline and thereby postpone coalition military action. Bush was having none of it: The talks would be scrapped, Bush said, if Iraq would not meet with Baker by January 3.

Domestic political signs within the United States were not consistent. Many members of Congress remained leery of war. In early December, House Democrats both insisted that Congress must approve any military action and accused Bush of rushing to war; by December 27, 100 members of the House formally urged Bush to give sanctions time to work. But public opinion polls suggested the president was in a stronger position than Democrats in Congress would admit: In early December, polls showed more than 60 percent of U.S. citizens supporting military action, and the percentage continued to grow as Hussein's intransigence became more and more apparent.

Meanwhile, in late December Pentagon planners worked at fine-tuning the delicate choreography of war. Coalition plans still called for a three-phase air campaign to be followed by a ground assault, but by now the land offensive had been redirected around the Iraqi west flank. Chairman Powell asked General Schwarzkopf when, if it were up to him, he would begin the air campaign; Schwarzkopf replied that the night of January 17 would be moonless and hence offer good cover for the initial attacks. He would attack, he told Powell, at 3 A.M. Saudi time on the seventeenth, which would be 7 P.M. Washington time, January 16. On December 29, Powell sent Schwarzkopf a warning order to prepare to begin hostilities at that time. On the evening of New Year's Day 1991, top U.S. officials were cloistered in the White House, reviewing the final war plans.[8]

Although the public was not aware of it, the Bush administration was giving strong indications to Washington insiders that war was now inevitable barring a last-minute Iraqi withdrawal. On December 17, according to Bob Woodward, National Security Adviser Brent Scowcroft told Congressman Les Aspin that Bush had essentially decided on war. The diplomatic efforts underway, Scowcroft reportedly said, were just "exercises." Four days later, Saudi ambassador Bandar visited the White House and reportedly found a serious, deliberate, resolute Bush, a changed man from his normal casual self. Bandar concluded that Bush was deadly serious about war.[9]

By January 4, 1991, the endgame was fully in place. Baghdad accepted the U.S. offer for talks, agreeing to bilateral negotiations between James Baker and Tariq Aziz in Geneva on January 9. Within a week, the world would know whether the crisis would be settled peacefully or whether the Middle East would again be plunged into war.

Human-Rights Violations in Kuwait

In late December, the London office of the human rights group Amnesty International released a scathing report on Iraqi human rights violations in occupied Kuwait. This document would become an important justification for coalition actions and was publicly cited by President Bush, members of the U.S. Congress, and leaders of other coalition nations. Its contents provide a horrifying portrait of a phenomenon as old as warfare: the excesses and evils of an occupying army.

"Widespread abuses of human rights," the report began, "have been perpetrated by Iraqi forces following the invasion of Kuwait on 2 August."[10] Shortly after the invasion, the report argued, Iraqi troops began a program of mass arrests. Subject to imprisonment were any members of the Kuwaiti military, foreign nationals living in Kuwait, and Iraqi exiles. The exiles, many suspected of belonging to groups banned on penalty of death in Iraq, faced the probability of torture and execution.

Soon after the invasion, many Kuwaitis apparently began showing their displeasure with various kinds of passive and active resistance. Some printed leaflets; others displayed Kuwaiti flags or photographs of the deposed emir; and still others, recalling a tactic used since Roman times, scrawled anti-Iraqi slogans on walls. Iraqi forces reacted harshly, at first arresting people on the street—whether or not they had any apparent connection to the opposition—and eventually raiding hundreds of homes. Hundreds, possibly thousands, of Kuwaiti women were raped in these attacks. Thousands of Kuwaitis were arrested, many beaten and otherwise tortured, and thousands were carted off to Iraq. As the direct Kuwaiti resistance mounted, so too did Iraqi reprisals: A killing of an Iraqi soldier could lead to mass, indiscriminate arrests or the destruction of homes. Some Kuwaitis later said that any Kuwaiti who bore the scars of torture was considered a potential source of evidence against Iraq and executed.

In one particularly gruesome section, the report summarized all the known means by which Iraqi soldiers tortured Kuwaitis in their custody. These included beatings, delivered with all manner of instruments from whips to rifle butts; prolonged beating of the soles of the feet, known as *falaqua*; suspending victims by the feet or by arms tied behind the back, sometimes beating them simultaneously; breaking of bones, sometimes by dropping victims from some height; using knives or other sharp objects to slash the victims; pulling out fingernails and toenails, cutting off tongues or ears, gouging out eyes, and even castration; administering electrical shocks; and injuring the victim's eyes using acidic liquids or cigarettes. In many cases prisoners would be forced to watch or listen to others being tortured.

The true horror of the Iraqi occupation only emerges in the personal stories related by the Amnesty International report. In them individual Kuwaitis relate the maltreatment and torture they suffered, often for virtually no reason. One example is the case of a thirty-two-year-old office clerk and father who was arrested for "food distribution"—buying and transporting food from a local cooperative, which the Iraqis charged was often done to aid the resistance.[11] On August 3, the man tried to bring one of his children to a local hospital but was turned away. Later he was stopped at a checkpoint, his food was confiscated, and he was taken to a local police station. He found about seventy other Kuwaitis there, some of whom he knew. Eventually the Iraqi guards summoned the clerk to the interrogation room.

Three Iraqis were waiting. "Are you happy with the situation in which you find yourselves?" one asked, as the man later related to Amnesty International interviewers.

The clerk had no reason to provoke trouble, and he answered simply. "Yes, we are fine."

"We are here to help you in the uprising," the Iraqi continued. When the Kuwaiti said he knew nothing of any uprising, another of the interrogators smashed him in the head with a rifle.

"I was immediately taken to another room," the man said later, "where I was subjected to torture for about one hour. They applied electricity to my fingers and genitals, and I was beaten with sticks. My friend whom I had seen earlier was brought into the room. One of the officers said 'Execute them,' but another officer replied, 'No, only one of them.' So they shot my friend there and then, in front of me. They shot me in my left leg."

Bleeding from his wound, the clerk was taken to a tiny cell, roughly five by eight feet, which he shared with several other victims of torture. The clerk remained there for five days, eating dry bread and nursing his wound.

Finally the Iraqis brought him out again. If he tried to leave Kuwait, he was told, he would be killed. To obtain his release, the clerk was forced to place his fingerprint on a prepared statement—one of thousands like it signed under great duress, denouncing the Kuwaiti royal family and pledging loyalty to Saddam Hussein. He was released, and he returned home to find his house ransacked, all his possessions, even his wife's wedding ring, looted by Iraqi soldiers. Just over a week later, ignoring the Iraqi warning, he took his family to Saudi Arabia.

To those familiar with such reports—and by December the world would know—the urgency of ending Iraq's occupation of Kuwait was plain. There were principles at stake, of course—important norms of international law that needed to be enforced. But there were also thousands of Kuwaitis suffering terribly at the hands of the Iraqi occupiers, and their suffering would not end until Saddam Hussein withdrew or was forced from Kuwait.

The *National Intelligence Estimate*

In late December, the U.S. intelligence community labored to squeeze dozens of different, and sometimes conflicting, opinions into the single "consensus" *National Intelligence Estimate* (NIE) speculating on whether the coalition military buildup would cause Saddam Hussein to withdraw. Faced with certain defeat, argued the report's majority (reportedly including the CIA and State Department), the Iraqi leadership would be irrational not to withdraw. It is likely that its authors investigated some of the possibilities for a last-minute Iraqi concession then being debated in public. Saddam might withdraw and keep Kuwait's two big oil-producing islands in the Gulf, some suggested; he might keep the disputed oil field along the Iraq-Kuwait border; he might pull out of half of Kuwait and demand negotiations. But whatever he did, the conventional wisdom said, he would do something to forestall the hammer blow of a coalition air campaign.

In a dissenting view, the DIA and its counterparts in the four military service intelligence agencies contended otherwise. To assume that Saddam would withdraw, they said, was once again projecting Western notions of rationality upon him. His invasion of Kuwait in itself was a strong indication that he viewed the world differently than did leaders in the West. Merely because analysts in the United States believed that war would be suicidal for Iraq did not mean that Saddam would share that view. Saddam might believe that if he could inflict serious casualties on U.S. forces, the American people would lose their taste for another distant military adventure.

In fact, if the authors of the dissent had wished, they could have pointed to one of the greatest minds in U.S. military history for support. General Robert E. Lee used a strategy much like the one imputed to Saddam: Knowing he could not win a prolonged war with the economically and numerically superior North, Lee hoped to demoralize the North's people with a series of bloody encounters. The Civil War was not universally popular in the North, and President Abraham Lincoln's political future was tenuous. If he could make the cost of war large and obvious, Lee thought, perhaps he could break the North's will to fight. It was a device much like that employed by Anwar Sadat in 1973 and again by Saddam in 1990–1991. Hussein could take little comfort, however, from the experience of his predecessors: Both had lost.

The DIA and military intelligence dissent was reflected, however, only in several footnotes to the NIE. The report's majority view was that Saddam would back down.[12]

Reasons for the Failure of Compellence

Obviously, the report was wrong. Despite the best U.S. efforts at intimidation and negotiation, compellence failed. Saddam did not leave Kuwait, and indeed his armies appeared to dig in deeper then ever. The threat to Saudi Arabia had subsided, but the perils of evicting the Iraqi army from Kuwait were growing—and the coalition's compellent threats were having no discernible impact. Once deterrence had failed, why did compellence not succeed?

As with deterrence, it is important first to know the subject of our inquiry. Thomas Schelling defines a compellent threat as one "intended to make an adversary do something," as opposed to deterrent threats, which aim "to keep him from starting something." Schelling's recommended strategy for compellence parallels his deterrence strategy. "Burn your bridges," he suggests; try to convince an aggressor that unless he backs down you have no choice but to attack him.[13]

There is no doubt that Bush did something similar. By doubling the U.S. troop deployment in the Gulf in November 1990, he created a situation that demanded either an Iraqi withdrawal or war within a few months; half a million U.S. troops could not be kept in the region indefinitely or even far into the hot summer season, and to pull some of them out before Iraq conceded would have involved a massive loss of face for the United States. Previously Bush had secured a resolution from the United Nations demanding an Iraqi withdrawal by January 15, once again tying his own hands; he could not wait long after the deadline passed before initiating military action. Moreover, through his expansive rhetoric and frequent reference to the critical interests at stake, Bush intentionally committed U.S. prestige to the eviction of Hussein's armies from Kuwait.

Despite all these efforts, and others—a crippling six-month economic blockade, the deployment of a massive coalition military force, the cultivation of unprecedented unanimity in the United Nations—Saddam did not budge. Later, after a month of the most intense air bombardment since 1945, Iraq's armies remained hunkered down in and around Kuwait absorbing devastating punishment but resolutely refusing to be *compelled* to withdraw. Compellence had obviously failed, and only a full-scale ground offensive would eventually free Kuwait.

Many of the reasons for compellence failure can be mined from our earlier analysis of the shortcomings of deterrence. Barriers to sending a deterrent signal can also constitute barriers to compellence signals: A democratic nation cannot promise to begin a war if its people will not support it. If a nation hoping to compel another needs the support of allies—for basing rights, supplies, or troops—and does not get it, compellence might be undermined. In this case, Hussein apparently believed that when push came to shove, neither the American people nor the coalition would stomach an actual war. Such is the danger and a common result of bluffing as a policy component: Because the United States could not be certain of how it or its allies would react, Hussein was able to believe he could judge better than U.S. leaders.

More frequently, however, it is the initial mind-set of the aggressor, rather than judgments made along the way, that dooms compellence. Having invaded a country or otherwise violated deterrence, an aggressor might view its own stakes in maintaining its gains as very great. Cognitive dissonance can exercise a powerful effect: Having chosen a bold course, an aggressor will be more likely than ever to reject evidence that the decision was wrong.

Cultural distinctions can also play a large role in the failure of compellence. Raphael Patai, author of twenty books on the Middle East, commented in his seminal work *The Arab Mind* about conflict resolution in Arab societies. "In every conflict," wrote Patai, Arabs "tend to feel that their honor is at stake, and that to give in, even as little as an inch, would diminish their self-respect and dignity. Even to take the first step toward ending a conflict would be regarded as a sign of weakness which, in turn, would greatly damage one's honor." For these reasons, it is nearly impossible for an Arab "to come to an agreement in direct confrontation with an opponent. Given the Arab tradition of invective and proclivity to boasting and verbal exaggeration, any face-to-face encounter between two adversaries is likely to aggravate the dispute rather than constitute a step toward its settlement." Patai's grim analysis was borne out in the confrontation between the UN coalition and Iraq. Hussein refused to give ground, and his intransigence led to war, a failure of deterrence as well as compellence.[14]

Classical deterrence theory also encourages a misunderstanding of aggressors' motivations by positing an overly narrow definition of *rationality*. In this sense, the DIA dissent to the government's NIE was absolutely correct. What may appear irrational to a Western leader might not to the leader of a third world state. The prototypical example in recent history is Anwar Sadat's initiation of the 1973 war: He did not hope to win but expected to gain political advantage even in military defeat. For Sadat, writes Robert Jervis, "losing battles was not necessarily incompatible with gaining his political objectives"; Jervis quotes Henry Kissinger as pointing out that the Western "definition of rationality did not take seriously the notion of starting an unwinnable war to restore self-respect."[15] To fulfill these goals, Egypt chose not a strategy for victory but one designed to maximize Israeli casualties—a "limited strategy of attrition warfare" built around the assumption that "even if Egypt sustained 50,000 casualties, it could absorb these losses, but if it inflicted 10,000 casualties, Israel would be forced to terminate the fighting."[16]

It is almost certain that similar presuppositions guided Saddam Hussein's willingness to let war come. Before the crisis began, he convinced himself that the United States would not respond to his aggression. In his February 24, 1990, speech, for example, Saddam Hussein made remarks that left doubt whether if push came to shove, he believed the United States would stand up to him. "Brothers, the weakness of a big body lies in its bulkiness," he told his military leaders. "All strong men have their Achilles' heel. Therefore, irrespective of our known stand on terror and terrorists, we saw that the United States as a superpower departed Lebanon immediately when some Marines were killed, the very men who are considered to be the most prominent symbol of its arrogance. The whole U.S. administration would have been called into question had the forces that conquered Panama continued to be engaged by the Panamanian Armed Forces. The United States has been defeated in some combat arenas for all the forces it possesses, and it has displayed signs of fatigue, frustration, and hesitation."[17] One could hardly imagine a more persuasive speech to justify risking war with the United States.

Even the prospect of actual war did not cause Hussein to back down, in all likelihood for very much the same reasons that Anwar Sadat accepted conflict in 1973. In his infamous July 25 interview with U.S. ambassador Glaspie, Saddam suggested that even the prospect of war would not deter him. The United States could attack Iraq, he said, but "do not push us to the point at which we cease to care. When we feel that you want to injure our pride and destroy the Iraqi's chance of a high standard of living, we will cease to care, and death will be our choice. Then we would not care if you fire a hundred missiles for each one we fired because, without pride, life would have no value."[18] As columnist Charles Krauthammer wrote the day after the war began, if Saddam could become "the first Arab ever to stand up to a superpower in war," he would be "in a position to demand parts of Kuwait, a lifting of the embargo and retention of his military power." For Saddam, capitulation "meant humiliation and—quite possibly, as often follows in the Arab world—death." War meant "a chance for victory. And with victory, glory."[19] Such views confounded Bush administration officials, who expected Hussein to back down.

Enlisting Congressional Support

In early January, the crisis moved forward on two simultaneous fronts: a debate in the U.S. Congress and direct U.S.-Iraqi talks in Geneva. Within the Bush administration there was a real debate over whether they should appeal directly for congressional support. Some officials, reportedly led by Secretary of Defense Cheney, feared risking a no vote. Congress could not be trusted to support the White House, they argued, and the ambiguity left by no congressional action would be better than an open split within the government. Others, including Chairman Powell, did not favor going to war without explicit congressional approval. The American people would not understand such a strategy, they argued; U.S. troops would lose morale when they recognized that their whole government was not behind them.[20]

By January 7, it was clear that Congress would take up the question. That day Speaker of the House Tom Foley announced that the House would debate a resolution authorizing President Bush to use force; eventually the Senate would decide to do so also. On January 10 the Congress would begin passing judgment on the administration's rush to war. The only remaining question was whether Bush would directly request the support of Congress, thereby implicitly admitting that he needed it.

Following the majority advice of his staff and cabinet, Bush decided the next day to send a letter to Congress. There were risks involved, he knew. But if Congress was going to debate the issue in any case, and if his request might help encourage a favorable response, Bush may have believed he had little choice. He wrote the first draft of the letter himself.

A Voice in Support of War

That same day, January 8, former president Richard Nixon forcefully joined the ranks of those defending Bush's policies. "It is time for some straight talk," Nixon argued in a nationwide editorial, "about why 400,000 young Americans spent Christmas in the deserts of Saudi Arabia and why in less than two weeks the United States may be once again at war."[21]

War would not be necessary, Nixon wrote, to promote democracy—Kuwait was far from that—or to end Saddam's cruelty. Rather, "We are in the Persian Gulf for two major reasons. First, Saddam has unlimited ambitions to dominate one of the most important strategic areas in the world." The Gulf, with its critical oil supplies, could not be allowed to come under the domination of a megalomaniac, Nixon contended.

The second rationale for war was one of principle. The world was entering a new order, and the principle of nonaggression needed to be firmly defended at this precedent-setting time. "We cannot be sure," Nixon admitted, "as many believe and hope, that we are entering into a new, post–cold war era where armed aggression will no longer be an instrument of national policy. But we can be sure that if Saddam profits from aggression, other potential aggressors in the world will be tempted to wage war against their neighbors."

"If we must go to war," Nixon concluded, "it will not be just a war about oil. It will not be a war about a tyrant's cruelty. It will not be a war about democracy. It will be a war about peace—not just peace in our time, but peace for our children and grandchildren in the years ahead."

Nixon held out little hope that Saddam would withdraw, that the crisis would be settled peacefully. The war he sought to justify now seemed increasingly inevitable.

The U.S.-Iraqi Meeting

On the evening of January 8, both Iraqi deputy prime minister and foreign minister Tariq Aziz and U.S. secretary of state James Baker arrived in Geneva for talks the following day. Aziz stopped and spoke with the press, saying he had arrived with an open mind. If there was talk of peace, he said, he would listen. But he also carried a stern warning: "If we hear the same talk that has been repeated during the past months"—the U.S. condemnations of Iraq and demands for a withdrawal—then, Aziz ominously pledged, "we will give the appropriate answer."[22]

Secretary Baker left the airport without comment.

The following morning at 11 A.M., the two men met at the Intercontinental Hotel in Geneva. Baker and Aziz, along with their delegations, entered the hotel's main meeting hall—the long, windowless Salon des Nations—by opposite doors, approached, and shook hands. A few minutes of media photographs followed, during which both men looked tense and declined to answer questions. Finally the media were shunted out, the doors were closed, and Baker and Aziz began what would become six-and-a-half hours of discussions. They sat opposite each other along what *New York Times* reporter Elaine Sciolino has described as "a makeshift conference table cobbled together from catering trestles."[23]

Iraq Awaits War

At about the same time, Ulrich Tildner, a journalist with the Vienna Domestic Service, broadcast a report based on information from Baghdad and other sources. Iraq, it seemed, was not concerned about the threat of war.[24]

"In Iraq," Tildner reported, "people are not aware how big the danger of war really is at present. Thus, little significance is being accorded to the meeting between Foreign Minister Tariq Aziz and U.S. Secretary of State James Baker. People trust in the strength of their own army and believe that U.S. President Bush will not realize his threats and order the troops concentrated in the region to attack. Above all, the young generation, trained during the leadership of the Ba'th Party and who have profited from Saddam Hussein's power, remains unimpressed by the threats of the anti-Iraq alliance. Saddam Hussein can and will make politics with the calmness of his subjects. Since no outbreak of a panic or a mass exodus from the capital Baghdad can be expected in the hours before the expiration of the UN deadline on Tuesday, Hussein will first go all out."

According to Tildner and other journalists recently or still in Baghdad, the Iraqi people viewed the prospect of war without great fear. They had survived a conflict with Iran, many Iraqis believed; they would survive this as well. There was some chance, Tildner speculated, that "Hussein will announce some kind of symbolic withdrawal of individual units from Kuwait at the last minute." But these would be only partial and would not presage a full withdrawal.

Hussein and the Iraqis gained some of their confidence from a judgment about President Bush. He was not as strong as he tried to appear, they said. "According to leading Iraqi politicians," Tildner reported, "U.S. President Bush is bluffing."

The Talks Fail

In Geneva, the Baker-Aziz meeting came to nothing. Baker attempted to deliver a letter from President Bush to Saddam Hussein, demanding in very blunt language that he withdraw from Kuwait or face the consequences. The original, in a sealed manila envelope, and one open copy for Aziz to read were placed on the table. Aziz read the message and, claiming that "the language in th[e] letter is not compatible to the language that should be used in correspondence between heads of state,"[25] refused to accept it. Both letters sat in the middle of the table throughout the talks, "a visible reminder," wrote Elaine Sciolino, "of the chasm between the two sides."[26] During the talks, Secretary Baker apparently attempted to persuade Aziz of the risks Iraq faced in war; the Iraqi foreign minister tried his best to show a dispassionate face, claiming Iraq was ready for whatever might happen.

Afterward both sides admitted that the talks had broken no ground or given any hope of ending the crisis short of war. "I heard nothing from Tariq Aziz," lamented Baker, "showing that the Iraqi position has become more flexible."

Top Iraqi officials continued to claim that they knew what they were doing, that they appreciated the risks involved of confronting the greatest military power in the world. "We have not made miscalculations," Tariq Aziz insisted at his press conference after the Baker talks. "We are very well aware of the situation; we have been very well aware of the situation from the very beginning. . . . We know what the deployment of your forces in the region means; we know what the resolutions you imposed on the Security Council mean; and we know all the facts about the situation—the political facts, the military facts, and the other facts. So talking about miscalculation is incorrect."

If coalition forces attacked, Aziz remarked almost casually, "we will not be surprised. We have our experience in war, and I told [Secretary Baker] that if the American administration decides to attack Iraqi militarily, Iraq will defend itself in a very bold manner." That boldness would in part be designed to draw Israel into the war. In response to a question about whether Iraq would attack Israel in the event of hostilities, Aziz replied unequivocally. "Yes," he said. "Absolutely yes."[27]

Saddam Hussein was even more blunt. In a January 9 speech to the Ba'th party broadcast over Iraqi media, Hussein said the Iraqi armed forces were ready for war. They would confront the forces of "infidelity and aggression," he said, and achieve a decisive victory. "If the Americans are involved," Saddam raged, "you will see how we will make them swim in their [own] blood."[28] In the following days, the last hope for peace apparently gone, the Iraqi press readied its people for war—all preparations were in place, Iraqi media argued; Bush was leading himself into an "inescapable trap"; the "mother of all battles" was near at hand, and it would lead to the liberation of the Islamic holy places.[29]

With an eerie calmness and a mystifying confidence, Iraq—its government and people alike—awaited war.

The Congressional Debate

The discussions of the war in the U.S. Congress were not nearly as serene. By January 10 both houses were deeply enmeshed in a sometimes acrimonious debate about one of the most critical pieces of legislation any of the members would consider during his or her time in Congress: a resolution authorizing the president of the United States to begin a war. There were few black-and-white issues or arguments those crucial days in Congress. Most of those who favored giving Bush war powers did so with notable reservations, and many of those who opposed the resolutions did so with regret and did not wish permanently to rule out the possibility of military action.

Still, the choice to be made was plain. The Bush administration was on a direct course for war, likely to begin within a few days of January 15 against an army of half a million in a distant corner of the globe. The question now was whether Congress would endorse or condemn that action.

Congressman Don Edwards of California would not support Bush. The bill authorizing force "is really a Pontius Pilate resolution that says that Congress is going to wash its hands of this matter and go home." Edwards favored continued reliance on sanctions—as did virtually all the Democrats and the few Republicans who opposed the resolution authorizing force. "War is too important," Edwards contended, "to go to war because we are impatient."[30] Sam Nunn's case in the Senate was much the same: He urged the administration not to rush a war; a few more months of sanctions might work to smoke Hussein out without a fight.[31] Others were concerned about the potential casualties: "Many experts maintain," worried Congresswoman Cardiss Collins of Illinois, "that the United States would suffer tens of thousands of casualties if we go to war. Numbers like that scare me."[32]

Others objected to the United States bearing the brunt of an international war. "The Netherlands gets 100 percent of its oil from the Persian Gulf," complained Congresswoman Barbara Boxer, yet they had contributed "no ground troops; Japan, 63 percent of its oil from the Persian Gulf, no ground troops; Spain, 59 percent of its oil from the Persian Gulf, no ground troops. . . . France gets 38 percent of its oil from the Persian Gulf, 8,400 ground troops; Italy, 36 percent of its oil from there, no ground troops. . . . Germany,

11 percent, no ground troops; the United States of America, 11 percent of its oil, 300,000 ground troops and a lot of our treasury and our budget."[33]

Those supporting the pro-Bush resolution referred to familiar arguments about checking aggression and protecting the world's oil supplies. California Congressman Robert Lagomarsino summed up the case well: "No one wants war. . . . But, if Saddam is not stopped now, if his aggressive designs are not frustrated, peacefully if possible, or if necessary by force, we will all pay a higher price later." Many apparently hoped that by sending a strong signal of resolve, Congress would complete the U.S. policy of compellence and force Hussein to withdraw. "Our bold, yet responsible, policy," said Lagomarsino, "is the right one with the best chance of achieving our goals peacefully."[34] Senator J. Bennett Johnston of Louisiana agreed: "The stronger the demonstration of force, of unity of resolve, of power in the hands of the President of the United States to go to war, then the better chance we have to avoid that war."[35]

Some members favoring the resolution pointed explicitly to the Iraqi nuclear program as a further justification for war. "The clock is ticking," said Congressman Duncan Hunter of California, "not only with respect to Saddam Hussein's chemical and biological weapons, but also nuclear weapons." Hunter related estimates that Iraq had 27 pounds of enriched uranium, enough for at least one bomb, and possibly supplies of plutonium and tritium as well. Hussein was "racing, just as Adolf Hitler was racing in World War II, to build a nuclear system." Hunter's strong implication was that war might be necessary to destroy Iraq's nuclear program.[36]

In the end, most of those in Congress who opposed the war were unwilling to undercut President Bush. With over a half-million U.S. troops in the Gulf or on their way there, a congressional rejection of Bush's policy would have been tantamount to a vote of no confidence, a crippling blow at presidential leadership and authority. Whether intentionally or by accident, George Bush had moved far and fast enough on the road to war so that Congress, to the extent that it had greater doubts about the enterprise, was unable to slow him down. He had marginalized Congress's role.

Not all members of Congress were happy with this result. Senator John Kerry of Massachusetts summed up the dilemma well. "I hear it from one person after another—'Well, I want to back up the President.' 'I do not want the President to look bad.' 'The President got us in this position. I am uncomfortable—but I cannot go against him.' . . . Are we supposed to go to war simply because one man—the President—makes a series of unilateral decisions that put us in a box—a box that makes that war, to a greater degree, inevitable? Are we supposed to go to war because once the President has announced something publicly, to reverse or question him is somehow detrimental to the Nation despite the fact [that] we are a coequal partner in government?"[37]

The majority of Congress apparently believed so. For on January 12, the House of Representatives voted 250 to 183 and the Senate 52 to 47 to approve resolutions authorizing President Bush to use force in turning back Saddam Hussein's aggression. The sense of relief in the White House was palpable throughout Washington.

Analyzing the Costs of War

As war became increasingly probable, military analysts outside the government began to speculate about what it would cost. A host of casualty estimates emerged, all based on the idea that the interests at stake in the Gulf had to be weighed on some political and moral scale against the number of Americans likely to die. Estimates of casualties varied widely, from a few thousand total casualties to over 50,000 dead alone. In the end, the political and military experts who used various methods of forecasting and techniques of military analysis enjoyed mixed success. There was no shortage of opinions of what would happen, both before and during the war. Some were wildly off the mark, others were eerily prescient, though the general public impression after the war was that most "experts" had been terribly wrong.

If we are to undertake a valid critique, it is important to distinguish between types of military analysis. Some do not involve forecasting at all: These are military exercises and war games, simulations that are run to give officers practice in making the real-time decisions of a war. They are not designed to predict what would actually happen in war but rather to raise some possible scenarios so that military leaders can practice responding to them. Such war games have in the past proved extremely useful. By coincidence, in July 1990 the U.S. Central Command was engaged in modeling a possible Iraqi thrust south, and many CENTCOM officials have said they were far more ready for war as a result of the exercise.

A second technique of analysis might be called quantitative modeling. Quantitative modelers attempt to come up with mathematical formulas to predict various aspects of war. The most famous such estimates in this war were of likely coalition and Iraqi casualties. Modeler Trevor Dupuy testified before Congress that his carefully developed equations led him to conclude that the United States and its allies would suffer 8,000–16,000 casualties, the Iraqis 60,000. Other estimates ranged from a few thousand coalition casualties to tens of thousands. These were obviously of little value and proved generally inaccurate, largely because the Iraqis did not put up much of a fight; their accuracy also depended heavily on when they were made—by the end of the air campaign, many commentators had revised their estimates of likely coalition casualties down dramatically. To the degree that these estimates affected policy, they did so only marginally. The quantitative aspect turned out to be not as important as subjective judgment.

This is the third area of military analysis—pure opinion, drawn from expertise. As will always be the case, these opinions were of varying accuracy: Few observers predicted how poorly the Iraqi army would do in battle; very few anticipated Saddam Hussein's string of miscalculations, beginning with the invasion of Kuwait itself. Still, many military experts predicted the coalition's tactics, from the air war to the flanking nature of the ground operation, with great precision; and a number of individual experts were right on a host of issues—from Saddam's intention to use force to Israel's decision to stay out of the war to the devastating effect of air power and the perfunctory nature of the ground campaign.

In short, when techniques of military analysis are used to inform decision-making and not to predict, their application is generally helpful. But despite the best efforts of statisticians to quantify the future, forecasting remains as much an art as a science. In this case many of the false predictions were based on a lack of knowledge of the Middle East and of the psychology of the Iraqi leader. The prescription for the future is clear: Use war games and exercises extensively (especially joint and combined ones), treat any quantitative forecasting with a large dose of skepticism, and work to improve the level of expertise within the U.S. government on *all* regions where a U.S. or allied intervention may be needed in the future.

The Last Hope for Peace

The last, faint hope for peace arrived in Baghdad on January 12 in the person of UN secretary general Javier Pérez de Cuellar.[38] That same day, the few remaining diplomats in the U.S. Embassy in Baghdad left Iraq for Germany on a chartered Iraqi Airways 727. The stage was set for war unless Pérez de Cuellar could produce some magical last-minute compromise.

But there was no last-minute magic to be had. Pérez de Cuellar met with Tariq Aziz and then, for over four hours, with Saddam Hussein. The secretary general had little bargaining power because he had no control over U.S. or coalition actions; the most he could do was try to persuade Hussein to take the first step, to indicate he would be willing to withdraw. As we have seen, such a compromise was anathema to the Iraqi leader. Not surprisingly, he once again rejected outside demands and pleas to end the crisis. Pérez de Cuellar left on January 13 having witnessed no hint of flexibility from Hussein.

The next morning, January 14, Iraq's National Assembly laid down its own marker. The U.S. Congress had voted to support its leader, and now Hussein's puppet assembly would do the same. It voted to endorse his policy of refusing any concession on Kuwait.

Justifications for War

As war approached, observers in the West began to take stock of their purpose, to reaffirm the justness of the cause. Many took comfort in historical analogies. Confronting Saddam's aggression, it began to be said, was justified by the lessons of history. And the most powerful lesson drawn that January related to the ultimate folly of appeasement, World War II. It had to do with the Italian invasion of Abyssinia.

Italy's 1935 invasion of Abyssinia had much in common with Saddam Hussein's attack on Kuwait. Frequent parallels have been drawn between Saddam Hussein and Adolf Hitler, but some argued that the Italian dictator Benito Mussolini would have been a better choice. In December 1934, anxious to fulfill his grandiose dreams of empire, Mussolini prepared to invade the African kingdom of Abyssinia—like Kuwait, a tiny nation of minimal concern to the world's great powers. Like Saddam, Mussolini was shocked at the international reaction: Britain assembled a coalition of nations, including Greece, Turkey, and France, to confront Italy and pledge a military response if Mussolini invaded. As today, the hope for a new world community capable of standing up to aggression—then called the League of Nations, today embodied by the United Nations—energized the response. Abyssinia was a member of the league, just as Kuwait is a member of the United Nations.

Like the UN coalition over half a century later, the British-led group slapped economic sanctions on Italy. Then as now, the critical commodity was oil: If Italian imports of the fuel could be stopped, the Italian economy might grind to a halt. And then as now, what was at stake was not so much clear national interests but the establishment of a precedent. The military historian A.J.P. Taylor notes that "the League action against Italy was not a common-sense extension of practical policies; it was a demonstration of principle pure and simple. No concrete 'interest' was at stake in Abyssinia—not even for Italy."[39]

In 1935, this attempt to establish a principle of nonaggression failed. The revelation of a secret British and French plan to avoid war by offering Italy concessions, including de facto control over Abyssinia, undermined the anti-Mussolini coalition—as similar concessions might have done to the anti-Iraq coalition in 1990. While Britain and France bickered, while the United States wavered in commitment to economic sanctions, Mussolini invaded in October 1935. After the attack, with Abyssinia still holding out, Britain did not abandon its crusade; it called for deeper economic sanctions, including an all-important oil embargo. But negotiations with other league members dragged on for months, and gradually it became clear that the league would not respond in any forceful manner to Mussolini's aggression.

In 1935, the cost of appeasing a dictator and avoiding war was high. The international community was fractured; A.J.P. Taylor notes that "The real death of the League was in December 1935, not in 1939 or 1945. One day it was a powerful body imposing sanctions, seemingly more effective than ever before; the next day it was an empty sham, everyone scuttling from it as quickly as possible." Meanwhile, Adolf Hitler "watched the conflict with sharp eyes, fearful that a triumphant League might next be used against Germany."[40]

When the league failed, explained Albert Speer, Hitler's close associate at the time, "Hitler concluded that both England and France were loath to take any risks and anxious to avoid any danger. Actions of his which later seemed reckless followed directly from such observations. The Western governments had, as he commented at the time, proved themselves weak and indecisive."[41] Five months later, in March 1936, Hitler seized the Rhineland.

With his invasion, Mussolini had struck a blow not only at an ancient African kingdom but also at the embryonic international community. The analogy to the present situation is striking, and the lesson many drew in January 1991 was that it would be just to evict Saddam Hussein from Kuwait. Had he succeeded, not only would his own regional ambitions have grown but other dictators would have learned that the world would cast a blind eye to aggression. As the great historian Michael Howard wrote on January 2, "The reasons then advanced [in 1935] for accepting that *fait accompli* now seem very familiar. War was unacceptable to the electorate, it would wreck our convalescent economy, Mussolini had after all a very reasonable case, Abyssinia was an undemocratic feudal state and not worth saving anyway. So we failed that test. In consequence we had to face others far more terrifying. We do not have to make the same mistake again."[42]

The Onset of War

By January 15, the date of the United Nations deadline for Iraq to withdraw from Kuwait, the stage for war had been set. U.S. and coalition air units had been alerted to attack and made final preparations for combat. Iraq's forces—many of them, the world would later find out, unhappy and unconvinced of their purpose—dug in and awaited an assault they expected soon. Thousands of miles apart, George Bush and Saddam Hussein had come to the same conclusion: The die was cast; the interests at stake, for both of them, demanded war.

As the United Nations deadline passed in New York, the 53rd Tactical Fighter Squadron, F-15s brought to the Gulf from Germany, celebrated in Saudi Arabia. Pilots and aircrew gathering around the squadron's operations desk—it was 8:00 in the morning, Saudi time—and gave a cheer. On the wall hung a handmade "official Iraqi 1991" calendar; the entry for January 15 read "Time's Up."[43]

Out on the flight line, Staff Sergeant Mike Thomas had set his watch alarm for 8 A.M. to remind him that the deadline had passed. Amid all the noise of planes warming up and taxiing, Thomas didn't hear his watch. Later he remembered that Iraq had now officially ignored the UN ultimatum. "I just had to stop and collect my thoughts," Thomas would tell a reporter. "Is today the day for war?"

Speaking with reporters, most members of the squadron displayed a quiet, mature confidence—a genuine fear of war but a desire to do a job well for which they had spent years training. Captain Mike Miller, a twenty-eight-year old Tennesseean, admitted, "I'm a little bit scared. I think if somebody tells you they're not, they're lying to you. But we've trained for this so much . . . that hopefully when I get out there and start pushing buttons and making things happen, everything comes as second nature."

"I'm facing it and handling it ten times better than I thought I would," related Air Force chaplain Mike Thornton. "I think that's the case with most of the troops."

Like the members of the 53rd, over a million people—soldiers and sailors, aircrew and marines, men and women, experienced combat veterans and green recruits, professional soldiers and reservists, Americans, coalition troops, and Iraqis alike—waited for the killing to begin.

By all accounts, January 16 was a calm day in Baghdad. Many in Iraq and elsewhere expected the coalition to wait at least a few days after the January 15 UN deadline before beginning military operations. No one knew what the night ahead held for them.

Publicly, the Iraqi government and many of its people remained firm. A Baghdad media broadcast that day suggested that the nation was prepared for war.[44] "Iraq's brave men at the front of rightness," the report boasted, "have their fingers on the trigger while awaiting the zero hour for engaging in the most honorable epic in history—the mother of battles."

The government and people of Israel were following the crisis with great interest. Several days earlier, Israeli media had broadcast a report detailing the current views of the Israeli Defense Forces, or IDF, on the Gulf situation. Their summary was as concise and accurate as any in those days before the war.[45]

"After the failure of the Geneva talks," said correspondent Karmela Menashe, "the defense establishment and the IDF believe that there is now a greater danger of war in the Gulf. Military elements say that in view of the stands presented by the two sides, a military move seems to be the only viable option open to realize the U.S. goals in the Gulf. War, they estimate, is now closer than ever."

Iraq's media later reported that on January 16, Saddam Hussein drafted a letter to George Bush, effectively a reply to the Bush ultimatum that Tariq Aziz had rejected in Geneva.[46] The letter was reportedly revised that evening by Iraq's Revolutionary Command Council just hours before Schwarzkopf's intended H-Hour. The letter did not mince words.

Saddam addressed his remarks to George Bush, "enemy of God and colleague of the devil. The glorious Iraqi people and I have listened thoroughly to your hysterical statements threatening terrible consequences for Iraq and threatening aggression and destruction if Iraq fails to comply with your terms of capitulation. Accursed be you and hopeless are your objectives." Iraq had "prepared [itself] very well for battle," Saddam claimed.

And yet, the Iraqi leader did not abandon the opportunity to press for one last attempt to end the crisis short of war. "Fear God," he advised Bush, "withdraw your armies and those of your allies from the land that is sacred to Arabs and Muslims. . . . Such is the recourse that has been open to you so far and is still open to you before the moment of aggression, for which you are planning, comes." Iraq had not attacked the United States, Saddam pointed out, calling for a fresh set of talks on Iraq's previous peace initiatives.

Such proposals were surprisingly conciliatory for a nation on the brink of war. One can detect a seed of doubt in these suggestions. For so long, the prospect of war with the United States had been for Saddam a distant, theoretical proposition; at arm's length, the war could have been viewed in a favorable light. Now that combat was imminent, however, was it possible that Saddam had second thoughts? Might he have appreciated at the last moment that his scoffing at U.S. will was misplaced, that President Bush would indeed force him from Kuwait? We cannot know; we may never know. Saddam had a prediction, however, of what war would bring: "The battle will be prolonged," he fumed, "and heavy blood will be shed."

Top Iraqi officials may have hoped that their renewed reference to a negotiated solution would delay the war, even at that late moment. Whatever chance the letter had of inspiring new talks, however, was lost by its timing. For it was not broadcast to the world until 7:30 in the morning Baghdad time, January 17. By that time the Gulf War had been under way for almost four hours.

5

The Air Campaign

At about midnight Saudi time on January 16, hundreds of coalition aircraft took to the skies to begin flights that would carry them to war. In their secure command post, Brigadier General Buster Glosson and Lieutenant General Chuck Horner watched the attack unfold on two huge radar screens. Many of the planes placed themselves under the guidance of airborne warning and control system (AWACS) aircraft; four of these AWACS planes prowled south of the Iraq-Saudi border keeping track of dozens of attack planes. Back in Riyadh, Glosson and Horner, the men who had supervised the planning of the imminent air campaign, watched and waited. "Time kind of stood still," a navy officer in the command post related later, "as you saw those little dots moving towards Iraq."[1]

On the runways, pilots were fully briefed and knew this mission was not a rehearsal. "The arming area was full," Captain Alan Miller, an F-15 fighter pilot, would say later. "The taxiways were full. The trail of airplanes back in their parking areas was all lined up with [F-15C] Eagle after Eagle after Eagle. . . . We thought it was going to be a fight like none we had ever imagined."[2]

U.S. leaders and pilots had reason to be worried. Confronting them in Iraq was an air defense network air force officials would later claim was far more imposing than the air defenses in Eastern Europe during the cold war. Iraq possessed 7,000 radar-guided missiles, 9,000 missiles with infrared guidance, 7,000 antiaircraft guns, and 800 fighters. (See Figure 5.1.) Neutralizing these defenses, both by attacking them directly and by smashing their command-and-control systems, would be a major objective of early air strikes.

Even before H-Hour—3 A.M., January 17 in the Gulf, the moment when the bulk of the first night's air strikes would begin—dozens of coalition aircraft and hundreds of troops were in action. (See Figure 5.2.) Special operations helicopters—MH-53J Pave Low choppers, designed to sneak quietly into enemy territory—led a flight of Apache attack helicopters from the 101st Airborne Division into Iraq to strike early warning radars. Later, just minutes before H-Hour, a single F-117A stealth fighter attacked an air defense control

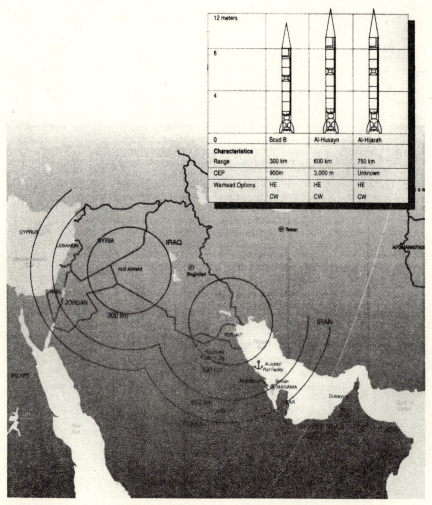

FIGURE 5.1   Iraqi Missile Capabilities. *Source:* Department of Defense, "The Conduct of the Persian Gulf War," Final Report to Congress, April 1992, p. 17.

center in southern Iraq. The two attacks may not have gone off perfectly timed to the second; apparently a warning was flashed to Baghdad. The first anti-aircraft shots seemed to be fired blindly in the Iraqi capital even before U.S. aircraft arrived overhead.[3]

U.S. special operations teams were also operating well inside Iraq. Dropped in by air, small groups of Green Berets and other special forces hid in small "spider" holes for days or roamed Iraqi territory in dune buggies and on foot, performing reconnaissance, stealing Iraqi military equipment for analysis back in Riyadh, intercepting communications, and doing other jobs. Now,

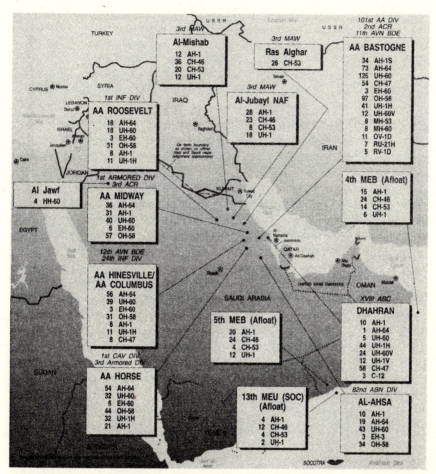

FIGURE 5.2   U.S. Rotary-Wing Aircraft Bed Down on January 16, 1991. (Note: Aircraft numbers and locations changed continuously.) *Source:* Department of Defense, "The Conduct of the Persian Gulf War," Final Report to Congress, April 1992, p. 144.

on the eve of the war, they sought out and attacked Iraqi radars and other targets important to the early stages of the air war.

When H-Hour arrived, other stealth fighters attacked a host of targets in Baghdad—communications facilities, command and control, military headquarters, and the electrical power grid feeding the military command-and-control network (see Figure 5.3). Stealth fighters would be the only coalition aircraft over Baghdad during the entire war; on that first night alone, F-117s hit 31 percent of the targets with only 2.5 percent of the aircraft used. Using precision-guided 2,000-pound bombs, the F-117s smashed building after

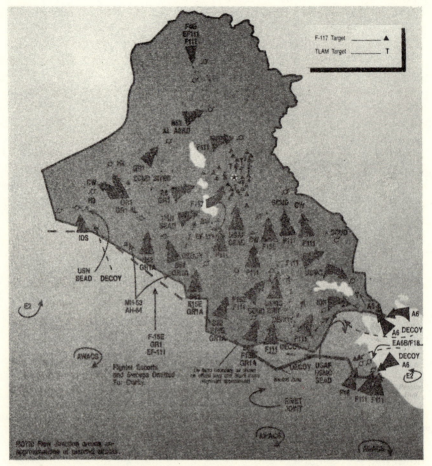

FIGURE 5.3   The First Wave (Planned): The first two hours and forty-six minutes.
Source: Department of Defense, "The Conduct of the Persian Gulf War," Final Report
to Congress, April 1992, p. 155.

building.[4] Videotapes of the attacks were shown to reporters just a few hours
later. In a Baghdad suburb, another stealth hit a site where the Iraqis were suspected of operating a U.S.-made Hawk missile battery captured from the Kuwaitis; if operational, the Hawks could have caused real problems for U.S.
planes.[5]

"You pick precisely which target you want," Col. Alton Whitley, commander of the 37th Tactical Fighter Wing, the stealth unit, said on his return
that morning. "You can want the men's room or you can want the ladies'
room." Whitley confirmed that the stealth fighters were invisible to Iraqi radars; the only antiaircraft fire that emerged was a random barrage shot up into

the sky in the hope of hitting something. Thousands of Iraqis, he reported, were fleeing Baghdad: "It was bumper to bumper leaving the city." Whitley gladly relayed that the stealths had flown without loss and performed superbly. "I saw a lot of old boys become young men last night," he said of his pilots.[6]

Hundreds of other strike missions were going according to plan as well. In northern Iraq, coalition attacks destroyed Iraqi air defense sites, electrical power plants, and chemical weapons industries. Out west F-15E Strike Eagles went after fixed and mobile Scud launchers, airfields, and other air defense sites. Just north of Kuwait similar targets were hit. Coalition attack aircraft benefited from the support of EF-111 Ravens, electronic warfare aircraft used to jam enemy radar, and F-4G Wild Weasels, fighter-bombers specially equipped to attack air defense radars. Iraqi air defense gunners soon learned the dangers of turning on their equipment: As soon as coalition aircraft detected a missile or gun-search radar, air force Wild Weasels or navy F-18 Hornets would sweep in firing high-speed antiradiation missiles (HARMs) designed to home in on the Iraqi radar signals. Dozens of air defense sites were destroyed using such tactics. Meanwhile F-15C fighters prowled the skies, ready to respond to any Iraqi planes that might try to intercept coalition air strikes.

During the first twenty-four hours of the war, the coalition would fly over 1,300 sorties, including over 800 flown by strike aircraft. Navy ships fired over 100 Tomahawks into Iraq. Although coalition leaders could not know it yet, the Iraqi air defense force and air force were already crippled, their communications disrupted, many of their commanders dead, dozens of air defense sites destroyed. Once Iraq's military lost the capability to respond to aerial attacks, it became extremely vulnerable: From its sanctuary in Saudi Arabia, the coalition could launch crushing air strikes day after day and wear down Iraq's ground forces until they broke. Building on the foundation laid on that first night, coalition air units would achieve complete air supremacy within days. In less than thirty minutes the coalition had created a tremendous momentum toward victory.

The High-Technology Warfare Revolution

Although it was barely under way, the coalition's air campaign against Iraq had already demonstrated that this war would be very different from past ones. Over the past decades there has been a true revolution in warfare, a product of high-technology weapons, communications, and command-and-control systems. The effects of technology—in precision-guided weapons, in stealthy delivery systems, in advanced sensor and targeting systems, in battle-management platforms—is transforming and, in fact, already has demonstrably transformed, the way in which armed forces conduct their operations.

Partly due to the reach and accuracy of modern deep-strike weapons—like the strike aircraft flying on that first night of the war—military thinkers have begun to argue that future battlefields will look very different from those of World War II. In the future, vast slow-moving military forces deployed along well-known front lines will be vulnerable to attacks by smart weapons launched from tens or even hundreds of miles away or dropped from attacking aircraft. As a result, modern armies are looking at concepts of nonlinear warfare in which smaller, fast-moving, more independent units maneuver around a battlefield, coalesce to attack enemy formations, then melt away into smaller component parts less vulnerable to smart weapons. As in war at sea, the focus will be not so much on seizing territory as on destroying enemy combat forces.

New tactics might resemble guerrilla warfare writ large: Smaller, agile, stealthy units stage hit-and-run raids with tanks, armored cars, artillery, and helicopters integrated with tactical air support as well as with infantry squads. And again, ground, air, and even naval forces are becoming increasingly interdependent as static military front lines become a thing of the past and ground units depend on their air and naval counterparts for intelligence, communications, and fire support. In the future, some contend, armies attempting to fight traditional, strictly linear wars will be overwhelmed and defeated. They will suffer the same fate as waves of infantry in World War I, as horse cavalry in 1939—and as the Iraqi army in 1991.

Besides the United States, no nation has more fully studied these ideas and attempted to work them into its military strategies than the former Soviet Union. In many ways, coalition operations in the Gulf War represented as much a confirmation of Soviet ambitions as U.S. doctrine. For years Soviet strategists, led by General Nikolai Ogarkov, have recognized, along with their U.S. and European counterparts, the importance of high-technology deep-strike weapons. They have described the development of smart weapons as a revolution in military affairs with implications comparable to those of nuclear weapons. Coalition forces demonstrated that Western armies have mastered concepts that Soviet planners have been investigating for decades: deception before ground operations begin, exploitation of space systems and aircraft for command and control, the use of special forces to disrupt an enemy's rear area, employment of airmobile troops (either parachutists or helicopter-borne) to establish strong points well behind the front line, devastating armored thrusts conducted by all-arms maneuver groups, and achievement of air superiority and use of air strikes to neutralize enemy movements.

In military affairs, however, theoretical recognition of changes in warfare is easier than building military forces capable of responding to them. More than any other nation, the United States has demonstrated the ability to *fight* and *win* wars based on such doctrines. This is a competitive advantage the United States should zealously guard.

The most convincing confirmation of the revolution in war was seen in the application of air power in the air campaign. The effects of what would become a six-week coalition air assault on Iraqi forces was devastating—thousands of tanks, armored personnel carriers, and artillery pieces were destroyed; perhaps tens of thousands of Iraqi soldiers were killed. In future contingencies, the enemies may not so completely abandon the skies to U.S. and allied aircraft. It therefore seems obvious that concentrated air power using modern precision weapons will remain a key U.S. advantage in any contingency operation and will, in circumstances similar to those in the Gulf, remain the dominant component of U.S. military capabilities in the forthcoming revolution in warfare.

In the context of that revolution, it is important to keep in mind the relative efficiency of precision-guided munitions launched by air versus those fired from the ground. A key element of emerging warfare is the notion of over-the-horizon targeting, which engages enemy forces even out of sight of ground-based sensor range. Battle-management technologies, warning and control systems, target attack sensors, and other systems discussed further on are used to find and target enemy units at long range. The question then becomes how best to hit them. In this war, ground-based over-the-horizon weapons such as the army tactical missile system (ATACMS) were used sparingly; air-launched precision weapons were one of the stars of the war. Again, stronger enemy air defenses, especially those including large numbers of interceptor aircraft, would make problematic a reliance on air-launched precision weapons alone. But in conventional wars where the air defense threat will be no greater than that found in Iraq—and that includes all but a very few conceivable such wars—a disproportionate reliance on tactical aircraft, helicopters, and cruise missiles for delivery of precision weapons may be warranted.

To control the operation of tactical aircraft, helicopters, cruise missiles, and other weapons and units, and indeed to manage the whole battlefield, coalition forces used command-and-control centers and battle-management systems to coordinate the ongoing battle. These functioned in essence as a far more advanced version of what the Soviets called a reconnaissance strike complex. On the modern battlefield, to identify an enemy target and bring precision weapons to bear has almost become tantamount to destroying it. The key is to establish a synergistic system of detection, targeting, and attack. Satellites, reconnaissance aircraft and drones, and other sources of intelligence locate enemy forces and track them. Battle-management aircraft and ground stations direct strike aircraft, ships, or ground maneuver units to meet the enemy. Weapons systems conduct the attack, and intelligence platforms are once more brought to bear, this time to perform battle-damage assessment. As was demonstrated conclusively in the Gulf War, such a process of real-time targeting and attack can destroy opposing armed forces at an amazing rate.

U.S. battle-management systems help commanders keep constant tabs on what forces and equipment are where on the battlefield and direct their units to achieve the best results rapidly and efficiently. In this war, for example, battle-management systems implementing a single air-tasking order helped choreograph the most intricate—and successful—air campaign in history. In the Gulf, the two primary battle-management platforms were the AWACS and the joint surveillance target attack radar system (JSTARS) aircraft. The former managed much of the air battle; the latter helped keep track of movements on the ground and direct U.S. land forces. Both proved to be remarkably effective, even though the latter was still in the development stage. In the future, battle-management systems will continue to provide a potentially decisive advantage to U.S. and allied forces. Refinements are still needed—for example, partly because JSTARS was pushed into the field years before its scheduled deployment date, it was capable of interaction only with a few high-level commands, and it could not communicate adequately with lower-level ground commands. Further development of battle-management systems will remain a priority.

In the early days of coalition air operations, space systems were already proving their worth in supporting coalition military operations in a wide variety of ways from detection to battle management. Throughout the war, global positioning system (GPS) satellites provided real-time navigational data to land, sea, and air units, which used over 5,000 GPS receivers. Communication satellites handled a good deal of the voice and data transmissions. Meteorological satellites offered critical weather data for planning military operations. And space warning systems gave indications of Iraqi missile launches. Desert Storm has been called the United States' first comprehensive space war, and it should serve as a catalyst for accelerating the development of tactical space applications. It is important that the U.S. military recognize the extent of its vulnerability as well: Iraq had no antisatellite weapons, or even primitive communications or surveillance satellites. Not all future adversaries will lack this equipment, and as U.S. forces become dependent upon satellites, they will become increasingly vulnerable to an adversary with rudimentary satellite communications and observation capabilities, and even to primitive antisatellite weapons.

Even from its first hours, the Gulf War also demonstrated the rising value of helicopters in modern warfare. In many ways helicopters are the perfect aircraft for nonlinear warfare. They provide both mobility and lethality, flying over terrain obstacles such as mountains and rivers, establishing new operational bases wherever circumstances dictate. Their ability to strike targets from great distance with precision weapons is a major asset to ground forces. During the ground war, on the coalition's far left flank, helicopters established several base areas and leapfrogged through them, creating an air bridge hundreds of miles long and penetrating deep into the Iraqi rear. Other helicopters performed battlefield and strategic interdiction—knocking out Iraqi air defense radars early in the air campaign. In the future, helicopters could evolve from specialized systems with limited application to much more flexible weapons capable of fulfilling a host of missions.

The early experience of the air war also confirmed the value of stealth technologies. U.S. F-117 stealth fighters flew hundreds of missions in the war without loss, dropping precision weapons and, at least at the outset of the war, destroying a disproportionate number of Iraqi targets hit. U.S. Tomahawk cruise missiles, stealthy weapons because of their small size, repeatedly slipped with impunity through Iraqi air defenses during daylight hours. A continued emphasis on stealth in U.S. tactical air systems is clearly warranted, though it is not clear that this war has demonstrated what the mix of U.S. combat aircraft should be between stealth and nonstealth types of aircraft.

By noon on January 17, Saudi time, the war had only been under way for nine hours. Already, however, the implications of high technology had become apparent. Coalition aircraft were striking targets more precisely and with greater effect than ever before possible. The evidence was already mounting: The revolution in warfare long trumpeted by military analysts was at hand. Iraq's doomed armed forces would soon learn that lesson in a very immediate way.

War-Plan Revisions

Originally the air campaign was meant to consist of three phases. The first would gain air superiority, interrupt Iraqi command and control, and hit such sites as chemical, nuclear, and biological weapons manufacturing plants and Scud missile sites. In the second phase, coalition aircraft would suppress air defenses in the Kuwaiti theater of operations and gain air supremacy. In the third phase, the focus of coalition attacks would shift to Iraqi ground forces in preparation for the coalition ground offensive. U.S. Air Force officers had specific ideas of how fast the air campaign should proceed, and how long it would take them to achieve each of their original objectives in the three phases.

But the smoothness of the initial strikes of the air campaign, due in part to Iraqi weaknesses and to the degree of surprise achieved by coalition aircraft during initial strikes, called for a revision of the original plans for the war. Perhaps most significant was that air superiority was established surprisingly quickly, allowing all phases of the air campaign to merge together.

The weakness of the Iraqi air force coupled with U.S. and coalition success did not mean there were no losses. By January 17, 8 aircraft had been lost. One, ironically, was from the first mission launched from USS *Saratoga*, the same ship whose pilots would boast the first air kills of the war. The plane was downed by a surface-to-air missile (SAM), providing a warning that, although

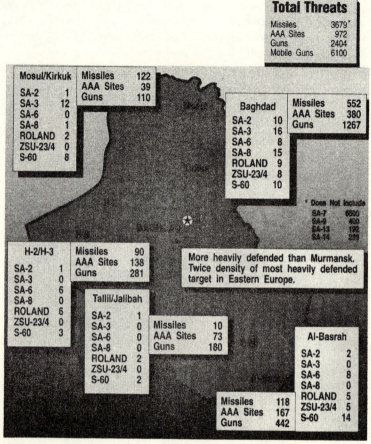

Total Threats	
Missiles	3679*
AAA Sites	972
Guns	2404
Mobile Guns	6100

Mosul/Kirkuk

		Missiles	122
SA-2	1	AAA Sites	39
SA-3	12	Guns	110
SA-6	0		
SA-8	1		
ROLAND	2		
ZSU-23/4	0		
S-60	8		

Baghdad

		Missiles	552
SA-2	10	AAA Sites	380
SA-3	16	Guns	1267
SA-6	8		
SA-8	15		
ROLAND	9		
ZSU-23/4	8		
S-60	10		

* Does Not include

SA-7	6500
SA-9	400
SA-13	192
SA-14	288

H-2/H-3

		Missiles	90
SA-2	1	AAA Sites	138
SA-3	0	Guns	281
SA-6	6		
SA-8	0		
ROLAND	6		
ZSU-23/4	0		
S-60	3		

More heavily defended than Murmansk. Twice density of most heavily defended target in Eastern Europe.

Tallil/Jalibah

		Missiles	10
SA-2	1	AAA Sites	73
SA-3	0	Guns	180
SA-6	0		
SA-8	0		
ROLAND	2		
ZSU-23/4	0		
S-60	2		

Al-Basrah

SA-2	2
SA-3	0
SA-6	8
SA-8	0
ROLAND	5
ZSU-23/4	5
S-60	14

Missiles	118
AAA Sites	167
Guns	442

FIGURE 5.4   Surface-to-Air Missile and Antiaircraft Artillery Threat. *Source:* Department of Defense, "The Conduct of the Persian Gulf War," Final Report to Congress, April 1992, p. 241.

the SAM threat was relatively low, SAMs could still be deadly (see Figure 5.4). Although the coalition did lose 8 planes the first night, that rate was surprisingly low; some air force analysts had anticipated losses as high as 150 aircraft for the first night alone.

Despite the early successes of the air campaign—successes soon broadcast to the world in the form of videotapes of precision weapons smashing Iraqi buildings, hardened aircraft shelters, and other targets—coalition air units soon encountered problems. Their most persistent foe proved to be not the Iraqis but the weather. During the Gulf War, Iraq experienced its worst weather in fourteen years. Predictions called for low cloud cover about 15 percent of the time, but in reality cloud cover set in about 40 percent of the time. The cloudy weather began on January 20, shortly after the campaign began. As many as 40 percent of the primary targets for the first ten days were lost, and aircraft, under strict orders not to drop their bombs without definite target identification, were forced to return to their bases without having dropped their bombs.

Besides fighting the weather, coalition air units were soon scurrying around in search of an elusive but potentially deadly target: Iraqi Scud missiles. Destruction of the Scuds was one of the top priorities of the air campaign plan, but the mobile missiles proved difficult to find. Coalition aircraft developed a number of different tactics for attacking the Scuds. F-16 fighter-bombers were placed on "box patrol," roaming the airspace around specific pieces of land and hunting for Scud launchers. Other aircraft learned to use their radars to detect the enormous trenches the Iraqis dug to conceal the missiles; once the radars had located a Scud trench, attack planes were directed in for the kill. Press reports after the war also suggested that special forces units participated in the Scud hunt.

The Scud threat became real on the second night of the war. Iraq launched nine of the missiles, eight of them at Israel as part of its announced intention to widen the conflict. Immediately the Scuds provoked a new minicrisis: Israel seemed ready to enter the war.

Israel had been especially wary of Iraq since even before the Gulf War began. On April 2, 1990, Saddam had vowed to burn half of Israel with chemical weapons if Israel launched a preemptive strike against Iraqi weapons production facilities.[7] A late May 1990 emergency summit meeting of the Arab League in Baghdad was the source of especially vitriolic anti-Israeli propaganda, which served only to increase Israeli anxiety regarding Iraq. When Iraq invaded Kuwait, many Israelis were skeptical of U.S. resolve in the Middle East—they did not expect the United States to take the kind of forceful action against Iraq that they viewed as necessary.

As the United States became increasingly determined to reverse the Iraqi aggression, however, it pressured Israel to keep quiet and allow U.S. coalition-building diplomacy with moderate Arab states to succeed. For the most part the Israelis complied with U.S. wishes, though they found it especially difficult in late summer 1990 when the United States announced plans to sell F-15s, Patriot missiles, and M1 tanks to Saudi Arabia.[8] Though Israel also began to benefit from Gulf tension through promises of increased U.S. economic aid and weapons sales, it was disturbed that the historical ratio of Arab to Israeli assistance was reversed in favor of the Arabs: For example, Egypt's $6.7 billion military debt to the United States was forgiven. As 1990 drew to a close, however, and it appeared that force would be used to solve the Gulf crisis, Israel found it increasingly difficult to keep quiet in the face of Iraqi threats to attack Israel if attacked by the United States. On December 5, Israeli foreign minister David Levy warned that Israel might attack and remove the Iraqi threat if the United States failed to do so.[9]

When Iraq's Scud missiles began to crash down on Israeli cities, many in Israel urged that the tiny nation respond as it always had—with overwhelming retaliatory force. An early crisis came on January 22, when a single incoming Scud missile escaped total destruction by an intercepting Patriot and went on to cause significant loss: 3 deaths, 96 other casualties, and the destruction of 900 people's homes. After the attack, Israeli defense minister Moshe Arens appeared on television to promise retaliation.[10] Many in Israel feared that if the policy of disproportionate retaliation were abandoned, Israel's future deterrent credibility would suffer serious damage. The natural desire to fight back at an aggressor must also have figured prominently in Israeli attitudes. For the moment, however, Israel waited.

It was fortunate that none of the Scuds fired at Israel were tipped with chemical warheads. Israeli patience wore increasingly thin as many feared that as Saddam became more desperate he would make good his threat to "burn half of Israel." Israeli military officers also became increasingly impatient with Allied efforts to hunt down and destroy the mobile Scud launchers. They felt that Allied pilots were insufficiently aggressive, that Israeli forces were more capable of eliminating this threat, and they chafed at being prevented from executing their plans for retaliation. The Israelis repeatedly put forward schemes for dealing with the Scuds, all of which were rejected by the United States.

The Israeli plans would also have been unacceptable to the Arab members of the coalition. Israel wanted to retaliate by attacking Scud sites in western Iraq with either air or both air and ground forces. To accomplish this mission with just air assets, they would have had to fly over Syria, Jordan, or Saudi Arabia. Placing special operations troops in Iraq would have caused even more difficulty, as this plan would have required a continuous air bridge to support the ground forces. In both cases, the cooperation of the Allies would be required in order to prevent Israeli and coalition forces from accidentally firing on each other. Regardless, the military difficulties paled in comparison to the political difficulties. It was too much to ask that the Arab members of the coalition be seen attacking an Arab state in concert with Israeli forces, even if, as some allowed, Israel had the right to defend itself. The United States preferred that Israel allow it to retaliate on behalf of its ally.

The Israelis did not retaliate. Several factors conspired to restrain them. First, the United States applied tremendous political pressure on the Israeli government both before and during the war. Repeated calls from U.S. State Department, Defense, and administration officials—as well as calls from President Bush to Israeli prime minister Yitzhak Shamir—kept up a constant chorus for restraint. Israeli defense minister Moshe Arens reportedly spoke with Secretary of Defense Cheney sixty times during the war.[11] Indeed, a special communications link, a sort of U.S.-Israeli hotline, was installed in the Pentagon just for this purpose. Additionally, as time passed the Israelis perceived that there was much political capital to be gained by restraint. Greater sympathy toward Israeli positions in an Arab-Israeli peace settlement, to say nothing of increased financial assistance in housing Soviet Jewish immigrants, were among the potential benefits.

Second, the United States provided additional Patriot missile batteries to Israel on top of the sets that had been sold before the war. Two Patriot batteries with U.S. crews arrived in Israel from Germany on Saturday, January 19. These missiles were equipped with advanced PAC-2 software, which made the Patriots more effective against Iraqi ballistic missiles. Israel's own Patriots, with PAC-1 software, were optimized for use against aircraft. Additionally, the presence of U.S. troops in Israel for the purpose of defending the Jewish state served to illustrate the U.S. commitment to Israel's security despite the circumstances of the moment, which required close cooperation with Arab militaries.

Operational constraints also served to restrain Israeli desire to strike back at Iraq. Information exchanges with the Israelis during the war must certainly have revealed that U.S. forces were already doing much of what Israel planned. It would be unacceptable, for example, to have both coalition and Israeli special operations forces roving the western Iraqi desert in search of Scuds—the potential for discovery and mistaken identity would be too great. Separate air forces performing the same mission would be equally unacceptable. Another method by which the United States may have discouraged the Israelis was by refusing to reveal the IFF (Identification Friend or Foe) codes being used by coalition aircraft. Unless the Israelis were given these codes, should they fly into Iraqi airspace their aircraft would become targets in the integrated allied air surveillance system. In the end, however, the United States adopted some Israeli recommendations regarding aerial pursuit of the Scud launchers.[12]

In all, 41 Scuds were fired at Israel. Three-quarters of these were fired in the first ten days, causing a great deal of material damage but mercifully few fatalities.[13] Scuds were fired at Israel right up until the beginning of the ground war despite extensive coalition efforts to locate and destroy Scud launchers. If nothing else, the air effort to destroy the Scuds demonstrated the difficulty of performing this mission and raised important questions with respect to ballistic missile proliferation and defenses.

Regardless, the effect of the Scuds upon the Israeli populace and the politics of the Middle East was profound. Though Iraq's missiles caused no military damage to Israel, they nearly succeeded in drawing the Israelis into the war. The sight of Palestinians cheering the incoming Scuds hardened Israeli resolve regarding occupied Arab lands and significantly complicated an already complex search for Middle East peace.

Bomb-Damage Assessment

Besides the weather and the need to hunt Scuds, another factor inhibiting the effectiveness of the air campaign—and one of the lessons of the war—was in the area of bomb-damage assessment, or BDA. Partly due to bad weather and partly because the United States relied on either satellite photos or aircraft reconnaissance pods, BDA timeliness and quality did not allow full exploitation of U.S. target acquisition and attack capabilities. Accurate BDA reports are necessary for effective military operations: They serve as a force multiplier, allowing military commanders to focus successive attacks on the most important remaining targets. The problem was not only that timely information was not always available but also that the services were not equipped to work well together in the intelligence field. Not enough thought had been given to presenting real-time BDA data to operational commanders and staff planners.

All branches of the U.S. military should pursue improvements in BDA capabilities. These can come in two varieties. The first would be to use information provided by cameras on aircraft making the actual attacks, which produced the stunning videos seen repeatedly on television during the war. Combined with precision weapons, bombsight cameras give an accurate report of whether a target was actually destroyed immediately on the return of the aircraft. Unfortunately, it appears that not all U.S. fighters and fighter-bombers possess such cameras—in part because not all carry smart munitions all the time and, when dropping dumb bombs, do not track the weapon to the target with a camera. Such a capability should be made more widely available, and the importance of such means should be recognized when future generations of aircraft and helicopters are designed.

Second, the military services should deploy new systems designed specifically to provide real-time intelligence and BDA from the battlefield. The best available candidates for such a mission are unmanned aerial vehicles (UAVs), small drone aircraft that can fly around a battlefield making video, infrared, and other observations and transmit them back to command posts. It has long been recognized that UAVs can make a major contribution to modern armies, and they were used extensively in the Gulf. By January 16, when Desert Shield was transformed into a raging Desert Storm, UAVs had already flown 230 missions and logged 650 hours over enemy territory. By the end of the war the drones had flown 530 missions and spent 1,700 hours aloft.

The performance of the roughly 30 UAVs in the Gulf nonetheless exceeded expectations. The UAVs—also known as remotely piloted vehicles, or RPVs—performed a host of missions. Army UAVs preflew routes that would be used by Apache helicopters in attacks on Iraqi positions; the Apache pilots watched the real-time video transmission from the UAV as it flew the exact route these same pilots would fly at night just hours later. Marine UAVs followed the progress of the Iraqi armored column that struck south at Khafji.

UAVs helped direct the fire of navy battleships' massive 16-inch guns. Some even managed to round up waving bands of Iraqi soldiers who wanted to surrender and guided them over to coalition forces.

In the future, UAVs could perform an even wider menu of roles. As mentioned above, they could become a primary source of real-time BDA. They could continue to provide intelligence and reconnaissance, as they did in the Gulf. But UAVs also have a promising combat role as well: In an era of precision weapons, UAVs are natural platforms for laser designation systems. In the future a fleet of UAVs could circle above a battlefield twenty-four hours a day, constantly designating targets for a rotating set of attack aircraft or for smart munitions fired from rocket launchers or artillery pieces to the rear. The army has in mind many such missions—and others, including limited air transport—for a future family of UAVs, as noted in its 1991 planning document. Drone aircraft will likely play an important role in future battle-management systems. It is imperative, however, that the military not gold-plate the UAV—pack it with so many technical gadgets that its cost, weight, and difficulty of repair rise dramatically.

War Improvisations

As the air war continued, U.S. pilots, mechanics, and electronics specialists encountered problems and seized opportunities. The F-16 onboard computer, it was discovered, was packed full of information. It couldn't accommodate new software, like programs designed to help aim and guide CBU-87 cluster bombs or a 30mm gun pod. The F-16s used those weapons anyway, though not as effectively as they might have. Some characterized the aircraft as a big computer game that needed more disk space.[14]

Meanwhile pilots of the big F-111 fighter-bombers learned new ways to kill tanks. They learned that if they flew attack missions at dusk and used infrared sensors, they could detect Iraqi tanks which, though dug-in, would be radiating the heat they had absorbed during the day. F-111s would speed over the sand, scanning the desert floor with their regular target acquisition radars, the weapons operator concentrating on the little screen in the cockpit. When the conventional radar gave indications of potential targets—raised peaks in the desert—the weapons operator would switch to infrared; hot spots indicated probable tanks. The rest went like a conventional precision-weapons attack: The weapons operator would fix his laser designator on the hot target; onboard computers would shoot a set of glide instructions and winglet settings to a laser-guided bomb in the plane's belly and release the weapon. A few seconds later, the Iraqi tank would be smashed with a direct hit on the top of its turret, an area of light armor. Pilots soon coined a phrase for the tactic—"tank plinking"—and with this tactic, air force units were reportedly destroying 100 to 150 Iraqi tanks per day before the ground war started.[15]

Early on, the first air-to-air clashes occurred between coalition and Iraqi jets. Later on day one, when the sun was up—and with it, U.S. pilots feared, Iraqi planes—two F-18s from the USS *Saratoga* in the Red Sea took off on a strike mission into western Iraq. Each of the F-18s carried four 2,000-pound bombs, but even with such a heavy load the aircraft is an agile performer, designed for fighter as well as attack missions. These FA-18s would perform both roles on the same flight.[16]

As the U.S. planes flew into Iraq, the *Saratoga*'s E-2C Hawkeye—the mini-AWACs radar plane embarked on U.S. aircraft carriers—spotted two Iraqi fighters speeding out to meet the F-18s. Following directions from the Hawkeye, the F-18s shifted course to meet the enemy fighters. "They were coming at us basically nose to nose," said one of the U.S. pilots later. The two groups of planes were closing at a combined speed of more than 1,300 miles per hour.

Each of the F-18 pilots locked his radar onto one of the Iraqi planes. Just a few seconds had passed since the initial warning. The U.S. pilots put aside their first-combat jitters and followed their training. They decided to let the approaching planes come to within visual range before firing to make certain they were indeed enemy. When the Iraqi planes—MiG-21s, as it turned out—could be seen, the U.S. pilots quickly checked for the telltale smoke or other signals that the Iraqis might be firing missiles. They were not. A few more seconds passed.

After what must have seemed a lifetime to the U.S. pilots, they finally decided to fire. Sparrow air-to-air missiles streaked out from under their wings. The shot was a tough one: When aircraft are closing head-on, the high intercept speed and small target presented by an approaching plane create difficulties for heat-seeking or radar-guided missiles. But the Sparrows found their mark, and both Iraqi planes exploded and crashed to the ground. About forty-five seconds had elapsed since the Hawkeye had first broadcast its warning. Other Iraqi planes had moved toward the area, but after the first two MiG-21s were destroyed and when the F-18s locked their target radars onto the second set of Iraqi aircraft, they fled. The F-18s continued on their mission, bringing thousands of pounds of death and destruction to Iraqi troops in western Iraq.

Across the Kuwait theater of operations, the momentum of the air campaign fed on its initial successes and rapidly built on the initial impression that a carefully laid plan was being more than capably executed. Almost immediately impatient observers became caught up in the sortie count–based presentation of the campaign, desperate for more information concerning the damage being done to Iraqi forces by all the endlessly airborne coalition aircraft.

The sense of brilliant orchestration was reinforced by CENTCOM briefers in Riyadh, who attempted to convey in more detail the objectives being pursued and the overall success rate. On Friday, January 18, coalition air commander Lieutenant General Charles Horner appeared on television to narrate two cockpit videotapes. One tape showed two laser-guided bombs demolishing a hardened aircraft shelter (HAS). The second showed how a U.S. F-117A pilot had dropped his bomb through the roof of the downtown Baghdad headquarters of the Iraqi air force, blowing the walls of the building out from inside. As the sortie count grew, coalition losses remained low, and even accidents occurred at a remarkably low rate, the sense of Allied technical superiority, professionalism, and expertise made the war against Iraq seem a decided issue from the first hour. Regardless, the slow rate of BDA discussed previously contributed to a sense of impatience regarding results.

Though militarily insignificant, the Iraqi Scud counterattack on January 18 forced one of the first changes in the carefully laid three-phase air campaign. Along with adapting to the bad weather and the overall merging of the three phases, the Scud campaign required improvisation to find the best mix of tactics and strike packages. In addition to F-16s on "box patrol," slower A-10 Warthogs conducted road reconnaissance, flying up and down travel routes in western Iraq hoping to catch the Iraqis playing a shell game with their Scuds. The A-10s were sometimes directed to their targets by E-8 JSTARS aircraft, which were able to detect the ground movement with their sensors. Though the coalition tactics were successful and significantly reduced the number of Scuds fired, they were unable entirely to prevent all launches.

January 17 saw the highest number of air-to-air engagements in the war as U.S. F-15s and FA-18s shot down 8 Iraqi aircraft. Only 2 Iraqi fighters were downed on the second day of the air campaign, but 6 on the third day.[17] The intensity of the air campaign appears to have sent the Iraqi air force into shock, as the number of their sorties declined rapidly from pre–January 17 levels. Indeed, they hardly flew at all. The lack of Iraqi activity could be explained in a number of ways. Their pilots could simply have been afraid of taking to skies filled with highly capable enemy aircraft. Second, the disruption of Iraqi command and control, combined with the effects of direct attacks on Iraqi air bases, may have kept the Iraqis from flying. (Trained largely by Soviet advisers, Iraqi pilots were probably highly dependent upon ground radar control for conducting interceptions of attacking aircraft. As with most third world air forces, too, they were not proficient at flying at night.) Third, Iraqi air force orders may have been to save their aircraft strength for the ground war—General Schwarzkopf suspected this might be the case as early as day three of the air campaign.[18] Regardless, the Iraqis' lack of activity was a welcome, if extremely puzzling, surprise to the coalition forces.

By the beginning of the second week of the war, however, the Iraqi flyers seem to have come out of shock and decided what to do: Fly to Iran.[19] On the tenth day of coalition attack, 27 Iraqi fighter aircraft escaped to their neighbor's airspace. Forty-eight more were to flee in the next three days.[20] This movement was probably in response to the Allied effort to destroy Iraqi aircraft in their hardened aircraft shelters. Using bombs designed to penetrate such structures, U.S. aircraft were slowly beginning to destroy the Iraqi air force even though it was not contesting control of the air. When flying to Iran, the Iraqis would take off and make a low-level beeline for the border, often making it across before the high-altitude coalition combat air patrol (CAP) could catch them. The escape route was later sealed when the coalition moved their combat air patrols into Iraqi airspace itself, reducing the Iraqis' reaction time.

Air Force captain Steve Tate, one of the first Allied pilots to down an Iraqi aircraft in air-to-air combat, later described a CAP mission over Iraqi territory flown on February 3: "Today we did a defensive counter-air, offensive counter-air kind of mission . . . up by the Iranian border." Tate and his flight were looking for Iraqi planes trying to fly to Iran. "They're trying to intercept these guys before they get to the border up there." By this time, however, airborne targets were scarce. "We didn't see any Iraqi airplanes airborne whatsoever, but we saw a lot of bombs being dropped out there today. . . . I've only seen one airplane airborne so far," said Tate, referring to his kill of the first night of the war, "and it wasn't airborne for very long."[21]

Regardless, the flight of the Iraqi air force was something of a surprise and the source of great debate. Some coalition analysts speculated that Iraq had reached an agreement with Iran under which the aircraft had been sent away for their own protection, to be returned after the war ended. A variation on this idea postulated that the aircraft would conduct an attack from Iran. Others felt that the pilots were defecting with their aircraft and that the "white-feather squadron" had no intention of either returning to Iraq or participating in the war. (This supposition was supported by rumors of the execution of the Iraqi air force commander.) Whatever the reason, a significant portion of the Iraqi air force removed itself from the battle, contributing to the sense that the Iraqis had conceded control of the air.

Not all Iraqi pilots were unwilling (or unable) to fight. On January 24, a Royal Saudi Air Force captain piloting a U.S.-made F-15 Eagle shot down a pair of Iraqi Mirage F-1s over the northern Gulf. Both Iraqi aircraft were loaded with the air-launched version of the Exocet antiship missile. Had they succeeded in attacking a coalition ship with their Exocets, at a minimum they would have caused a significant number of casualties. (In 1987, during the Iran-Iraq war, an Iraqi F-1 had accidentally fired two Exocets at USS *Stark,* a frigate on patrol duty in the Gulf. Both missiles hit the ship, and although they did not sink it, 37 sailors lost their lives.)

Regardless, by the second week of the campaign the Allied air forces had turned their attention increasingly to interdicting Iraqi supply routes. By this time the Iraqi "strategic" targets, such as the nuclear, chemical, and biological weapons production facilities, as well as Iraqi command-and-control centers, had been repeatedly bombed. The Iraqi air force had become irrelevant, and their medium- and high-altitude air defenses had been almost completely suppressed. Air search and targeting radars for the defending surface-to-air missiles sites were hit with Allied anti-radiation missiles. Indeed, by January 24 radar activity had fallen by 90 percent.[22] Antiaircraft fire was thereafter limited to unguided ballistic shots for large SAMs, infrared-guided shoulder-fired SAMs, and uncoordinated gunfire.

A record number of sorties to date, 2,700, were flown on January 25, and 236 Tomahawk missiles had been launched by that date. Also on the twenty-fifth, coalition forces discovered a vast oil spill contaminating the northern Gulf. The source of the spill was soon identified as Kuwait's Mina Al Ahmadi oil terminal facility, occupied by the Iraqis. The twenty-mile-long spill was created when the Iraqis deliberately opened pipelines leading into the Gulf from storage tanks ashore. This unorthodox tactic on the part of Saddam Hussein caused considerable consternation, as it was feared that the growing oil slick could foul the intakes of Saudi Arabian desalinization plants. Coalition troops, as well as large numbers of Saudi civilians, were dependent upon these plants for potable water. Two days later, on the twenty-seventh, U.S. FB-111s halted the flow of oil by dropping laser-guided bombs on pipeline system manifolds.[23] The attack also was an attempt to ignite the oil and burn as much of it as possible before it caused even greater environmental damage.

Meanwhile, the coalition aircraft loss rate continued to be low. The eleventh U.S. aircraft lost, a marine AV-8B piloted by Captain Michael Berryman, was shot down on January 28 after three days of no combat losses. His was the coalition's eighteenth such loss, though several more aircraft had been lost in noncombat accidents. If shot down or forced to abandon their aircraft, Allied aviators suffered one of three fates: They were either killed, captured, or rescued. Information regarding those killed often had to wait for the end of hostilities. (Indeed, Iraq released the remains of 12 coalition dead on March 13, 8 of whom were Britons. Most were probably aircrew from the 6 low-flying Tornado fighter-bombers lost attacking Iraqi airfields.) Special operations forces (SOF) deployed in northern Saudi Arabia formed search-and-rescue teams specifically tasked to find downed pilots in Iraq. Employing helicopters guarded by A-10s and F-15s, these SOF flyers conducted several dramatic rescues.

Those unfortunate aircrew captured by the Iraqis were few. In violation of Geneva conventions regarding the treatment of prisoners, however, those who were captured were paraded in public, beaten, and made the feature of a clumsy Iraqi propaganda ploy.[24] The prisoners were displayed on television programs critical of the war and bore obvious signs of mistreatment; the Iraqi effort to solicit sympathy backfired as world public opinion was repulsed by Iraqi brutality. Fortunately, the aircrew did not lose their freedom for long and were all safely returned at the conclusion of hostilities.

As January drew to a close Iraq launched small ground offensives across the Kuwaiti-Saudi border. The largest of these attacks, at Khafji, resulted in the Iraqis' taking the town on the twenty-ninth. Though the Iraqis had to be driven out with ground forces, the full force of the division-size attack was broken as the Iraqis were harassed by coalition aircraft. U.S. Air Force AC-130 gunships destroyed 4 tanks and 13 other vehicles on the night of January 29–30.[25] (The AC-130 is a transport aircraft specially configured for ground attack. It has 4 guns of various calibers and precision aiming equipment that allows it to target objects on the ground with great accuracy.) The combination of coalition air and ground forces soon drove the Iraqis back to their lines in Kuwait, never again to attempt an offensive in the face of coalition strength.

Indeed, two weeks after the start of the air campaign, Department of Defense statistics revealed the extent of damage done to Iraqi warfighting capacity: Twenty-six Iraqi leadership targets had been repeatedly bombed, forcing Saddam Hussein to run the war from inadequate facilities in mobile command vehicles. A quarter of Iraqi electrical generating equipment was inoperative, while a further 50 percent was degraded. As a result, Iraqi communications, industry, transportation, and public services were virtually nonexistent. Over 800 sorties had been directed at 29 air defense centers, reducing them to rubble.

Thirty-eight of 44 targeted Iraqi airfields had been bombed in over 1,300 strikes. Nine of those airfields were considered inoperative. Over 70 hardened aircraft shelters had been destroyed, forcing the Iraqis to hide their aircraft in residential areas (where they knew they would not be bombed) or fly them to Iran. Over 1,500 strikes had been flown against the 30 known fixed SCUD launch sites and known Iraqi missile production facilities. Both sets of targets were considered destroyed.

So-called strategic targets in Iraq had by this time been repeatedly attacked. All 31 nuclear, chemical, and biological facilities targeted had been bombed in over 535 sorties. (This total included a significant number of Tomahawk missile strikes.) All of Iraq's known nuclear facilities were considered destroyed, including the Baghdad Nuclear Research Center.

Finally, in the interdiction effort, 33 of 36 targeted railroad and highway bridges had been bombed in over 790 sorties, further isolating the Iraqi army in Kuwait. The Iraqis compensated as best they could by building pontoon bridges, but these too were soon identified and attacked. As a result of the bombing, highway traffic was greatly diminished, and CENTCOM estimated that the quantity of supplies reaching the Iraqi army in the Kuwaiti theater of operations (KTO) had been reduced from 20,000 to 2,000 tons a day. Republican Guard forces were receiving increasing amounts of attention as the skies became more safe for the lumbering B-52s. On January 30, 28 B-52s dropped 470 tons of bombs on the guard. As the days passed, more and more attention would be devoted to Iraqi ground forces as the air campaign shifted its emphasis to what was described as "battlefield preparation."[26]

The Importance of
Highly Trained Military Personnel

Perhaps the most misleading lesson currently being drawn from the Gulf War is that it was won by technological superiority alone. Night after night television reports treated the U.S. public to stunning images produced by smart weapons: videocamera-equipped missiles transmitting final pictures as they dove into military or industrial buildings, laser-guided bombs slamming into bunkers and bridges, rapierlike cruise missiles winging their way to targets in Baghdad past the rolling cameras of the international media. Without doubt, precision weapons such as those played a major role in the war. But they were only *part* of the reason for the stunning coalition victory. There was much more to this conflict than smart weapons, and we should not rush too quickly to embrace the idea that such weapons alone decided the war.

In another place, at another time, and against another enemy, high-tech smart weapons might not play as large a role as they did in the Gulf War—they may even play a limited role. In the Gulf War it often seemed that Saddam Hussein was planning and executing his strategy to put U.S. precision weapons on display. He began a conflict in a largely flat and featureless terrain easily scanned for activity by U.S. satellites and aircraft, at a time of year when the United States would be able to wage warfare unencumbered by bad weather. Once he had created this target-rich and smart bomb-friendly environment, Saddam sat back, waited for us to initiate the war and cripple his air defenses, and then allowed us to conduct a devastating month-long air campaign from the invulnerable sanctuary of Saudi Arabia and other surrounding nations. Finally, he did not feed or supply his troops adequately; his arbitrary and brutal decisions (beginning with the choice to invade Kuwait in the first place) undercut his commands and demoralized his troops—they had very little to fight for.

Unfortunately, we cannot count on finding such cooperative adversaries in all future wars. In Korea, for example, the army of the Communist North has spent forty years moving much of its hardware and many of its command posts and personnel underground. This strategic advantage is compounded by the mountainous terrain throughout much of the peninsula and seasonal rains, fog, and clouds: The North Korean army is probably much less susceptible to an onslaught of smart weapons than was Iraq's. Other areas where U.S. military forces might be called to fight, such as Eastern Europe, Southeast Asia, and Latin America, are actually hostile to technological warfare. In Korea, moreover, if war begins we will likely be facing a ground battle from the first day, immensely complicating the U.S. and South Korean military task in general and the employment of smart weapons in particular.

Apart from technology, then, what did win the war? The key U.S. and co-alition advantage in influencing the character of the war was personnel. Desert Storm proved, among other things, that the U.S. all-volunteer force is militarily competent: U.S. soldiers, sailors, air force, and marines performed superbly in conditions that were often far worse than the short casualty lists suggest. This was in the end a war won by people, not machines—a fact apparent even in the early days of the air campaign.

The quality of the people in the U.S. military today is in part the result of a reaction to the disastrous experience of the 1970s, when the military was demoralized from Vietnam and lacking in pride and social esteem. Drug abuse and intraservice tensions were rife, readiness rates and training scores low. Determined to rid themselves of this "hollow" force, leaders of the U.S. armed forces embarked in the 1980s on a comprehensive program of discipline, training, and rebuilding the military's pride in itself. New doctrines were developed and new equipment was on the way; these were necessary, but alone they would not be sufficient for the rebuilding of our forces. Motivation, professionalism, and combat readiness were the watchwords; a renewed emphasis on leadership at all levels and new specialized instruction, training bases and technologies, and constant maintenance and exercises were the tools of rebuilding.

Particularly notable has been the continuing focus on leadership, which lies at the heart of any military organization. Numerous advanced training schools have been established to inculcate principles of leadership and to test their students on its practice. Some of these schools serve officers, particularly in ranks most likely to be in command of a battalion, ship, or squadron; others concentrate on noncommissioned officers—the experienced sergeants and petty officers who form the core of a well-trained fighting force. Talk of replacing leaders with "managers" in modern armies was abandoned, and new emphasis was placed on training military leaders—warriors competent in the business of combat.

Leadership is an especially important quality in the U.S. military, which has always relied on small-unit initiative much more than has its Soviet counterpart or armies patterned on the Soviet model. Centralized, authoritarian states fight as they govern—with orders usually given from the top and transmitted through rigid lines of command to units in the field that enjoy neither the authority nor the ability to react quickly and flexibly to events. The quality of improvisation, of seizing propitious moments in battle and exploiting them, has always been a hallmark of the armies of democratic states (though undemocratic ones can have it too—German troops in World War II were renowned for their small-unit flexibility). Such improvisation demands superb leadership from the squadron, small combat ship, or platoon level on up.

The results of this reinvigoration of the U.S. military became clear in the Gulf War. U.S. personnel quality was consistently high in all campaigns, both at the level of combat leader and foot soldier, pilot, or sailor. Coalition forces displayed great operational flexibility, including unit initiative and battlefield innovation. Air units used their smart weapons in ways not by the book; quick-thinking air force officers soon had F-111 aircraft, not designed as battlefield strike aircraft, dropping massive 500-pound bombs directly on top of individual Iraqi tanks. The ground forces innovated as well: Breaching techniques used to punch holes through the Iraqi lines were developed from existing techniques; full-scale models of the Iraqi defenses were constructed, and U.S. specialists in doctrine and tactics devised new ways of perforating them.

David Gergen of *U.S. News and World Report* has written of this "great revival" in the U.S. military. The emphasis on education is particularly great: "No other body in America" besides the military, Gergen argues, "places greater emphasis on sharpening the mind." The military academies have entrance requirements more demanding than many exclusive private universities. Once in the military, the commitment to education continues: "By the end of a 20-year career, an officer has usually devoted five or six years to study" in schools "that not only stress traditional military doctrine but also widen and deepen an officer's understanding of American political life, international affairs and grand strategy." As we have seen, the military's commitment to education is matched by its focus on leadership skills. Gergen notes that "David Campbell, a psychologist with the Center for Creative Leadership, has found that in tests of his seminar classes of military brass and business managers, the military officers score the highest of any group on leadership skills, decisiveness, dominance, self-assurance, achievement orientation and psychological health."[27]

Training in general also played a critical role in improving the effectiveness and combat readiness of the U.S. armed forces. Training comes in many sizes and flavors: It can be classroom instruction in high-tech warfare, on-the-job instruction about equipment or tactics, or live-fire exercises in the California desert with soldiers crawling on their bellies through barbed wire. The box-office hit *Top Gun* depicted a few scattered air combat sequences, but for the most part it was about training—the Top Gun school and its method of creating the most realistic air-to-air combat instruction possible. In the end, the training worked: in this war, like no other before it, troops without combat experience had justified confidence in their ability to fight.

An example of modern training can be found at the National Training Center. Located in the California desert, the center is host to dozens of military units every year, U.S. combat forces that rotate through for a taste of the closest thing they will get to war outside real combat. Resident at the center is the Opposing Force, or OpFor, soldiers taught to simulate Soviet or Soviet-style tactics. The OpFor, equipped with captured Soviet equipment or U.S.

equipment modified to look like it, takes on the visiting U.S. units in mock battles played out across the massive base. The visitors usually lose—it's meant to be that way—and they learn from their mistakes without having to do so in combat. Many soldiers interviewed in the field later remarked that this sort of realistic training was what best prepared them for war; many also said that the OpFor actually employed Soviet-style tactics better than the Iraqis themselves. The navy and air force have their own training areas—the navy uses Guantánamo Bay in Cuba as a center for a great deal of readiness drills, and the air force maintains a number of combat simulation ranges—for many years using huge live-fire ranges in the Philippines to stage mock air raids and dogfights—as well as the more well known Red Flag and Desert Flag exercises. Pilots in Desert Storm said the first air attacks were mirror images of Red Flag, which had prepared them well for the operations.

Training also means exercises, in the Middle East and elsewhere. U.S. forces often go on maneuvers and joint exercises on their own, but even more important are combined exercises with current or potential allies; the air forces, armies or navies of two or more nations can work together in a simulated combat environment and work out problems that might arise in war. In the early 1980s the United States began a series of binational exercises with the Egyptians called Bright Star, in which dozens of U.S. Air Force aircraft and thousands of U.S. troops were brought into the Middle East to engage in simulated combat side by side with Egyptian forces in a desert environment. Similarly in Korea, the United States annually deploys aircraft and thousands of troops to the South to work with U.S. forces already there as well as South Korean units in mock battles. The navy conducts simulations with its partners in NATO and other theaters, testing communications and tactics. The efficiency, camaraderie, and personal relationships built by such exercises contribute immensely to combined combat effectiveness when the forces are later merged during a crisis or war. Even the logistics of moving a corps out of one theater and into another are practiced in the annual REFORGER exercise, a capability that proved crucial to the deployment of VII Corps from Europe to Saudi Arabia in forty-five days.

Finally, as with weaponry, training in the U.S. armed forces today employs high technology. Even the simplest field maneuvers might now take advantage of advanced lasers fitted to guns to simulate the firing of a weapon; soldiers wear laser detectors and if hit must be treated as mock casualties and removed from the exercise through tactical treatment and evacuation systems. U.S. aircrew use space-age flight simulators to become accustomed to their aircraft and its weapons; tankers use systems much like a video game for target practice; navy gunners and missile operators practice their trades on similar equipment. And of course, such advanced training equipment is particularly important today. The smart weapons that did so much damage to Saddam Hussein's war machine did not build themselves, or maintain themselves, or deliver themselves to the target areas. Highly trained, technologically competent U.S. soldiers, sailors, aircrew and marines did all of that and more. If high-tech weapons are growing in their importance in modern warfare—and they clearly are—then training is growing in importance right along with them. The U.S. advantage in training technologies is at least as great, and as important, as its advantage in weaponry.

None of this training is free. Like any other military activity, it costs money and cannot therefore escape debates about fiscal priorities within the Defense Department. The annual cost of maintaining the National Training Center might buy a dozen tanks, or a couple of attack planes, or several dozen smart weapons. Training is more than something the military just "does"; it is an investment, in this case in the military's human capital, and as such must compete with other investments—in research and development, in high-tech weapons, in basic fighting equipment.

Secretary of Defense Richard Cheney recognizes this and has rightly placed great emphasis on maintaining quality personnel even as the U.S. military is reduced in size by 25 percent or more in the coming years. Cheney's commitment is admirable, but as time passes, as more bases and defense production lines are closed and more weapons systems canceled, the temptation will be strong to begin neglecting military people in favor of weapons. Buying weapons creates jobs and energizes the economies of a large number of congressional districts; training offers those benefits at only a very few locations.

Yet given the importance of high-quality personnel, one lesson of the war in the Gulf is that training investments must be protected, in terms of both the money and time spent on them. There is no point in having a "hollow" force armed with the most modern missiles and laser-guided bombs if it is not motivated to fight, if its leaders cannot lead, if its technicians cannot maintain their equipment, and if its troops are not schooled in the basic aspects of warfare. We must remain on guard against a military long on equipment and short on competence.

The U.S. Navy's Contribution

Though the U.S. Air Force dominated the air war, overshadowing both allied air forces and the contribution of other U.S. services, no discussion of the air campaign would be complete without a consideration of the contribution made by naval aircraft. Such a consideration is especially necessary in light of the controversy that grew up after the war surrounding their role. When we consider the naval component, there is also an opportunity to discuss the overall campaign at sea. Though naval aviation dominated the maritime effort, it far from represented the full naval effort.

Even as the confrontation in the Gulf began, naval forces on the scene demonstrated U.S. resolve by establishing a preliminary air defense screen between Iran and the Arabian Peninsula, keeping watch on Teheran's neutrality in the conflict. A cruiser equipped with the high-tech Aegis radar system and aircraft carriers positioned less than forty-eight hours away demonstrated once again the value of a forward U.S. presence in areas of vital concern. Because the Iraqi naval threat was minimal, coalition naval forces secured the KTO on three sides without serious opposition. U.S. naval forces of the Middle East Task Force formed the early core around which Allied nations could tangibly and visibly join the growing coalition effort to isolate Saddam Hussein. Throughout the war, the coalition naval blockade clearly demonstrated the political and military effectiveness of building on such long-standing military relationships.

Among the operational lessons of the embargo is the fact that the embargo apparently did reinforce Hussein's predisposition to hold the Iraqi army in static deployments to avoid wear and tear on its equipment. The embargo continued throughout 1992 as the coalition's best tool for wielding political leverage.

As with air and ground forces, the Gulf War highlighted needed areas of improvement in U.S. naval capabilities that would contribute significantly to the new U.S. contingencies strategy. After the need for strategic sealift, perhaps the next most prominent need is in the area of mine countermeasures. The Gulf War was the second indication of a major shortcoming—in the Gulf reflagging operation in the late 1980s, World War II–era mines gave U.S. naval forces real problems. Existing plans to remedy this deficiency have not yet reached fruition. After the war, U.S. Central Command (CENTCOM) head General Norman Schwarzkopf told the Congress that the United States has a "very, very antiquated minesweeping fleet and very, very small numbers that frankly just couldn't get the job done."

The performance of U.S. carrier aviation in the war also merits close examination. Carrier-based aircraft flew some 18,000 missions through early March 1991, dropped more than 11 million pounds of bombs, and fired over 600 air-to-ground missiles. Regardless of the counts used to influence the debate on the proportional contribution of carrier-based aircraft versus land-based, carrier aircraft were less effective in the aggregate than their land-based counterparts for the missions required by this air campaign. This was true partly because naval ordnance was often not optimal for the task at hand; carriers had only a limited number of precision munitions available. Other contributing factors may have been an inadequate communications link between the carriers and those managing the air campaign and the fact that carrier aircraft often had to fly farther to their targets than land-based aircraft, which placed a burden on limited tanker support.

It is possible to outline several clear conclusions about aircraft carriers from the Gulf experience; some emphasize their importance, others demonstrate their limitations. For example, as the first major combat vessels on the scene,

USS *Independence* and USS *Eisenhower* played a major role in sending a robust military and political signal of U.S. resolve. Had the Iraqis carried their attack into Saudi Arabia after a brief pause in August, U.S. carrier-based aviation would have been critical for attacking the advancing Iraqi columns. As noted earlier, in this war the coalition base of operations boasted very modern, well-equipped airfields capable of supporting hundreds of land-based tactical aircraft. This will not always be the case, and when it is not, carrier aviation will be even more important.

However, as demonstrated in the Gulf, the contribution of carrier-based aircraft to any major land campaign is significantly constrained by their limited numbers. Their offensive power, although impressive, is necessarily constrained by competing requirements to provide fleet defense and engage in antisurface combatant operations. Where maritime combat occurs, of course, carriers will be indispensable.

The lessons derived from the war suggest neither that carrier aviation is perfect nor that it should be abandoned, but they do point toward one major reform. Some carrier-based aircraft lack important capabilities that would have allowed them to use more precision weapons oriented toward the land attack mission—laser designators, for example. The requirements of our new military strategy involve a shift in focus from the Soviet Union to regional contingencies, where U.S. naval forces will need to concentrate more on restricted water operations and support of land operations and less on deep-water navy-on-navy confrontations. In the future, the navy will have to increase its capability to conduct sustained, precision strike operations over land.

Preparations for the Ground War

During the first week of February 1991, questions were being raised over the efficiency and effectiveness of the air campaign. When evidence began surfacing that the campaign was actually as much as nine days off schedule, President Bush started to prepare the U.S. public for a ground war by stating that coalition goals would not be won by air power alone. Despite initial glowing reports, the weather and other factors had taken their toll on the ability of the coalition air force to accomplish its objectives.

By the end of the first week of February, the air campaign had become almost routine. Central Command briefings from Riyadh and Pentagon Defense Department briefings spoke of the continued high sortie rate and the rapidly increasing total number of sorties. There were, however, several highlights. The Department of Defense (DoD) announced on February 2 that all Iraqi naval vessels capable of firing missiles had been destroyed. Henceforth, the Iraqi navy was considered combat ineffective.[28] On the third, DoD announced that 65 more HASs had been destroyed, further limiting the options Iraq had for preserving its air force.[29] Increasing damage was being inflicted on Iraqi armor, supply lines, and Republican Guard forces. Even after the first week of February, speculation was intense as to when the ground campaign would begin. Speculation was fueled by an imminent trip of senior Defense Department officials to the KTO.

On the February 8, British defense minister Tom King gave the first official account of the toll taken in Iraqi armor—over 600 tanks. The Central Command briefer in Riyadh later confirmed the numbers, adding that the Allied forces were not waiting to cross a specific threshold before initiating ground combat—they would not necessarily start or wait, for example, when 75 percent of Iraqi armor was destroyed.[30] Also on February 8, Secretary of Defense Cheney and Chairman Powell arrived in Saudi Arabia for discussions with General Schwarzkopf regarding the course of the war, further fueling speculation that a ground war was imminent. Cheney and Powell were to return to Washington with the general's opinions and advise the president.

Indeed, at the end of the third week of the air campaign the Allies were looking for ways to further increase its effectiveness. During the flight to Saudi Arabia Secretary Cheney suggested that select marine amphibious or army ground forces be added to the campaign in an effort to draw the Iraqis out of their prepared positions and make them more vulnerable to the air force. A third possibility would be a raid into Iraq from helicopter assault teams from the 101st Airborne Division.[31] Whatever tactics were used, it seemed clear that coalition commanders were not yet ready for a major armored assault because the last of VII Corps' equipment had only recently been unloaded in Saudi Arabia. The decision was made to continue with air attack alone and be patient regarding the rate of Iraqi army attrition.

So the air campaign proceeded apace. On February 8, 2,500 sorties were flown, bringing the total to 55,000. Thirteen more Iraqi aircraft fled to Iran, bringing the total to 121 Iraqi fighters and 26 transport aircraft. AWACs planes, able to measure the amount of Iranian flight activity, reported that the defecting Iraqi planes were idle. In Kuwait and southern Iraq, Iraqi soldiers continued to surrender, walking south to the Allied lines. On the ninth, the number of Iraqi tanks destroyed was increased to 750, and 650 of 3,000 artillery pieces and an estimated 400 armored personnel carriers were reported destroyed. The sortie count rose by another 2,000.

Naval aircraft continued to contribute to the overall campaign. As with Iraqi aircraft, surviving vessels of the Iraqi navy were fleeing to Iran. Few completed their voyages. On February 10, U.S. Navy A-6s destroyed a pair of Iraqi patrol boats in the northern Gulf, and on the eleventh a British Royal Navy Lynx helicopter flying from the guided-missile destroyer HMS *Cardiff* fired two Sea Skua missiles at a 75-foot Iraqi patrol craft, leaving it on fire and sinking. British and U.S. shipboard helicopters were to cooperate extensively in the surveillance and control of the northern Gulf. U.S. helicopters, although possessed of a superior search radar, lacked missiles like the British Sea Skua. Armed with the small air-to-surface missiles, the British helicopters were more able to engage Iraqi naval targets.

Concluding their visit to Saudi Arabia, Cheney and Powell returned to the United States on the tenth and stated that there was a limit to what could be achieved using air power.[32] Regardless, they gave no impression of what recommendations they would give to the president concerning the direction of the air war. In retrospect it seems clear that their recommendation was to continue the campaign without adding ground elements. In an October 11 Pentagon press briefing, Joint Staff Director of Operations Lieutenant General Thomas Kelly stated that Allied air forces had not yet reached the point of diminishing returns. Nevertheless, as February progressed the perception that a ground war was imminent grew steadily.

The countdown was soon to be overshadowed by a tragic event. Early Wednesday morning, February 13, U.S. F-117 stealth fighter-bombers dropped a pair of laser-guided bombs onto a fortified Iraqi shelter in downtown Baghdad. The bombs scored direct hits, penetrating the heavily fortified roof and exploding within. Unexpectedly, the attack produced a large number of Iraqi civilian casualties—over 400 deaths according to Iraqi accounts. (Western media were able to confirm 100 deaths when visiting the site.)[33] The Iraqis claimed that the United States had deliberately attacked a civilian bomb shelter—statements they supported with televised pictures of civilian casualties. U.S. military representatives heatedly denied the Iraqi allegations.

The televised reports of the attack and the effect they had would call into question the wisdom of prolonging the air war. In a careful response to Iraqi claims that the bunker was a civilian air-raid shelter, U.S. military officials produced drawings made from satellite photos and other evidence drawn from intelligence sources to present their case that the facility was being used for military purposes as a command-and-control center. They pointed out that the bunker had a camouflage-painted roof and a security fence, features that did not support the Iraqi claim. Coalition briefers reiterated that great effort and extreme care went into the selection of targets and that in no way were Iraqi civilians being targeted. If they had believed that civilians were sharing a military facility, that facility would not have been bombed. Still, the event contributed to the feeling that the air campaign had indeed begun to meet the point of diminishing returns and that a ground war was needed to end the conflict quickly. This feeling was reinforced two days later when Iraq stated it was ready to negotiate based on the UN resolutions seeking to resolve the Gulf crisis.

February 13 saw 2,800 Allied sorties (as the coalition began consistently pushing towards the 3,000-sortie-per-day mark) and by the next day the number of Iraqi weapons destroyed had gone up significantly. Briefings given in Washington indicated that nearly one-third of Iraqi armor and artillery in the Kuwait theater of operations had been destroyed: Thirteen hundred tanks, 1,100 artillery pieces, and 800 other armored vehicles. The increased totals were said to reflect a shift in emphasis in targeting precision munitions to individual pieces of Iraqi hardware—a result of the so-called tank plinking. The Iraqi army was described as being "quickly and utterly shattered."[34]

A variety of powerful weapons aided coalition air forces in the destruction of the Iraqi army. One of these was the BLU-82 "Daisy Cutter" bomb, a 14,000-pound behemoth last used in the Vietnam War. Employed mostly for psychological effect, the weapon was dropped out the cargo doors of C-130 aircraft to clear paths through frontline Iraqi trenchlines and obstacles. The Daisy Cutter explosions, reportedly, were spectacular. Use of the weapon was coupled with the dropping of propaganda leaflets warning Iraqi troops that they were to be the target of the most powerful conventional weapon in the U.S. arsenal. According to numerous reports, these warnings induced a large number of Iraqi troops to surrender.

A second weapon developed for use during the war was the GBU-28 laser-guided bomb. As the air campaign progressed, certain Iraqi hardened shelters proved capable of withstanding hits from U.S. penetrating bombs. In order to overcome this problem, the 4,700-pound GBU-28 was machined from surplus 203mm cannon barrels and fitted with a nose cone, laser-guidance system, and fin set. When test-dropped in the Nevada desert, one GBU-28 penetrated over 100 feet into the earth. A second broke through over 22 feet of concrete during a sled test. After being shipped to Iraq, the only two weapons employed were dropped on a bunker complex at the Al Taji military airfield north of Baghdad. "At Taji Bunker No. 1, the raid's primary target, a bomb hit the site squarely, causing a small puff of smoke to blow out one of several entrances. . . . About 7 sec. later, there was a large secondary explosion that destroyed the site."[35]

Though the GBU-28s were developed to handle tough targets, the Daisy Cutters were being dropped in anticipation of the coming ground campaign. Other events indicated that the climax was near. On February 14, a fourth aircraft carrier, USS *America*, entered the Gulf, also in preparation for the coming ground war.[36] As the air war continued apace, there was a continued shift in emphasis from Iraqi strategic to tactical targets in the southern Kuwait theater of operations. As shown in Figure 5.5, coalition air forces continued to maintain a high sortie rate. Indeed, the fifth and sixth weeks of the air war seemed little more than an increasing sortie total and ever-growing accounts of Iraqi equipment destroyed. In late February General Schwarzkopf conducted a ninety-minute interview in which he characterized the Iraqi army as on the verge of collapse. Increasing reports of skirmishes, raids, and other ground activity broadcast the imminence of the ground war.

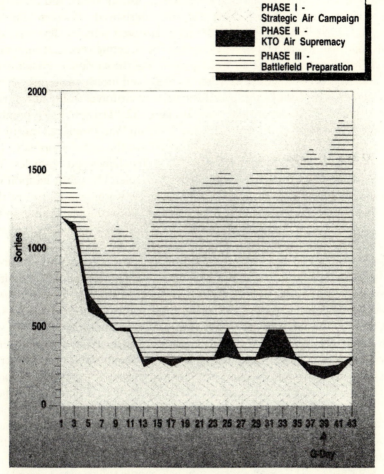

FIGURE 5.5   Coalition Air Campaign: Combat Sorties by Phase—Actual Execution. (Note: Phase IV aircraft sorties are included in Phase III sortie depiction.) *Source:* Department of Defense, "The Conduct of the Persian Gulf War," Final Report to Congress, April 1992, p. 135.

The Effectiveness of the Air Campaign

In the final analysis, the coalition's air campaign was a stunning success.[37] Coalition aircraft flew 109,876 sorties, dropped 88,500 tons of bombs (6,520 tons of them precision weapons), and shot down 35 Iraqi planes in air-to-air combat. Of 594 Iraqi aircraft shelters identified at the outset of the conflict, 375 were destroyed.

The F-117 stealth fighters flew over 1,300 sorties consisting of 6,900 hours of flying time and dropped 2,000 tons of bombs. F-15 air superiority fighters flew 5,900 sorties and kept Iraqi aircraft away from coalition strikes; F-15E attack versions flew another 2,200 sorties, attacking Scud missiles, tanks, airfields, and roads. The 144 tough A-10 ground-attack planes flew 8,100 sorties through heavy antiaircraft fire and attacked a host of Iraqi equipment. Bigger F-111s flew over 4,000 strike missions and "plinked" their way to 1,500 confirmed tank kills. Another attack aircraft, the F-16, proved a workhorse of the war, flying over 12,500 missions. The lumbering B-52s flew over 1,600 missions on their own and dropped a vast amount of bombs—almost 26,000 tons, about 30 percent of all bombs dropped during the war. Navy and marine corps A-6s, A-7s, AV-8Bs, and FA-18s did their part, flying over 17,000 missions.

Tomahawk cruise missiles, JSTARS and AWACS battle-management aircraft, EF-111 Raven and EA-6B Prowler jammers, and a fleet of KC-10 and KC-135 tankers provided the support needed to multiply the destructive power of the attack aircraft and make the air war such a resounding success. TR-1s, RF-4s, and a host of air force, navy, and army electronic intelligence-collection aircraft provided the information to give the campaign direction. Allied aircraft provided additional mass, special capabilities and munitions, and flexibility that also contributed to the overall success.

Even if it was not true, as USAF general Merrill McPeak suggested, that the air campaign against Iraq was the first time in history that a field army was defeated by air power, it is widely agreed that in this case it created the conditions for a rapid, low-casualty ground phase.

6

One Hundred Hours

As midnight on February 23 passed and the early morning of February 24 arrived in the Gulf, a half-million-strong coalition force prepared for the final battles of the Gulf War. (See Figures 6.1 and 6.2.) At 4:00 in the morning on the twenty-fourth, General Schwarzkopf's ground phase would begin—thousands of tanks and other military vehicles and hundreds of thousands of ground troops tearing through the Iraqi lines, attempting to encircle and defeat the massive Iraqi army. Coalition aircraft had waged a devastating air campaign against the Iraqis for over a month, but Schwarzkopf and his aides still had major worries. What if Saddam was hoarding his strength for the ground battle? The Iraqi fortifications around Kuwait were said to be formidable, and behind the Iraqi lines thousands of Regular Army and Republican Guard tanks waited to meet any coalition advances.

Many coalition ground officers also feared that Hussein would use chemical weapons during the decisive ground battles to come. Iraqi forces could deliver them with artillery, aircraft, or Scud missiles and had chemical mines as well. Schwarzkopf's ultimate nightmare was of his beloved troops hung up amid Iraqi minefields, barbed wire, and bunkers, pounded mercilessly with nerve gas and other chemical and biological weapons.

The final outcome of the war was hardly in doubt; it had not been since January 18. The only question left was at what cost the victory would be won. Early on the morning of February 24, many in the coalition feared that cost might be high.

Marine Battles

In fact, by February some coalition ground troops had already had their first taste of battle. On the night of January 29–30, dozens of Iraqi tanks and thousands of troops crossed the border into Saudi Arabia. The Iraqi tanks approached Saudi positions with their turrets reversed, a possible signal that the Iraqis intended to give up. "Apparently they want to surrender," said Major

Craig Huddleston, a U.S. Marine officer in the area monitoring the Iraqi movements. "They have their turrets reversed and they are not indicating any hostile intention."[1]

"We've got to play this close to our vest," Huddleston told his men. He was concerned that the marines not misjudge the Iraqi intention and either kill surrendering soldiers or fall victim to a ruse. "We don't want to blow this one."

Very quickly, however, it became clear that the Iraqis were full of fight. Ten minutes after his first hopeful remarks, Major Huddleston told reporters that the Iraqi units "have engaged the Saudi forces in combat, and we're going to kill them." "They probably ought to call 911 right now," Huddleston said later. "I expect we're going to expel them rather violently. . . . We're going to spank them rather hard."

Huddleston was not speaking idly. Within hours a powerful array of fire-power was brought to bear on the Iraqi columns. Saudi troops absorbed the brunt of the assault, but they were supported by Saudi and U.S. marine artillery, marine Cobra attack helicopters, AV-8 Harrier ground attack jets, air force A-10 close support aircraft, and navy A-6 strike planes. Out in the open and moving, the Iraqi vehicles made perfect targets for every weapon the coalition used. Dozens of Iraqi tanks were destroyed, hundreds of Iraqi soldiers undoubtedly killed. The fight was so one-sided that the next day one marine officer would boast, "We kicked their asses"; another looked forward to the possibility of finding more Iraqi units out in the open: "I hope they keep attacking us, the dumb f---s."

A handful of Iraqi tanks and several hundred soldiers did make it into the deserted town of Khafji, however, and holed up to repel Saudi and U.S. attacks. Before the Iraqis stormed in, twelve marines had gone into Khafji to watch the border from empty buildings in the abandoned town. When the Iraqi units arrived, the marines were asked if they wanted to leave, but they decided to stay to direct artillery fire onto the enemy that surrounded them.[2]

One group of marines huddled on the second floor of an empty apartment building. Some Iraqi troops had come in on the ground floor and were walking around talking and passing by the bottom of the staircase in view of the marines. Rather than allow themselves to be captured, the marines had decided to set off a claymore mine in the staircase, even though the explosion would undoubtedly bring other Iraqis rushing to their position. Another marine directed artillery fire at targets so close the explosions sent shrapnel into his thigh. "I'd be lying," said Corporal Chuck Ingraham, "if I said dying didn't come across my mind." By February 1, however, Khafji had been cleared of Iraqis and all twelve men were safe.

Khafji was not the only battle fought that night. All along the border, Iraqi units came forward to probe coalition positions. In many cases U.S. Marine Light Armored Vehicles (LAVs)—lightly protected armored cars with ma-

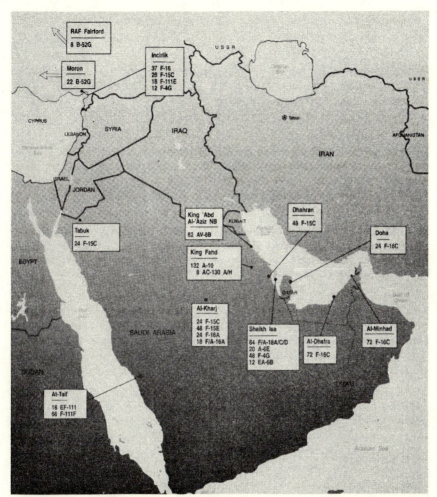

FIGURE 6.1   Coalition Land-based "Shooters" on February 24, 1991. (Note: Aircraft numbers and locations changed continuously.) *Source:* Department of Defense, "The Conduct of the Persian Gulf War," Final Report to Congress, April 1992, p. 142.

chine guns and TOW antitank missiles—deployed in front of the main lines as a screening force absorbed the brunt of these probes. Marine LAVs destroyed a number of Iraqi tanks with missiles and sent others scurrying for cover. Saudi and Qatari troops bore primary responsibility for expelling the Iraqis from Khafji.

By February 1, Saddam Hussein's desultory little ground offensive was over. Iraq had lost several dozen tanks—42 in the battle for Khafji alone—and hundreds of prisoners. It was a preview of what would come.

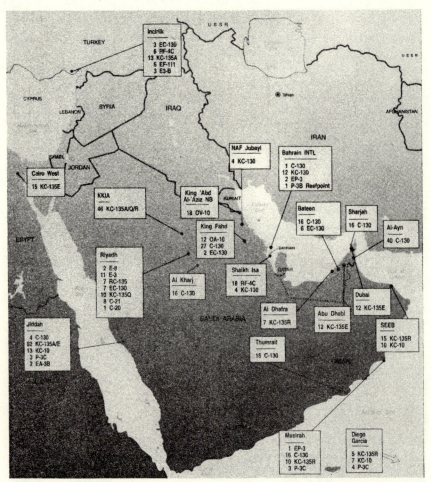

FIGURE 6.2 Coalition Land-based Support Aircraft on February 24. (Note: Aircraft numbers and locations changed continuously.) *Source:* Department of Defense, "The Conduct of the Persian Gulf War," Final Report to Congress, April 1992, p. 143.

U.S. Ground Forces

The coalition strategy for the ground campaign (see Figure 6.3) was a simple concept: Outflank the Iraqi forces in Kuwait by pushing into southern Iraq far to the west and then turn east to engage the backbone of Hussein's army—the eight divisions of the Republican Guard. But in execution it was exceedingly complex. On the extreme left of the coalition's front, XVIII Corps units, the French 6th Light Armored Division with components of the U.S. 82nd Airborne Division, were to seize Iraq's As Salman air base and establish a

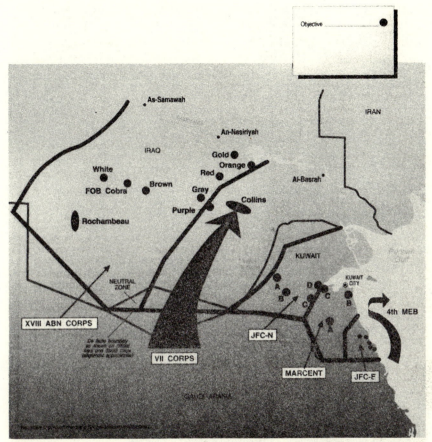

FIGURE 6.3   Ground Offensive Campaign Concept of Operations. *Source:* Depart-ment of Defense, "The Conduct of the Persian Gulf War," Final Report to Congress, April 1992, p. 91.

screen to protect the coalition's flank. To their right, another unit of XVIII Corps, the 101st Air Assault, was to leapfrog to the Euphrates River, where it would cut the major Iraqi highway running through the river valley. This ac-tion would isolate the Iraqi forces in Kuwait and southern Iraq from supplies and reinforcements as well as block their major avenue of retreat. The 24th Mechanized Division, along with the 3rd Armored Cavalry Regiment (ACR), was to drive over 100 miles to the Euphrates River, also to block the retreat of Iraqi forces, then continue their attack eastward toward Basrah with the intent of destroying the Republican Guard.[3]

Next to XVIII Corps was VII Corps, comprising the 2nd Armored Cavalry Regiment, the 1st Infantry Division (the famous Big Red One), the U.S. 1st and 3rd armored divisions, the British 1st Armored Division (including the 7th Brigade—the Desert Rats of World War II fame) and later, after conducting a feint elsewhere, the 1st Cavalry Division (of only two brigades). This corps was the heaviest on the coalition front; it drew the principal mission of attacking to the left of the Saddam Line in front of Kuwait and most of the Iraqi forces, turning the Iraqi defenses, and eventually enveloping the Iraqi forces. Orders to VII Corps unit commanders were to concentrate on destroying enemy armor and artillery and bypass Iraqi infantry. As one U.S. colonel observed, "We didn't involve ourselves in unimportant fights. We concentrated on the objective, which was the Republican Guard."[4]

Other groups of coalition forces were spread throughout the theater. Joint Forces Command-North (JFC-N), situated to the right of VII Corps, consisted of the 3rd Egyptian Mechanized Division and the 4th Egyptian Armored, the 9th Syrian Armored Division, an Egyptian Ranger Regiment, the 45th Syrian Commando Regiment, the 20th Mechanized Brigade of the Royal Saudi Land Forces (RSLF), the 4th Armored Brigade of the RSLF, and two brigades of exiled Kuwaiti soldiers, the Shaheed and Al-Tahir brigades.

The 1st Marine Expeditionary Force contained two marine divisions, the 1st and 2nd, and one U.S. Army armored brigade—the 1st, or "Tiger," Brigade of the 2nd Armored Division. The marines would attack between the two groups of Arab forces, in the "heel" area of the Kuwait-Saudi border.

On the extreme right of the coalition front, on the Gulf coast, was the Joint Forces Command-East (JFC-E). JFC-E included Task Force Omar (the 10th Infantry Brigade of the RSLF, a motorized infantry battalion from the United Arab Emirates, and an Omani motorized infantry battalion); Task Force Othman, with the Saudi 8th Mechanized Brigade, a Bahraini infantry unit and the Kuwaiti Al-Fatah Brigade; and Task Force Abu Bakr, comprising the 2nd Saudi National Guard Motorized Infantry Brigade and a Qatari mechanized battalion.[5]

Iraqi Ground Forces

Facing the coalition were 43 Iraqi divisions: 7 Republican Guard, and 36 regular. Twelve of the 43 divisions were armored, some were mechanized, and the majority were infantry. The Iraqi army totaled roughly a half-million men, with over 5,000 tanks and 3,000 pieces of artillery. Most of this massive force was hunkered down behind obstacles stretching the 138-mile length of the Saudi-Kuwaiti border. Dug-in behind minefields, barbed wire, oil-filled trenches, and an earthen berm, the Iraqi divisions awaited the coalition attack as illustrated in Figure 6.4.

Individual Iraqi soldiers, too, awaited the ground war. In the Kuwaiti desert, a young Iraqi soldier named Hassam Malek Mohammad Mardy sat in his bunker and prayed for an end to the conflict. "I am like a prisoner," Mardy

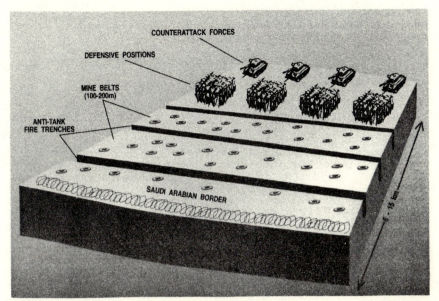

FIGURE 6.4   Iraqi Defense in Depth. *Source:* Department of Defense, "The Conduct of the Persian Gulf War," Final Report to Congress, April 1992, p. 350.

wrote in his diary. "My stomach is sick. I live unhappy, alone, all day long," he wrote February 24. "May God make this problem easy. May it be solved quickly."[6]

Huddled six feet underground in dark, steaming bunkers, thousands of Iraqi soldiers like Mardy had endured weeks of aerial bombardment. Some ate spare rations of canned beans, fruit, and other food; others had exhausted their stocks, their supply lines smashed by coalition aircraft. Indeed, in contrast to conditions experienced in the war against Iran, many Iraqi soldiers were reduced to eating no more than a handful of rice and drinking a mouthful of water per day. Adding to their discomfort was the moral and sometimes physical abandonment by their officers.

"What do you want of me, life, you traitor?" Mardy wrote that day. "I am your friend, and you have done these things to me."

As revealed by prisoner-of-war interviews after the Gulf War was over, many of the Iraqi troops in and around Kuwait did not understand their cause and had no particular desire to be there. They did not agree with Saddam Hussein's expansionist ambitions. The cream of Iraq's youth had been dragged from family, friends, jobs, school; division after division, brigade after brigade, hundreds of thousands of Iraqi fathers, brothers, sons, and husbands were dispatched to Kuwait to fulfill the personal ambitions of a brutal dictator. Thousands had already died—General Schwarzkopf would later estimate that, by the time of the ground war, many Iraqi units in Kuwait were at half to one-quarter their original strength and many of the rest had been wounded or had deserted. (See Figure 6.5.) Some of those who remained and did not support the cause were cajoled, propagandized, and in some cases tortured. "I hear their screams," one Iraqi wrote on January 12 of his comrades who didn't support the cause. "God be with them. Send us help."

Hassam Malek Mohammed Mardy enjoyed no special advantage over his fellow Iraqi soldiers. In the end, he shared the fate of many of them: Shortly after the ground war began, he died, shot three times through the head.

"I open my eyes and cry, sitting, thinking, 'Oh God, will you accept me?' " read one of his final diary entries. "I close my eyes and remember. Then I cry again. There is sand on my face. It is about to cover me. It is my destiny. I want to shout in my loudest voice but life doesn't follow me."

Preparations for Battle

More than three weeks before the ground offensive, vast numbers of coalition forces had shifted west along the Iraq–Saudi Arabia border as shown in Figure 6.6. This jog to the left was masked by the coalition air campaign, which completely frustrated Iraq's attempts to locate its enemies. General Schwarzkopf and his top staff had made the decision to go around the Iraqi flank, at the same time attacking it head-on. U.S. and other coalition divisions moved west to get outside the main Iraqi defensive lines; VII Corps moved over 150 miles west and XVIII Airborne Corps moved 250 miles west.

The size of the logistical undertaking necessary to support these movements was phenomenal. Major General Gus Pagonis, chief logistician for the theater, superintended the move of more than 250,000 men and more than 1,000 tanks an average of 200 miles, often over unimproved roads that were hardly more than tracks in the desert.[7] Roads leading to coalition staging areas were lined with trucks, bumper to bumper, twenty-four hours a day. Convoys were so tightly packed that at any point along the tap line (a road servicing the Trans Arabian Pipeline) trucks were passing every fifteen seconds. Supply units stockpiled enough food and war supplies for sixty days: 5,000 tons of ammunition, 550,000 tons of fuel, 300,000 tons of water and 80,000 MREs (meals, ready-to-eat) per division.

Many units used the move west as an exercise for the real thing, maneuvering in formation and even crossing practice berms established to resemble that dividing the Saudi-Iraqi border. The 24th Mechanized covered more than 320 miles in ten days, moving 25,000 men, 1,793 tracked and 6,560 wheeled vehicles (fully loaded with fuel and ammunition) with only one accident. In the end more than a quarter of a million soldiers were in place hundreds of miles into Saudi Arabia.

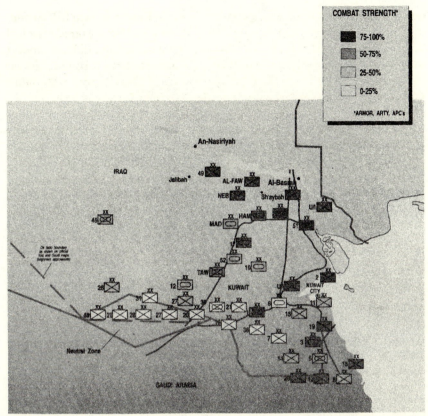

FIGURE 6.5 Intelligence Assessment, February 23. *Source:* Department of Defense, "The Conduct of the Persian Gulf War," Final Report to Congress, April 1992, p. 355.

Iraqi forces apparently knew nothing of these moves. Coalition aircraft made sure no Iraqi planes got off the ground, and without satellites like the ones employed by the coalition, Iraqi commanders had no way of looking into Saudi territory. Coalition forces did their best to deceive the Iraqis, aggressively patrolling and conducting feints all along the border to create confusion about where the attack would originate. At sea, thousands of marines embarked for an amphibious invasion that would never come—but one that did tempt the Iraqis to build many of their defensive emplacements in Kuwait facing toward the Gulf, useless when the coalition struck from the south.[8] Indeed, six Iraqi divisions were oriented to defend against attack from the sea. A second marine force, Task Force Troy, deceived the Iraqis by other means: Broadcasting tank noises over loudspeakers and deploying dummy tanks and artillery pieces, Task Force Troy sought to convince its opponents that an en-

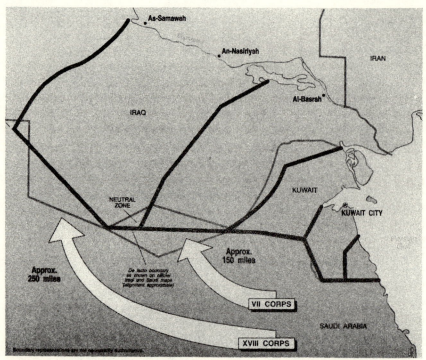

FIGURE 6.6   The Shift West. *Source:* Department of Defense, "The Conduct of the Persian Gulf War," Final Report to Congress, April 1992, p. 342.

tire marine division was preparing to attack in a place where in fact no marine division existed. In the days before the attack, coalition units scouted for promising targets. Iraq's artillery commanded a great deal of attention, both because it was capable of firing chemical warheads and because the Iraqis counted on it as a decisive component of their army, able to pour devastating fire down onto coalition attack columns. Iraqi artillery was in some cases longer-ranged than that of U.S. forces; some of the Iraqis' Austrian and South African–made guns could shoot far beyond U.S. 155-millimeter weapons. Regardless, U.S. artillery units used radars capable of tracking individual Iraqi shells and following them back to their points of origin to pinpoint enemy artillery positions; hundreds of Iraqi guns were destroyed by their vastly more accurate and efficient U.S. counterparts before the ground campaign even began. Coalition aircraft also made Iraqi artillery units a favorite target in the weeks and days before the ground war.

As G-Day approached, coalition units conducted their final preparations. Surveillance teams crept to within 3000 feet of the sand berm at the Saudi-Iraqi border and dug in to watch enemy movements and track the strength of Iraqi defenses. Others were far deeper, even to the Euphrates valley. Weak points identified by intelligence would be exploited days later; in some cases scouts found gaping holes in the Iraqi defenses through which coalition tank units drove without opposition. In the East, marine units began cross-border raids on G minus one, knocking out 18 Iraqi tanks and taking almost 150 prisoners. Reconnaissance and probing raids along the border penetrated as far as 15 miles into Iraq. Night-flying helicopters flew up and down the Iraqi lines, attacking the positions with rocket and machine-gun fire.

On both sides of the line, all was in place. The mother of all battles was about to commence.

Coalition-Building

As U.S. forces prepared to begin the ground campaign, they did so in the company of numerous coalition allies. A previous chapter has already stressed the importance of the multilateral support to the coalition, how the United States could not have put its forces in place to force Hussein from Kuwait without the help of friends and allies. In the future, therefore, the United States will probably fight its wars in the company of some form of coalition.

Multilateral assistance was almost as important to winning the war as it was to getting in position to win it. Although U.S. forces made up the bulk of coalition land, air, and naval units, other countries played important political as well as military roles in the war. Current and prospective treaty relationships will therefore remain important to future U.S. military operations.

In contingencies outside Europe, however, the United States will rely less on established treaty arrangements than on ad hoc short-term groupings of nations who share a set of common interests narrower than a formal alliance. This calls for renewed study of coalitions themselves—what they are, how effective they might be, in what forms they might come together. In many cases—as in the Gulf—coalitions will have a larger political than military role. In either case, U.S. military and political leaders must reexamine the issue of coalition-building: How was it done in this case? Could it be done that way in the future, or will George Bush's personal touch be hard to replace? What tools are most important in laying the groundwork for coalitions?

In this case, the groundwork for the coalition was laid in part by a critical element of U.S. foreign and defense policy: security assistance. Both politically and militarily, U.S. military assistance and sales had created a strong foundation for the joint effort required by Iraq's aggression. Without the strong bilateral relationships built up over many years, it is not at all clear whether our Arab coalition partners would have felt able to rely on the United States, or that Israel would have heeded U.S. requests to stay out of the war.

At the political level, when the Gulf Cooperation Council formally requested U.S. intervention to respond to Iraq's invasion of Kuwait, it did so against a background of trust based in part upon long-standing military cooperation. Many members of the coalition have received large U.S. grants or military sales since the 1950s: Egypt had received over $13 billion in security assistance since 1976, Saudi Arabia had purchased over $66 billion in equipment since 1953, Kuwait nearly $4 billion since 1971, and Oman, Bahrain, and Qatar had also purchased some equipment. Many officers and enlisted men of the Arab forces, especially in the Saudi military, had received U.S. training; U.S. officers have actually managed the development of the Saudi National Guard for many years. And of course the U.S. relationship with Israel is close and long-standing—Israel has received almost $29 billion in direct military aid since 1954 and has been a centerpiece of U.S. Middle East policy during that period.

The importance of the personal contacts and relationships built up through such cooperation should not be underestimated. In addition to weapons sales, security assistance, and U.S. training, Gulf states also benefited from close and extended contact with forward-deployed U.S. military forces. The Joint Task Force Middle East had been operating in the Gulf escorting reflagged Kuwaiti tankers since the summer of 1987. Exercises, other training drills, and courtesy calls between Gulf Arab and U.S. (as well as British and French) military officers prior to 1990 contributed immensely to facilitating later efforts in the war against Iraq. When top regional military leaders know and trust their U.S. counterparts, the prospect for cooperation is improved.

Militarily, too, security assistance aided the coalition war effort significantly. Apart from Syria, most of the Arab coalition members depended upon U.S. security assistance and arms sales for a significant element of their defense posture. Coalition forces were able to avail themselves of extensive Saudi basing facilities, many of which were designed and built under the supervision of the U.S. Army Corps of Engineers in configurations well suited for U.S. weapons in the Saudi arsenal. If this sizable logistical base had not been available, the nature of the war would have been very different.

One of the first lessons being touted from the war was that the United States must put in place severe constraints on future arms sales to the Middle East. Obviously, there is an important role for arms control to play, particularly to constrain development of weapons of mass destruction—chemical, biological, and nuclear bombs. At the same time, however, it must not be forgotten that moderate military aid and sales can be used to build relationships that help ensure war never occurs. The lesson of the war is not that all arms transfers are bad; rather, it is that the U.S. government, along with the governments of other arms exporters (particularly in Europe), must work toward a better balance between arms sales and arms control.

The Ground Campaign Begins

The ground offensive began at four o'clock in the morning Gulf time on Sunday, February 24, when elements of the 1st Marine Division quickly breached the first two lines of the famed Hussein Line and drove toward the Al Jaber military air base. (See Figure 6.7.) On their right, the Saudi and Gulf Cooperation Council forces of JFC-E began their attack at 8 A.M., seizing their initial objectives and moving toward the second line of the Iraqi defenses. This attack by I MEF (the 1st Marine Expeditionary Force, comprising the 1st and 2nd Marine Divisions) and JFC-E into southern Kuwait, along with the supporting movement of several naval ships closer to shore (including the battleship *Wisconsin*), gave the impression that the major Allied line of advance was toward Kuwait City. Meanwhile, to the west, the vast armored and airborne forces of VII and XVIII corps were in the final stages of preparing their advance toward what would become the real center of the battle—the Iraqi Republican Guard.

The coalition attack drove into Kuwait in four supporting thrusts. The road for I MEF was scouted by a pair of marine battalion-sized units that had infiltrated into Kuwait the night of February 22. Task Forces Grizzly and Taro located obstacles, minefields, and other defenses as they prepared the way for the main attack. This attack came at 4 A.M. when the 1st Marine Division began what General Schwarzkopf would later describe as a "classic breaching operation," rapidly clearing the first two lines of sand berms and minefields and driving toward Kuwait's Ahmed Al Jaber airfield. Along the way, the marines defeated several armored counterattacks in the Al Wafrah and Umm Gudair oilfields and by the end of the day had captured 8,000 enemy prisoners of war (EPWs).

The 2nd Marine Division was on the left of the marine sector and faced the densest array of minefields and defensive obstacles. Supported by the army's Tiger Brigade, the marines had to pass through successive belts of assorted antitank and antipersonnel mines, deadly areas covered by Iraqi artillery fire. The 6th Marine Regiment led the way into Kuwait, firing MICLICs, or mine-clearing line charges, which cleared pathways through minefields for vehicles to follow. (MICLICs worked by flinging a ropelike tube of explosives several hundred feet into a minefield. The tube would then explode, setting off the target mines and neutralizing the minefield.) The marines began their clearing operations at 5:30 A.M.; slightly less than eight hours later the Tiger Brigade passed through the breaches. Iraqi artillery was active during the breaching operations but was inaccurate and could not shift fire into the areas being breached. U.S. counterbattery fire proved highly effective.[9] To the right of the marines, the Saudi, Kuwaiti, and other Arab troops composing JFC-E cut six lanes in the dense Iraqi defensive belt near the coast and began advancing at 8 A.M., capturing initial objectives.[10] On the marines' left, the Egyptians and the Syrians advanced more slowly, encountering difficulty crossing Iraqi defensive barriers, particularly the fire trenches (a type of Iraqi barrier defense: a trench filled with ignited oil). While the easternmost element of VII Corps completed the activity in the vicinity of Kuwait proper, the 1st Cavalry Division conducted a feint toward the Wadi Al-Batin to fool the Iraqis into believ-

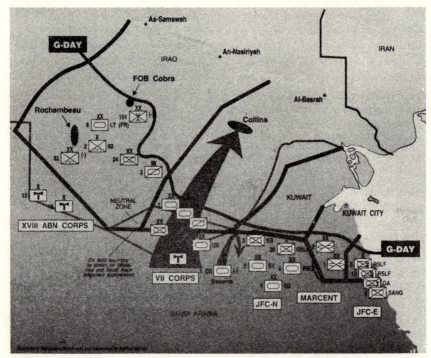

FIGURE 6.7   G-Day February 24. *Source:* Department of Defense, "The Conduct of the Persian Gulf War," Final Report to Congress, April 1992, p. 360.

ing they had correctly guessed a second avenue of coalition advance. Driving up one of the few terrain features of the theater, the 1st Cavalry assisted maritime forces in deceiving the Iraqis into thinking Kuwait itself would be the focus of main effort. In the process, the 48th, 31st, 25th, and 27th Iraqi infantry divisions were pinned, their attention turned uselessly southward.

Far to the west, elements of XVIII Airborne Corps also began their assault on the morning of the twenty-fourth. At 7:25 A.M., the 1st Brigade and 1st Battalion, 2nd Brigade of the 101st Airborne lifted off with 67 Apaches, 30 Chinooks, and 10 Hueys.[11] Their objective: to seize Forward Operating Base (FOB) Cobra, eighty miles into Iraq, or roughly half the distance to the Euphrates River. FOB Cobra would be the place from which the 101st would leapfrog into the Euphrates River valley and cut off the retreat of Iraqi forces escaping Kuwait. The first group of Blackhawk helicopters landed unopposed in Objective Cobra forty-one minutes after taking off. Once deployed in FOB Cobra, 101st troopers immediately began setting up helicopter refueling equipment.

Near the landing zone, however, some Iraqis were fighting back. As units of the 101st consolidated their position at FOB Cobra and began screening to the north, it became clear that up to a battalion-sized force was standing in the way. Air force A-10s and army AH-1s were engaging the Iraqis as Capt. John Russell's infantry company moved forward. Watching the action, Russell said of the entrenched Iraqis: "It became obvious we were going to have to do something."[12] The solution was the division's 105mm helicopter-deployed howitzers. Once the guns started shelling the ridge, surrendering Iraqis quickly began to appear.

The entire attack of XVIII Corps was far to the west of the Iraqi obstacle belt. Ground forces on the far left consisted of the French 6th Light Armored Division ("Division Daguet," mostly made up of the French rapid-deployment force), supported by elements of the U.S. 82nd Airborne. Beginning their attack at 5:30 A.M., the French drove toward their initial objective, code-named Rochambeau. Approximately twenty-five km into Iraq, Objective Rochambeau was occupied by nightfall and a large number of Iraqi prisoners were taken in the surrounding area. As French ground forces consolidated their hold on Rochambeau, they prepared for the next day's assault on the Iraqi town of As Salman, sixty miles into enemy territory and defended by the Iraqi 45th Infantry Division.

On XVIII Corps' right wing, the 24th Mechanized Infantry Division, alongside the 3rd Armored Cavalry Regiment, pressed its attack after being notified of the morning successes of the 101st and French 6th LAD. Crossing the line of departure at 3 P.M., the 24th drove almost unopposed into Iraqi territory.[13] Its mission was to drive to Iraq's Highway 8, which runs parallel to the Euphrates River, then to turn right and follow the two arteries toward Basrah. (Basrah is Iraq's second largest city, situated on the Shatt al-Arab waterway, the confluence of the Tigris and Euphrates rivers. It is a heavily militarized garrison town and was a center of conflict in the Iran-Iraq war.) Along the way the 24th was to destroy any fleeing Iraqi forces. Just outside of Basrah it was to halt and prevent any Iraqi forces still in the Kuwait theater of operations from leaving.

Originally, it had not been planned for VII Corps to attack until twenty-four hours after the initial assaults. The overwhelming success of the initial advances of the marines, JFC-E, and XVIII airborne corps, however, caused General Schwarzkopf to accelerate the timetable, ordering VII Corps to attack fifteen hours ahead of schedule.[14] At 3:00 in the afternoon VII Corps began the major attack of Operation Desert Saber. The 1st Infantry Division (the Big Red One, so-called because of its shoulder insignia), breached the Iraqi obstacles, began to clear the path for others to follow, and set off in the direction of the enemy 26th Infantry Division. Expecting trouble with mines, the M1 tanks of the 1st Infantry Division had been fitted with mine plows; as the attack progressed, however, they found that the Iraqis had not placed any mines forward of their main defensive line.[15] Further to the west, the 2nd Armored Cavalry Regiment (ACR) swept unopposed into Iraq, scouting the way for the 1st and 3rd armored divisions.

In reality, however, a large part of this component of VII Corps had already penetrated into Iraq. As early as February 23, the 2nd ACR, driving through a gap between the Iraqi 26th and 46th infantry divisions and encountering no resistance, had advanced twelve miles in order to cover engineers whose job it was to cut forty-three lanes through the ten-foot sand berm marking the Saudi-Iraqi border.[16] Resistance during this part of 2nd ACR's advance was almost nonexistent; the only casualty suffered by the unit was when a souvenir-hunter tossed an unexploded shell into his vehicle. It went off, injuring another soldier.[17]

On the 2nd Armored Cavalry Regiment's own right flank was the 3rd Armored Division, which began breaching operations at 3 P.M., quickly passing through the berm and into southern Iraq. With the 2nd Armored Cavalry and the 1st Infantry in front, and the 1st and 3rd armored divisions in tow, VII Corps attacked to the west of the Wadi Al-Batin, advancing rapidly and overrunning most Iraqi units with very little resistance. Most of the Iraqi forces contacted in the first day were dug-in dismounted infantry. The greatest problem they posed was what to do with them once they had surrendered en masse. One Iraqi soldier reportedly complained to a trooper, "Why did it take so long for you to get here? We were ready to surrender weeks ago."[18] (See Figure 6.8.)

The official history of the 2nd Armored Cavalry described its Gulf War mission in particularly colorful terms: "holding the Republican Guard's nose so that the rest of VII Corps could kick them in the ass." In planning the ground war, sectors of advance were demarcated on maps with successive "phase lines" marching into enemy territory. The 2nd Armored Cavalry phase lines were named for brands of beer, the first, still within Saudi Arabia, named Sharps (a nonalcoholic brew) out of deference to Saudi sensibilities.[19] The 2nd Armored Cavalry covered more than twenty-five miles in the first two hours, capturing several hundred prisoners. By the end of February 24, VII Corps had done more than simply fix the Iraqi forces and find their weaknesses. It had begun to exploit the deception that General Schwarzkopf had so carefully planned. As VII Corps drove north into Iraq, the fate of the Republican Guard became ever more tightly sealed.

As VII Corps and the rest of the coalition forces advanced, several developments, both expected and unexpected, increased their confidence in the final outcome of the ground war. First, the relative ease with which the Iraqi defensive barriers were passed allowed the coalition forces to move into an area where they could exploit their greater mobility in a war of maneuver against the Iraqis. The Iraqis' greatest anticipated advantage, that of fighting a defensive battle, was quickly nullified. Second, the formidable Iraqi artillery was nowhere to be seen. Although the Allies knew from experience at Khafji that

FIGURE 6.8   Samples of Pyschological Leaflets Dropped During Operation Desert
Storm. The Arabic script on the reverse of the 25 dinar note (with Saddam Hussein's
likeness) reads, "If you want to escape the killing, be safe, and return to your families,
do the following things: (1) Remove the magazines from your weapons; (2) Put your
weapon over your left shoulder with the barrel pointed down; (3) Put your hands over
your head; (4) Approach military positions slowly. Note: Beware of the minefields
sown along the border. Now, use this safe conduct pass. The Iraqi soldiers who are carrying this pass have indicated their desire for friendship, to cease resistance, and to
withdraw from the battlefield." *Source:* Department of Defense, "The Conduct of the
Persian Gulf War," Final Report to Congress, April 1992, p. 187.

Iraqi artillery was overrated, its failure to cover the front lines with fire during
Allied breaching operations greatly reduced its potential impact on the campaign. Meanwhile, U.S. artillery impressed with both its quality and quantity.
       Third, the tremendous number of surrendering Iraqis posed something of
a problem for the advancing coalition forces. It soon became apparent that the
Iraqi infantry divisions, for the most part, had little fight in them—though the
armored and mechanized units of the Republican Guard would behave otherwise. Indeed, surrendering Iraqis slowed the allied advance far more than the
Iraqis who chose to fight. A secondary problem caused by the large number of
surrendering Iraqis was that they nearly overwhelmed Allied intelligence assets
with work. Most of the U.S. military intelligence units were full of first-class
linguists—unfortunately, however, they were fluent in Czech, German, or
Russian, not Arabic. To interrogate Iraqi EPWs, the United States relied on

Kuwaiti students.[20] Regardless, the first grilling conducted by the intelligence unit assigned to the 2nd Armored Cavalry was in Russian because the Americans questioned an Iraqi major who had trained in Leningrad.[21]

The final development, and an issue that had received both wide debate and careful attention prior to the ground war, was the use of chemical weapons. As with Iraqi artillery, chemical attack could have vastly complicated coalition obstacle-breaching operations. (Indeed, artillery would have been the most likely means of delivery.) Regardless, there was great relief among the Allies that no chemicals were used while their forces drove through the first two defensive lines; as forces advanced, however, they did find stockpiles of chemical weapons.[22] These stockpiles were not very large, apparently, and Iraqi intent with respect to their use is unclear. In truth, however, the Iraqis may have been more afraid of fighting on a chemical battlefield than were coalition forces. Their fear could be explained in a variety of ways: concern that Allied retaliation would be severe, a lack of equipment for self-protection should something go wrong, or simply unwillingness to complicate what many may have already regarded as a decided issue. There is a great difference between gassing masses of unprotected Iranian infantry and trying the same thing with a trained army prepared to absorb and fight through such an attack.

Nonlinear Warfare

The coalition's use of airpower, precision weapons, airmobile attacks, and armored strikes deep into the enemy's rear confirmed another emerging trend in land warfare. Current doctrine has already raised the issue of the balance between the close and deep battles: In modern ground combat, the objective is not merely to meet the enemy along a static front but to engage and destroy forces and equipment well into the enemy's rear. As noted earlier, many analysts of war have argued that the high-technology battlefield will be less linear. The war in the Gulf confirmed this trend and went a long way toward justifying the decades-long investment in certain kinds of high-technology weapons systems as mentioned previously, as well as battle-management systems, survivable and deployable armor, and training and leadership development necessary to make it all work.

This was also perhaps the first truly twenty-four-hour-a-day ground war in history. Advances in night-vision equipment, including thermal imagery, now make it possible for U.S. ground units to fight nonstop, unencumbered by darkness or weather. Human beings are not as adaptable to this sort of warfare as equipment is; it is difficult to imagine a unit fighting much more than forty-eight to sixty straight hours, particularly on a fast-paced modern battlefield. Aircrews or personnel divisions on ships can be more easily rotated than ground-combat units, and the army and marines will have to give some thought to what might have happened had the ground battle lasted round-the-clock for 1,000 or 5,000 hours rather than 100.

There is also an important question from the perspective of weapons-system reliability. In the aftermath of the war it is easy to scoff at those who doubted the reliability of U.S. high-technology weapons; during this war, the operational readiness rates for these weapons were higher even than in peacetime. Those rates were probably at least as much a function, however, of vastly expanded maintenance operations and the brief duration of the war as they were of the inherent reliability of the weapons. This is a question that can and should be conclusively resolved by a careful analysis of maintenance data from the Gulf. Continued attention to the potential fragility of high-technology weapons systems is undoubtedly warranted.

The Gulf War also demonstrated beyond doubt the crucial role that special operations forces (SOF) have to play in this revolution toward nonlinear ground warfare. During the Gulf War, SOF conducted an amazing array of missions throughout the theater: laser-designating targets for U.S. aircraft, searching for mobile Scud missile launchers, collecting intelligence, cutting lines of communication, helping organize resistance inside Kuwait, and other missions. SOF units also possess important civil affairs capabilities, a key mission area given the degree to which political considerations intruded in the latter stages of the war. Given SOF performance in the Gulf, the emphasis on SOF within the Department of Defense should increase; even after the creation of a distinct Special Operations Command by Congress, SOF capabilities remain too low on the list of mission priorities.

Rapidly deployable land combat power will form an essential component of U.S. contingency response forces, as it did in the Gulf War. We cannot count on having five months to build up our capabilities in the next war. The U.S. Army is currently looking at modular force projection packages based around a rapid-deployment core of six brigades; the Department of Defense's new mobility goal includes acquiring enough sealift to transport those forces, the equivalent of two divisions with sustainment—a total of over 50,000 personnel—anywhere in the world within thirty days. Early-arriving tactical fighter squadrons and helicopter units can help boost the firepower and striking range of U.S. rapid-deployment forces. Meanwhile the marines proved once again their ability to deploy all-arms combat teams rapidly to far-flung locales, partly with the use of maritime prepositioning. Within several years, the United States is likely to possess fairly robust, strategically mobile contingency forces. But these will be useless under a contingencies strategy unless the glaring shortages in strategic mobility manifested in the Gulf War are corrected.

Day Two

The second day of the ground war dawned with the 1st Marine Division in possession of Al Jaber airfield. Other elements of the division had advanced to within ten miles of Kuwait City. These accomplishments came only after the marines had repulsed a number of Iraqi armored counterattacks on February 24 and into the early morning of the twenty-fifth. These engagements took place in a hellish environment: The burning wells of the Kuwaiti oil fields produced a dense black smoke that combined with fog from the freakish and unseasonal weather and almost totally obscured the battlefield. Regardless, the marines continued their advance on the twenty-fifth, destroying or capturing between 175 and 200 tanks.[23] With marine air and naval forces able to perform the deception mission, the 5th Marine Expeditionary Brigade, deployed in the Gulf, off-loaded from its ships to become the reserve for the two marine divisions on shore.

On the marine's left and right flanks JFC-N and JFC-E continued to assist in the assault on Iraqi III Corps, the force holding Kuwait proper. (See Figure 6.9.) JFC-E continued its advance up the coastline, securing its objectives against minimal resistance and at little cost. (Indeed, the opposing Iraqi force, elements of the 5th Mechanized Division, which had fought at Khafji, had apparently had enough of fighting and quickly surrendered.) The progress of JFC-E was inhibited more than anything else by the large number of Iraqis surrendering to fellow Arabs. On the marine's left flank the JFC-N continued its attack as well. The Egyptian forces, still struggling among the fire trenches, nevertheless secured a five-square-mile front. JFC-N did not, however, completely clear the second line of obstacles until late on February 25. The Egyptian 3rd Mechanized Division then advanced to the north, taking over 1,500 Iraqis as prisoners. As they attacked, the Egyptian 4th and Syrian 9th armored divisions prepared to follow through the breaches.

Operating from Tactical Assembly Area (TAA) Campbell, approximately fifty miles southeast of the Saudi town of Rafha and south of the Iraqi border, the 101st Air Assault Division began deep interdiction operations in the Euphrates valley. FOB Cobra served as the source of fuel and supplies for the armada of helicopters that was by now flying all over southern Iraq. Without FOB Cobra, helicopters carrying out their missions in southern Iraq would not have had the range to return to base in Saudi Arabia. The next objective of the 101st was to land all three of the 3rd Brigade's infantry battalions just south of the Euphrates River near the town of Al Khidr, at Area of Operations (AO) Eagle, while heavier forces including artillery, antitank companies, and engineers landed twenty-five miles further south at Landing Zone (LZ) Sand.[24] The mechanized force would then drive north to join with the air-assault troops. The assault began at noon on the twenty-fifth when 4 CH-47s carrying 8 TOW-equipped HMMWVs (high-speed, multipurpose, multiwheeled vehicles, the modern version of the jeep) took off from the rear in Saudi Arabia for LZ Sand. By the end of the evening, 66 H-60 Blackhawk helicopters had delivered 1,000 troops to AO Eagle, where they took up positions blocking any Iraqi retreat along Highway 8. The two forces linked up after the heavy forces drove north. Their day still not over, the engineers ren-

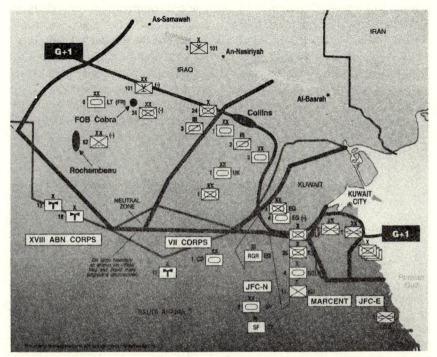

FIGURE 6.9   G + 1, February 25. *Source:* Department of Defense, "The Conduct of the Persian Gulf War," Final Report to Congress, April 1992, p. 377.

dered the highway unusable by blowing a large hole in it in one place and destroying a bridge in another.[25]

Also on February 25, VII Corps began making more serious contact with Iraqi mechanized and armored units. The 1st Infantry Division moved forward and destroyed brigades of the Iraqi 26th Infantry Division as the day progressed. The British 1st Armored Division passed through the breach made by the U.S. 1st Infantry at noon on the twenty-fifth and promptly attacked the Iraqi 12th and 52nd armored divisions.[26] These divisions were part of the Iraqi reserve meant to fill holes in the Saddam Line made by coalition thrusts. By the end of the day the British forces were to destroy 200 tanks, 100 APCs, and 100 artillery pieces and take over 5,000 Iraqis prisoner.

The 2nd Cavalry was meanwhile carrying out the cavalry scouting mission, attempting to fix the Republican Guard for the U.S. 1st and 3rd armored divisions. "Fixing" an enemy force involves both locating it and engaging it sufficiently to prevent it from moving away. These divisions, with the 2nd Armored Cavalry in the vanguard, continued to drive north toward the Euphrates, turning the Iraqi lines by gradually shifting east. In the early afternoon the 1st Armored on the far left and the 3rd Armored (between the 1st

Armored and the 2nd ACR) encountered entrenched infantry. (The 2nd
ACR, which began the offensive between the 1st and 3rd armored divisions
[ADs], had earlier shifted to a more easterly course while the 3rd AD continued to the northeast. As a result, 2nd ACR passed to the south and right of
the 3rd Armored and ended up between the 3rd Armored and 1st Infantry as
VII Corps came around in its "left hook.") The U.S. armored formations
were not appreciably slowed down by the entrenched Iraqis. In the afternoon
the 1st Armored came up against a reinforced Iraqi infantry brigade defending a logistics post near the town of Al Busayyah, engaging the Iraqis with the
help of their own Apache helicopters and air force aircraft. By early morning
on the twenty-sixth, the logistics center was destroyed.[27]

At sea, naval vessels approached the coast and continued to tie down 10
Iraqi divisions through feints and demonstrations. Aircraft deployed aboard
amphibious ships conducted strike missions against Kuwait's Faylaka and
Bubiyan islands and a simulated helicopter assault on Kuwaiti beaches.[28]
These feints were not only successful in deceiving the Iraqi high command,
their intended target, but coalition journalists, who reported that the Allies
had made an amphibious landing near Kuwait City.

By February 26, the rout of Iraqi forces in Kuwait had begun as more than
1,000 military and stolen vehicles clogged the four-lane highway leading
north from Kuwait City. The convoy was a potpourri of hot-wired cars, including Cadillacs, vans, fire engines, police cars, and even a milk truck.[29]
These vehicles were not only loaded with fleeing Iraqi troops but "ample evidence of the looting of Kuwait: televisions, video recorders, jewelry, silver-
ware, scarves, an electric piano and gold watches."[30] With JSTARS aircraft
monitoring the movement of the fleeing Iraqis, their northbound forces were
repeatedly struck by coalition air attacks. USAF A-10 Thunderbolts made the
first strike at the head and rear of the convoy during the night of February 25–
26. The next morning A-6E Intruders from USS *Ranger* began a series of attacks against what one pilot described as "like the road to Daytona Beach at
spring break."[31] Strikes were reportedly being launched so feverishly that
"ordnance crew members were loading whatever bombs happened to be closest to the flight deck."[32]

Coalition plans were being executed well ahead of schedule. During the
first two days of the ground war, resistance had generally been light. By the afternoon of the twenty-sixth, however, occasionally sharp conflicts became
much more frequent, particularly as units of VII Corps began to make contact
with the Republican Guard. (See Figure 6.10.) By the twenty-sixth, the
weather also had again deteriorated. What had been stiff breezes on the
twenty-fifth developed into a *shamal,* or dust storm, on the twenty-sixth. Visibility, already poor, was to become even worse. It was in such an environment

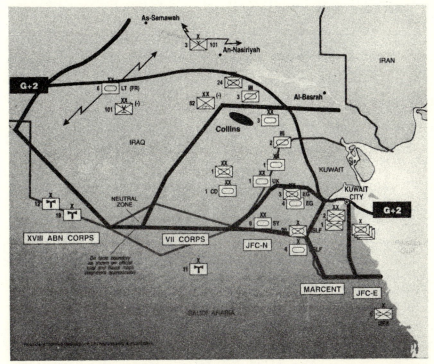

FIGURE 6.10 G + 2, February 26. *Source:* Department of Defense, "The Conduct of the Persian Gulf War," Final Report to Congress, April 1992, p. 389.

that the coalition armored formations were to meet Saddam's elite forces.

One such clash occurred in the afternoon, February 26, when Alpha Troop of the 4th Squadron of the 7th Calvary (1st Calvary Division) stumbled into the Tawakalna Armored Division of the Republican Guard. At 1530, scouts in the lead Bradley armored infantry fighting vehicles of Alpha troop began to detect hot spots through their thermal sights. As the troop crossed over a low ridge, suddenly before them stretched a massive Iraqi force of T-72s and BMP armored personnel carriers. Immediately the Bradleys opened fire with their TOW (tube-launched, optically tracked, wire-guided) missiles. One was hit by a T-72 as it started to pull back. Alpha's command sergeant, Ronald Sneed (a veteran of Vietnam), leapt from his vehicle to check on the disabled Bradley—later, Sneed would declare that "he had never faced a more intense 45 minutes than he was now facing." As Sneed ran toward the other Bradley, a round from a T-72 landed ten feet away, blowing him to the ground. Sneed regained his feet and climbed into the disabled vehicle. Inside Sneed found two of the crew members severely injured. Meanwhile, three more Bradleys had been hit and "the radio nets were frantic with pleas for a medic" as the Bradleys withdrew behind the ridge. The engagement had only lasted a few minutes, but in that time nine soldiers were wounded and two had been killed. The troop was credited with destroying 18 BMPs and 6 T-72s.[33]

Another such clash was the Battle of 73 Easting, which occurred when elements of the 2nd Armored Cavalry Regiment ran into units of the Republican Guard at a spot in the desert named only with a map reference. Second Armored Cavalry scouts first contacted elements of the Tawakalna Division when they fixed the Iraqis along their southern flank late in the afternoon of the twenty-sixth. I troop immediately attacked eastward through two lines of T-72s, destroying tanks, Armored Personnel Carriers (APCs), bunkers, and ZSU-23-4 self-propelled antiaircraft guns as they went. To the north, E troop of the 2nd Squadron destroyed more than 20 T-72s as they punched through the Iraqi lines.

The E and G troops, however, may have had the most action. As they moved east, they came upon a major armored force made up of more components of the Republican Guard Tawakalna Division and the regular Iraqi army 12th Armored Division. As darkness approached, E and G troops engaged successive groups of Iraqi tanks trying to escape the encirclement prepared for them. None succeeded. These elements of 2nd Armored Cavalry were joined in their attack on the Tawakalna by the 3rd Armored Division, which had been pushing steadily eastward during the twenty-fifth and twenty-sixth. When a cavalry squadron (scouting unit) from the 3rd Armored ran into the Tawakalna at 6:20 P.M., the U.S. troops reported to VII Corps commander Lieutenant General Fred Franks that the decisive corps engagement he was looking for was at hand. Thirty-eight hours of continuous combat with the Republican Guard was to follow.[34]

The rapidity of VII and XVIII corps' advance, however, meant that they risked soon outpacing their supplies. To keep the armored units moving, Chinook helicopters carrying huge bladders of fuel set up refueling stations at the leading edge of the advance. Fortunately, great stocks of supplies had been moved west along with the combat forces prior to the opening of the ground war. Only with such stockpiles could a modern armored division be kept supplied. To stock FOB Cobra, the 101st had sent a scouting team into southern Iraq the third week of February to clear a main supply route through enemy territory; now Task Force Citadel, a 700-vehicle convoy, sped through the desert to the base on February 24 and 25, carrying more desperately needed supplies.

Elsewhere on the twenty-sixth, the marines advanced against minimal resistance, the 1st Marine Division seizing Kuwait City International Airport early in the morning following a stiff clash with Iraqi armored units deployed nearby. Meanwhile, the 2nd Marine Division and the Tiger Brigade completed their seizure of key road intersections and principal objectives along the high ground (the Mutala Ridge) west and northwest of Kuwait City, effectively isolating the city.[35]

The Tiger Brigade was sent north with 45 of its M1A1s toward Mutala to catch the rear of the Iraqi forces retreating from Kuwait City. A *Newsweek* reporter riding with the 2nd Brigade described the M1A1s "like nothing so much as great dinosaurs sniffing for prey . . . their big 120 mm guns swinging restlessly from side to side."[36] Driving at twenty-five miles per hour along the highway, the brigade scattered the few Iraqi forces before it, not even stopping to pick up prisoners: "Huddled groups of green-uniformed soldiers waving white rags of surrender stood, bewildered, while tanks roared by." The brigade reached Mutala around 4 P.M. and immediately attacked the rearguard of the Iraqi forces. For the next several minutes, U.S. armored troops were engaged in a wild melee with Iraqi T-55s. After the short but intense firefight, the 2nd Brigade succeeded in overwhelming the Iraqi rearguard, which abandoned its tanks and fled into the desert.[37]

Meanwhile, the JFC-E, which had been enjoying so much success that its boundaries of operation were increased twice, had reached the southern edges of Kuwait City. There it halted to coordinate its entrance to the city with units of the JFC-N, which was slightly behind schedule, still conducting its sixty-mile drive to Kuwait's second military airfield, Ali Al Salem air base.[38]

In addition to 2nd Armored Calvary Regiment and 3rd Armored Division, the rest of VII Corps maintained its pressure on the mechanized and armored units of the Republican Guard.[39] The British 1st Armored Division, as the right pivot of this attack, was tasked to drive across the middle of Kuwait eastward toward the Mutala Ridge, which dominated Kuwait City. Reinforced by U.S. VII Corps artillery, as the British 1st Armored moved forward it enveloped and cut off the Iraqi forces to the south still entrenched on the Kuwait-Saudi border.

The rapidly developing tactical situation and the imminent main battle with the Republican Guard necessitated some realignment of Allied forces on the third day of the ground campaign. With the Saddam Line now well in the rear of VII Corps, the U.S. 1st Infantry Division was ordered to leave a battalion in the breach area as a precaution and move the remainder of the division northeast to participate in the attack on the Republican Guard. The 1st Cavalry Division, no longer needed for the deception mission, was released from theater reserve midmorning on the twenty-sixth. From its position near the Wadi Al-Batin, it was directed to take up a position on the left flank of the 1st U.S. Armored Division 155 miles to the north and attack eastward.[40] The cavalry moved quickly to carry out these demanding orders and enter the fight.

In XVIII Corps the 24th Mechanized, after a drive of 124 miles, reached the Euphrates River at 2 P.M. on February 26, completing the envelopment of

Iraqi forces in the Kuwait theater. Together with elements of the 101st Airborne Division, the 24th Mechanized now controlled long stretches of Highway 8. On the far left, the French 6th Light Armored Division secured the airfield at As Salman and established a screen from the Euphrates River to the Iraqi-Saudi border, a distance of over 118 miles. By sunset on the twenty-sixth, 30,000 Iraqis had become prisoners and 26 of 42 Iraqi divisions in the KTO had been destroyed; the coalition had created mass confusion in Iraqi command lines and driven most of the Iraqi army into retreat.[41]

By the afternoon of the twenty-seventh, the 24th Mechanized had turned east, capturing the Tallil and Jallibah airports in southern Iraq, and had begun its attack toward Basrah. It soon engaged elements of the Nebuchadnezzar Division (which was forced to retreat) and overran one of the Iraqi's principal theater logistics bases, containing over 1,300 bunkers full of supplies.[42]

As the number and intensity of clashes with Iraqi forces increased during the twenty-sixth and twenty-seventh, so, unfortunately, did casualties due to friendly fire. Nine soldiers of the 3rd Battalion of the U.K.'s Royal Regiment of Fusiliers, for example, were killed when mistakenly attacked by coalition aircraft.[43] Most of the friendly fire incidents were to take place on the twenty-sixth and twenty-seventh, when U.S. tanks would mistakenly fire on their own forces during close-in battles with the Republican Guard fighting in conditions of poor visibility. After the war, it was determined that 35 of 148 battlefield deaths were the result of friendly fire incidents.[44]

The Ground War Strategy

In the Gulf War, the United States did have effective high-tech weapons, it enjoyed the support of a broad coalition, and it had well-led, highly motivated, and competent troops. Those elements provided three components of victory. A fourth is found in the means by which those coalition forces were employed: military strategy. Once again Saddam obliged by playing directly into our hands—he filled Kuwait with his best troops and turned it into a bulging salient of military equipment virtually begging to be smashed from the air and surrounded on the ground. The coalition air campaign was anticipated by everyone outside Baghdad given the coalition's huge technological advantage and the devastating effects of modern airpower. Once the conflict moved to a ground phase, the fact that the coalition would strike around the Iraqi right flank (and the coalition's left) was a foregone conclusion to everyone except Saddam; in the pace and expertness of the movement, however, we administered a tactical shock from which Iraq's troops and leaders never recovered.

All elements of U.S. and coalition military power had a role in the overall strategy, which was to isolate Saddam and deprive his forces of supplies through a naval blockade, disrupt his command and smash his military forces from the air, and finally move forward and retake the land of Kuwait. It was on the ground, however, where the coalition made the purest use of a discrete military strategy. The idea of striking deeply around an enemy flank is probably as old as warfare, but in the modern age the importance of maneuver has been reaffirmed. U.S. deep-strike doctrines were born in the post-Vietnam focus on Europe: Outnumbered and faced with the wartime possibility of wave after wave of Soviet invaders, U.S. and NATO strategists hit upon a novel idea—why not destroy those follow-on waves before they reached the battle zone while engaging the first wave in a more traditional close battle of tank against tank? NATO forces set about to do just that, developing and purchasing advanced tactical strike aircraft, short-range ballistic missiles (similar to but far more advanced than Iraq's Scud), long-range rocket artillery, and other weapons to attack Soviet second, third, and fourth waves (or "echelons") before they got anywhere near the inter-German border. Meanwhile, NATO's tank and infantry divisions would be busy stopping the Soviet first wave. Eventually such doctrines came to be known as Follow-On Forces Attack, or FOFA.

The evolution of similar thinking within the U.S. military produced the AirLand Battle doctrine, which was actually developed before FOFA. Like FOFA, it is a strategy designed to counter numerous echelons of enemy forces. The U.S. Army recognized that it could not fight a battle against a numerically superior foe merely at the front line; eventually, mass and numbers would prevail. The solution: Engage enemy forces that have not yet reached the front line—through airmobile operations on helicopters, long-range artillery, and regular armored and mechanized units striking deep into the enemy rear.

In Operation Desert Saber, we saw a battlefield application of very similar ideas, supported by the weapons designed to execute the doctrine of FOFA and AirLand Battle. The basic AirLand Battle distinction between close and deep fighting was present: The bold flank moves by coalition armored and heliborne troops were designed not merely to encircle the Iraqi forces in Kuwait but also to produce a fight with the huge Republican Guard tank units lying in reserve. If coalition forces could engage them deeply, the Iraqi units would never be able to participate in the battle at the front line on the Saudi-Kuwaiti border. This is much like the way in which NATO would attempt to get in between Soviet echelons and destroy the supporting ones. The major *difference* between Desert Saber and U.S. tactics in Europe relates to the division of labor between the close and deep battles. The close battle allowed coalition forces to punch through the Iraqi defenses and engage Saddam's troops at the front line and was much less complicated than close battle would be, for example, in the more compartmented terrain of Europe; the issue of synchronizing close battle with deeper attacks against Iraqi reinforcing units never arose, allowing coalition units to keep up an exceptionally high momentum and speed of operations for the entire 100 hours of the ground battle.

Other elements of the coalition attack mirrored state-of-the-art U.S. and NATO strategy. Fast-moving tank columns punched through the enemy's flank and moved to encircle the main body of Saddam's troops. Helicopter-borne airmobile troops leapfrogged through various desert supply bases deep into the enemy's rear areas, seizing bridges over the Euphrates and later the Tigris and blocking the major corridors of retreat. Special forces units operated throughout enemy territory, sabotaging communications and assisting in the encirclement effort. All the while disparate coalition forces remained in close touch via battle-management platforms—the AWACS and JSTARS aircraft, each carrying radars and computers to monitor and direct the air and ground battles, respectively. Fighter-bombers and attack helicopters prowled the battlefield looking for enemy movement and responding to requests for air support from coalition ground units.

As should be obvious from this description, even these "ground" tactics depend on crucial assistance from air units—space-based satellites for intelligence and communications, flying battle-management centers, and, of course, close air support during the battle. AirLand Battle, as suggested by its name, is a *joint* doctrine, mutually developed between the U.S. Army and Air Force, which have signed a memorandum of understanding on the doctrine. In this operation, even the navy played an important role in the ground war—firing sea-launched cruise missiles at heavily defended Iraqi targets, firing huge 16-inch battleship guns in support of troops ashore, flying hundreds of close air-support missions. Even the ground war was truly a joint operation, meshing the capabilities of all U.S. military services.

This strategy allowed us to rely more on finesse than brute force, substituting manuever and battlefield position for raw firepower and numbers. The flank move was supported by a grand deception: massive exercises, widely televised, by U.S. Marine forces off the Kuwaiti shore gave the impression in the weeks before the ground war that U.S. planners intended to make an amphibious assault on Kuwait's Gulf coast. After the war U.S. reporters toured Kuwait City and found hundreds of Iraqi battle positions facing out to sea, abandoned in haste when it became clear that the coalition attack was coming from a different quarter. The empty posts, many still filled with mountains of weapons, ammunition, and supplies, stood as mute testimony that Iraqi leaders had indeed been fooled. If the coalition had attempted to drive directly through Kuwait and to launch a sea-based attack, the nature of the war's ground phase—though not its outcome—would have been very different. Casualties would likely have been far higher.

Through the application of strategy, then, coalition leaders maximized their own advantages and minimized Iraqi ones; they did the unexpected, threw the Iraqis off their rhythm, disrupted the expected pattern of events. Against a centralized, inflexible army, and combined with a destruction of the enemy's communications, such tactics can be devastating. Most Iraqi forces simply abandoned their cause, surrendering or fleeing before or during the ground war. Some Iraqi units did mount counterattacks, but they were uncoordinated; indeed, many Iraqi units that did attempt to fight wandered around the battlefield blind and were often caught in the flank or rear by U.S. or British tankers who knew exactly where the Iraqis were. Coalition strategy established the context in which its high-tech weapons would have the greatest effect, in which coalition advantages would be leveraged to best advantage against Iraqi liabilities.

As successful as this application of strategy was, it—like the improvement in military personnel during the 1980s—was not achieved without a price. In this case, the price was not so much monetary as bureaucratic; traditional advocates of head-on attrition warfare were only defeated after "a guerrillalike battle that a small cadre of staff officers and planners fought over a decade within the Army and the Marine Corps."[45] Only after stiff resistance by maverick officers in all services, disparagingly called maneuverists or Jedi Knights by conservative colleagues but eventually backed by far-sighted generals, was the bullish "active defense" of the army's FM 100-5 doctrine rewritten into the sleek AirLand Battle. One lesson of the Gulf War is clearly that maneuver warfare can slice inflexible enemies to pieces, destroy their morale, and keep friendly casualties to an absolute minimum. There should be no backtracking from the progress established in AirLand Battle.

Attacks on the Republican Guard

During the night of February 26–27, General Franks of VII Corps launched his major attack against three mechanized divisions of the Republican Guard: the Tawakalna, the Medina and the Hammurabi.[46] Five divisions of VII Corps and the 24th Mechanized from XVIII Corps fell on the Republican Guard. On the twenty-seventh, VII Corps' attack progressively gained momentum as it systematically destroyed Iraq's armored formations. Across a 100-mile wide front, the five-division formation moved eastward, destroying everything in its path.

On the right flank and southernmost end of the moving wall of coalition armor, the Challenger tanks of the British 1st Armored Division finished off the remaining elements of Iraq's 52nd Armored. This action completed the encirclement of three Iraqi infantry divisions, still oriented against an attack from the south, and cut off their avenue of retreat. The British 1st Armored then directed its advance toward Highway 8 just north of Kuwait City and the Mutala Ridge, which they were to seize before the cease-fire was announced.

North of the British was the U.S. 1st Infantry Division. During the night of the February 26–27 this unit executed the very difficult manuever of a night passage *through* the lines of the 2nd Armored Cavalry Regiment. As the commander of the 2nd ACR, Col. Donald Holder, observed, "It was a combination of good training and good luck that we didn't shoot them up and they didn't shoot us up."[47] To make sure that 2nd Cavalry vehicles were not misidentified, the cavalry were given explicit orders: "Chem-lite your rear ends, get inside and stay." One lieutenant in the 2nd ACR commented, "We were lit up like Christmas trees."[48] As the twenty-seventh dawned the 1st Infantry moved forward from the 2nd Cavalry's lines, overran two brigades from the Iraqi 12th Armored Division, continued its advance toward the main highway leading north out of Kuwait City toward Basrah, and ran into soldiers of the 10th Iraqi Armored Division abandoning their positions and equipment.[49] (See Figure 6.11.) As evening approached on February 27, the 1st Infantry reached and cut the Kuwait-Basrah highway and began attacking north along that axis. Having allowed the 1st Infantry to "play through," the 2nd Cavalry followed behind it and saw no further combat.

Also on the twenty-seventh, the 3rd Armored Division completed its destruction of the Tawakalna Division while the 1st Armored Division attacked Iraqi forces to the northeast of the 3rd. They fought through the right flank of the Tawakalna Division, a brigade from the Republican Guard's Adnan Infantry Division, and a brigade from the Medina Armored Division. During their eastward movement, the 1st Armored passed through what had been an Iraqi logistics base: "Trucks had run off the roadway and now lay in battered heaps, some ripped apart by tank rounds, others crashed head on into poles and even into one another amid what must have been the terror and confusion of this five hour fight."[50]

All remaining Republican Guard forces, the objective of the VII Corps, were by now moving northward in full retreat. "The Corps pushed on, with the 1st Cavalry Division now following the 1st Armored in the north and the 2nd Cavalry Regiment backing the 1st Infantry in the center."[51] Involving over 3,500 tanks on the Allied side alone, VII Corps' tank battles constituted the largest armored engagements since World War II. Indeed, they were much larger than most tank battles of that war: four times larger than the famous Battle of El Alamein, for example, where 1,200 British tanks faced 520 tanks from the Afrika Korps.[52] As one nineteen-year-old gunner of an M1A1 in the 1st Armored Division described the scene, it was "like a movie from World War II—you look to your left and to your right and everybody is firing in line."[53] The advance of VII Corps was so swift that several units of the Iraqi divisions were caught in their fixed positions facing south and were taken on their flank. As a brigade commander in the 3rd Armored Division explained: "You will see some tanks out there with holes shot in their backs."[54]

The Last Hours

The remainder of the ground war following VII Corps' attack on the Republican Guard can be described as exploitation and pursuit against rapidly disinte-

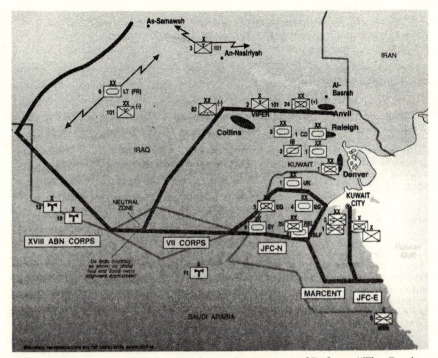

FIGURE 6.11   G + 3, February 27. *Source:* Department of Defense, "The Conduct of the Persian Gulf War," Final Report to Congress, April 1992, p. 400.

grating resistance. When notified that the cease-fire order was imminent (at 5 P.M. on the twenty-seventh), the 1st Armored planned an artillery attack for a final assault on elements of the Medina Republican Guard Division. This attack began at 5:30 A.M. on the twenty-eighth, with a simultaneous employment of MLRS (Multiple Launch Rocket System) rockets and 203mm and 155mm artillery rounds. It was immediately followed up with an Apache helicopter attack.[55]

Ground maneuver elements of the 1st Armored then descended upon the Iraqis, making contact with elements of the Medina Division in the vicinity of Kuwait's northwestern border with Iraq. 1st Armored troops destroyed two brigades of the Medina Division, as well as other Iraqi forces fleeing northward out of Kuwait, before the cease-fire went into effect at 8:00 A.M. on the twenty-eighth. The division then took up defensive positions along the Kuwait-Iraq border.[56] Because of the cease-fire, the 1st Armored and other elements of VII Corps were denied the opportunity to complete their final attack, concluding a double envelopment of the Republican Guard.

Elsewhere, JFC-E and JFC-N coordinated their linkup and liberated Kuwait City from the south and west respectively. Dramatic telecasts showed the

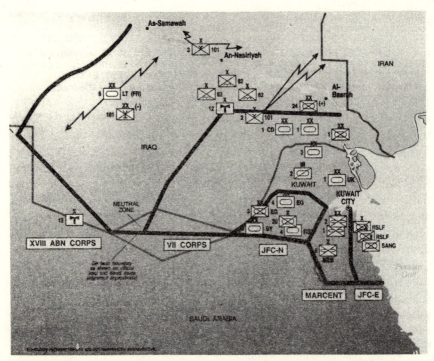

FIGURE 6.12   G + 4, February 28. *Source:* Department of Defense, "The Conduct of the Persian Gulf War," Final Report to Congress, April 1992, p. 408.

world the joy of the Kuwaiti people as their capital was liberated by Arab coalition forces. U.S. Marines secured the international airport and the high ground around Kuwait City. Moving north and west, forces of XVIII Corps continued their mission of securing the left flank and preventing the retreat of Iraqi forces. The U.S. 101st and 24th divisions continued to intercept fleeing Iraqi soldiers moving along Highway 8 while to their west the French found their area of responsibility quiet enough to begin mine-clearing operations.

At 8 A.M. on February 28 (G+4), exactly one hundred hours since the beginning of Operation Desert Saber, offensive operations ended as the presidential order for the cessation of operations took effect. (See Figure 6.12.) The war's end brought relief to hundreds of thousands of soldiers throughout the theater. A twenty-four-year-old gunner of a Bradley in the 1st Armored described the scene in his vehicle: "We wiped the sweat from our eyes, shook each other's hands and then we made some coffee."[57] For four straight days and nights (without sleep) in chemical-weapons suits, the coalition forces had battled the Iraqi army into submission while traveling hundreds of miles. They destroyed thousands of Iraqi tanks, armored personnel carriers, and artillery pieces in perhaps the most fast-paced blitzkrieg in history. Enemy prisoners of war were estimated at over 58,000 with estimates of Iraqi casualties varying widely between 25,000 and 100,000. The coalition, in contrast, lost fewer than 200 due to enemy action, and less than 2,000 were wounded. Only a handful of coalition tanks were lost in combat.

The cease-fire did not signal the complete cessation of fighting because Iraqi forces broke the agreement in several incidents. One such incident occurred on March 1 when a bus full of Iraqi soldiers opened fire after being stopped at a checkpoint by soldiers of the 24th Mechanized Infantry Division. The U.S. soldiers returned fire, destroying the bus, killing four Iraqis, and capturing nine others.[58] The major violation of the cease-fire occurred on March 2 at 6:30 A.M. when a large enemy column entered the security zone of the 24th Mechanized near the oil fields of Rumaylah. This column was attacked by M1A1s, Apaches and Bradleys from the 24th, and more than 187 Iraqi armored vehicles, 43 pieces of artillery and 400 wheeled vehicles were destroyed.[59]

Immediately after the announcement of the cease-fire, coalition forces were told to destroy all enemy equipment in their sectors as well as continue to monitor enemy forces. These were orders with which the troops were all too happy to comply as they collected vast quantities of Iraqi war material for destruction and shipment home for intelligence exploitation. Care of civilians became another responsibility as violent unrest in Iraq sent refugees streaming toward the Allied sanctuary in occupied Iraq. The coalition forces provided as much help as they could. For the Americans, policing and caring for refugees was a temporary and wearisome task to be completed prior to their ultimate goal: deployment home.

7

The Gulf War and U.S. Military Strategy

On March 3, 1991, coalition and Iraqi military leaders met at an airfield in Safwan, Iraq, just north of the Kuwaiti border. Before the meeting, General Norman Schwarzkopf sounded a tough line. "I'm not here to give them anything," he made clear. "I'm here to tell them exactly what they need to do."[1] Once at the meeting, according to the official Department of Defense interim report on the war, the Iraqis "appeared hostile."[2]

The officers held a ninety-minute meeting in a patch of barren desert surrounded by hulking U.S. armored vehicles and the charred hulls of burned-out Iraqi tanks. The Iraqi representatives agreed to all the terms of United Nations Resolution 686, pledging to abandon their ambitions on Kuwait and take a host of other steps demanded by the international community.

At the meeting, the head of the Iraqi delegation and the Iraqi vice chief of staff, Lieutenant General Sultan Hashim Ahmad Al-Jabburi, asked for an estimate of the number of Iraqi prisoners in coalition hands. Coalition officers said they were not entirely certain, that they were still counting. So far, however, they had counted over 58,000. "Lieutenant General Al-Jabburi," related the DoD interim report, "appeared stunned."

Later, General Schwarzkopf proposed that the two sides separate their forces by at least a kilometer, to prevent inadvertent clashes. The Iraqis agreed. General Schwarzkopf then proposed a specific division line well into Iraq at the tip of the U.S. and coalition front lines. General Al-Jabburi complained that the line was drawn well behind Iraqi lines; when informed that this was not, in fact, behind Iraqi lines but at the forefront of the coalition's advance, he "again appeared stunned."

After these two events, the DoD report continues, "the Iraqi attitude was noticeably more subdued."

159

U.S. diplomats, meanwhile, began what would become a months-long campaign to use the opportunity of Iraq's defeat to assemble an international conference in the Middle East. Secretary of State Baker headed for the Middle East in the first week of March to pursue a regional peace initiative. He was going, he said, primarily to listen; he would travel "without a blueprint."[3] President Bush and Secretary Baker hoped to use the newfound U.S. regional leverage and the cooperative attitude of the moderate Arab states to promote new agreements. U.S. diplomats also hoped to expand Washington's area of concern to draw in such issues as the rich-poor gap in the Arab world, which became a clarion call for Saddam Hussein during the Gulf crisis.

The Gulf War was over; a complicated and frustrating period of postwar diplomacy had begun.

Post–Cold War Defense Planning

From 1989–1992, the context for U.S. military planning changed dramatically and perhaps irrevocably. The Soviet Communist threat to U.S. interests, in Europe and elsewhere, has disappeared with the newborn, but fragile, democracies in Russia and Eastern Europe. Rather than being engaged in one major, unambiguous declared war against a well-studied adversary, the U.S. military will confront many threats of varying scope and importance ranging from the proliferation of weapons of mass destruction to armed attacks against U.S. friends or allies in the developing world. The stated purpose of the U.S. military has therefore already shifted from an anti-Soviet bulwark in Europe and elsewhere to a third world contingency force and may shift again to some form of combination rapid-deployment and peacekeeping force. Although the United States will undoubtedly leave some forces deployed in Europe and other locations, its primary military task will be to respond to troublemakers in the third world—like Saddam Hussein.

When it was first announced in the spring of 1991, this new military strategy focusing on crisis responses seemed relatively straightforward. U.S. interests, and those of our allies, are global, and regional instabilities could be readily foreseen and would pose a far less catastrophic threat to U.S. interests than earlier Soviet aggression. When looked at more closely, however, the strategy of regional contingencies betrays just as many difficulties and potential missteps as did containment. We are talking, after all, about a sea change in international politics, and as a result in U.S. foreign policy and military strategy. Such a radical transformation is bound to produce difficulties.

In simplest terms, a strategy is a method of reconciling means and ends. Every military strategy is therefore by nature a challenge—to find the best ways of applying resources toward military objectives, which in turn contribute to political ends. And strategy cannot be unilateral or static; it is derived from the interaction of at least two parties in which the goals and actions of each are determined in part by the behavior of the others. The new U.S. military strategy is no different. The passing of the cold war has not removed the challenge from strategy; it has merely redefined almost all the basic elements—potential adversaries, political goals (and thus military objectives)—while hinting strongly that new ways of reconciling means and ends are now available and needed.

Chapter 1 looked at changing U.S. foreign policy and the context for the Gulf War. Here we will consider one of the war's most distinct legacies: a new military strategy.

Emphasis on Regional Contingencies

In response to the waning of the Soviet threat, U.S. military planners have instituted a broad-based revision of strategy. For forty years that strategy had a single focus: containment of Soviet military and, at times, political expansion. Now, with the threat of Soviet expansion largely dissipated, the U.S. military is gradually adopting a strategy focused on regional contingencies.[4] This policy views the major threats to U.S. interests as arising not primarily from a central (read Soviet) threat but from spirals of regional instability or from a number of aggressive regional hegemons such as Iraq and North Korea.[5]

This new strategy involves a fundamental shift in emphasis, a sea change from the geostrategy and military doctrines of the cold war. "U.S. global strategy," one recent study noted,

> is evolving from a modified version of containment to a doctrine providing responses to lesser but worldwide contingencies. U.S. thinking will shift from a potential "one-and-a-half war" scenario, involving Europe and one other region, to the need to deal with up to two simultaneous contingencies in different regions. The larger of the two would be a conflict on the scale of a Middle Eastern or Korean war, involving up to two corps of U.S. ground forces and a corresponding level of air and naval commitments. A European commitment in the future may also fit into this large contingency. . . . The smaller contingency in the "two contingency" strategy might be a variety of low-intensity conflict, such as rapid intervention on the scale of Grenada or Panama.

The strategy would be in service of a U.S. defense policy emphasizing regional stability, in which the United States would play a key role—"not as a world policeman enforcing the hegemony of its own laws, but as a militiaman of sorts, called from a militarily relaxed posture to respond, in concert with its allies, to specific crises for limited periods of time."[6]

The Gulf War indeed represented a test case of these post–cold war concepts. As pointed out in the introductory chapter, the conflict was distinct in many ways. But in terms of its basic nature—representing as it did a shift in concern from the Soviet Union and its clients to a non-Soviet contingency— war leaders nevertheless applied new strategic concepts that are becoming the foundations of U.S. military strategy. Drawing lessons from the war is largely an attempt to assess the coherence between that strategy and the specific force structures, weapons systems, and operational and tactical schemes used on the battlefield.

Already there are hints that this new strategy will be no less controversial and no easier to implement than was containment. U.S. defense planners will face a challenging array of military, political, and economic problems and uncertainties in attempting to implement it in the years ahead, more than might have been assumed when the strategy was first promulgated. The most difficult challenge has already been noted in the *1991 Joint Military Net Assessment:* A series of contingency plans for each possible regional crisis is by itself neither a strategy nor a satisfactory substitute for military strategy. Missing is the definitive political statement of U.S. interests and objectives in the various regions of the globe and some indication of both a willingness to exert U.S. influence and of applicable priorities among the contending world regions. Until consensus on such policies has been forged—and we should remember that after the last war, it took the United States five years to hammer out the doctrine of containment—the new military strategy will continue to evolve.

While certain elements of any military strategy pertain largely to war, a nation's strategy has great importance in peacetime as well. Between wars, military strategies help guide the type and quantities of military equipment nations procure and the size of military forces they maintain. Unfortunately, throughout U.S. history strategy-force mismatches are all too common, and we run the risk of another period of strategic incoherence today. The ongoing build-down of U.S. military capabilities is simply not being guided by informed discussion of the connections between strategy, political guidance, battlefield operations and tactics, force size, and the kinds of weapons and other military equipment we obtain.

Not everything can be a priority for a defense establishment so strapped for resources; there is a clear need for priorities. Should the United States modernize its forces toward mid-intensity warfare against growing regional hegemons and sources of instability? Or is the greater threat to U.S. national security a range of transnational issues such as the narco-trafficking that is so visibly destroying segments of U.S. society, and against which the Department of Defense should emphasize military capabilities at the low end of the conflict spectrum? Indeed, one can easily make the case that priorities for the build-down of the 1990s are even more important than priorities would have been for the buildup of the 1980s; as the April 1989 CSIS report *Defense Eco-*

nomics for the 1990s argued, "Building up without a strategy is foolish; building down without one could be disastrous."[7]

Maintenance of Residual Forces

In formulating some coherent strategy for defense cuts, the most important—and most frequently neglected—issue has to do with the effectiveness of the residual military forces. At the end of every major war, the United States has allowed its military institutions to fall into disrepair. Interwar U.S. militaries have been ineffective, unprofessional, poorly trained, and of low morale.[8] As a result, and this is well worth remembering, the United States has done poorly in the initial battles of virtually all its major conflicts.[9] A military strategy predicated on fighting quick regional wars demands high-readiness forces because the military may be forced to enter such conflicts on short notice.

Despite this fact, now that the cold war is over, we risk making the same mistake again. Initial debates on defense reductions have focused almost entirely on numbers: budget figures, numbers of divisions and aircraft carriers and fighter wings. The task of maintaining *effectiveness*—a well-trained, highly motivated military establishment whose personnel, leaders, and equipment are truly ready for war—is far more than an exercise in quantification. But the task has fallen almost entirely to the military services, and it is not clear that they will be able to carry it out. Pressures brought to bear on the U.S. military from both the executive branch and Congress are already straining at its fabric of cohesiveness and professionalism.

The issue that we term "effectiveness" is also variously discussed in terms of "readiness" or its opposite, "hollowness." The prototypical recent example occurred in the 1970s, when the post-Vietnam U.S. military, riddled by drugs and a crushing lack of incentive, could not have been described as a combat-ready force. Such a lack of effectiveness, though stemming from different causes, is in fact a common peacetime phenomenon in the U.S. military; recall that before World War II U.S. troops had to train with wooden rifles and still had horse cavalry.

The task is complicated by the fact that effectiveness today requires much more than operational readiness and training among the different services. To be effective in the 1990s, U.S. forces will need more than a collection of individually effective units. Warfare today is a seamless activity in which ground, air, and naval units must operate as a cohesive team. This was dramatically seen in the Gulf War, in which the combination of a naval blockade, air power, ground forces, advanced artillery and missile systems, and battle-management and command technologies proved devastating. Military effectiveness now demands the ability to operate jointly with other services, to integrate high-technology intelligence and command-and-control systems, and in some cases to conduct multilateral operations with allies.

The problem today is that there are too many demands on the military for it to be able to preserve these elements of effectiveness. From the executive branch come two pressures: demands to retain hundreds of thousands of troops deployed abroad to support foreign commitments and demands to keep too much force structure (the Base Force).[10] From Congress come a number of bad political decisions. Three are particularly troublesome in the early stages of the build-down: overemphasis on guard and reserve force structure, unwillingness to close domestic bases the military says it does not need, and pork barreling on all manner of equipment, facilities, and weapons that DoD does not want. Meanwhile, the anticipated economic recovery would make recruitment and retention more difficult; and as defense spending declines, pulling down with it the level of training activity, the image of the military will suffer.

Chairman of the Joint Chiefs of Staff Colin Powell has frequently declared his intention to preserve an effective military, even at the price of force structure. His intention, and that of the service chiefs with similar priorities, is admirable. But it is not clear that other policymakers in Washington recognize the connection between the new military strategy's emphasis on crisis response and force projection and the need for a highly effective military. If the U.S. military once again becomes a hollow force, our military strategy will be a hollow doctrine as well.

Crisis Response and Forward Presence

Another potential disjunction is arising between two elements of the formal U.S. military strategy itself—crisis response and forward presence. (Its other two pillars are nuclear deterrence/defense and reconstitution.) It is increasingly apparent that Congress is not persuaded by the Bush administration's arguments for continued forward presence of U.S. military forces. If our strategy is one of crisis response and regional contingencies, some in Congress are legitimately asking, what role is there for U.S. troops permanently deployed abroad? With the growing opposition to all spending on foreign commitments—even extending to money spent in support of United Nations peacekeeping and humanitarian operations—the traditional U.S. reliance on forward-deployed forces is coming under renewed scrutiny. And two elements of the military strategy are increasingly being viewed as contradictory. In fact, crisis response and forward presence are mutually dependent, two sides of the same strategic coin—an argument that is not being made in the current debate.

Forward-presence forces support U.S. contingency operations in a number of important ways. In some cases they will actually provide the troops for the operation—in the Gulf War, for example, an entire U.S. corps was deployed from Europe, and such redeployments are an explicit rationale for a continued U.S. presence on the Continent. Forward presence is critical to effectiveness, providing a forum for training and planning in partnership with potential allies. Again in the Gulf War, U.S., British, and French forces used procedures, tactics, and interoperable equipment drawn from forty years of NATO experience.

In terms of logistics, too, forward presence makes a difference. Not only does it provide a worldwide network of bases from which military operations could be launched but it also encourages the creation of logistical infrastructures in possible contingency areas. Drawing a last example from the Gulf War, the huge (and largely secret) military infrastructure built up in Saudi Arabia, partly through U.S. security assistance programs, proved essential in handling the massive influx of troops and equipment during Operation Desert Shield.

U.S. forces deployed abroad will in turn depend on our crisis-response capabilities. As the number of U.S. forces overseas diminishes, no single example of U.S. forward presence is likely to be self-sufficient. Indeed, the United States seems to be moving more and more in the direction of global tripwires—small forces deployed in areas of concern to demonstrate a U.S. commitment but unable by themselves, or even in combination with local allies, to provide effective deterrence. An example can be found in Korea, where ongoing troop reductions may leave well under 10,000 U.S. troops in place by the mid- to late 1990s. Such a force (roughly one combat brigade and a few tactical air squadrons) would be critically dependent on early reinforcement and support, a function that could only be performed by highly ready, strategically mobile units—exactly the qualities of a force optimized for crisis response.

Forward presence and crisis response support each other in one other way: A robust commitment to one makes it less likely the other will be challenged. By maintaining U.S. forces abroad in regions of our global security interests, the United States can help deter aggressors or troublemakers, thereby reducing the risk of a contingency into which crisis-response forces would have to be sent. And by maintaining powerful and strategically mobile power-projection forces, we can help avoid regional challenges to deterrence by making clear our ability to supply and reinforce our reserve units rapidly and effectively.

When examined closely, then, the two most immediately relevant elements of U.S. strategy, forward presence and crisis response, are necessarily complementary. Increasingly, however, they are competing for attention and resources. If the new military strategy is to be effective, the Department of Defense must convey a sense of synergy between its two key pillars of general-purpose forces.

Maintaining Modern Systems

U.S. defense policymakers charged with implementing a strategy oriented to regional contingencies must also determine an effective rate of modernization for U.S. conventional capabilities. In the past, the modernization of U.S. tanks, aircraft, naval vessels, and other military equipment was tied to a familiar benchmark—the leading edge of Soviet technology. Given the decline in the Soviet threat, a slower rate of U.S. modernization is now acceptable. Even if regional aggressors have top-of-the-line equipment from the former Soviet Union, they will not possess the comparable military professionalism required to operate it (as demonstrated by Iraq's performance in the Gulf War). The level of U.S. technology required to prevail in contingency operations, therefore, is certainly lower than in the Soviet case.

Interestingly, the rationale for high-technology weapons shifted subtly during the Gulf War. Previously, technology had been promoted as the West's solution to overwhelming Soviet numbers. But Soviet preponderance has now disappeared in a cloud of economic disintegration and arms control, and in regional contingencies the United States and its allies can eventually (notwithstanding constraints on U.S. strategic lift, which will limit the speed of any buildup) expect to enjoy at least numerical parity and, in some cases, overwhelming superiority. But the U.S. advantage in military technology became something else in the Gulf War: a tool for saving U.S. and Allied lives. Military leaders recognized this, as did the American people, who may now demand similar high-technology applications in future conflicts. Stealth fighters were able to operate without loss, Iraqi armored columns were destroyed at a considerable distance before they could engage U.S. ground forces, and, in general, the war was managed to minimize U.S. casualties. (As we also learned, of course, this new technology is as dangerous as it is powerful and can inadvertently cause Allied as well as enemy casualties.)

In the past, a U.S. military leader might have objected that although reducing losses was an admirable and most desirable goal, it was to be viewed in the context of the higher goal of victory. Indeed, the traditional criticism of U.S. military strategy has been that it is too heavily dependent on attrition and brute force and does not take advantage of maneuver and guile. At Antietam the Union and Confederate armies lost over 26,000 men in a single day; the U.S. Marines suffered almost 25,000 killed and wounded in seizing the eight square miles of the island of Iwo Jima. By the 1970s, the military was experimenting with more flexible doctrines such as AirLand Battle, a variant of which proved successful in the Gulf War; but the primary purpose of these maneuver-oriented doctrines was to obtain victory, not reduce casualties.

The scale of casualties deemed acceptable will vary with the nature of the war. But it is a vitally important question whether U.S. citizens will accept farflung military operations if U.S. casualties are high. There was great concern in Washington—and great hope in Baghdad—that U.S. public support for the Gulf War would evaporate when the first 10,000 Americans fell in battle. And if, as in this case, the *outcome* of the war is never in doubt and the only question is how many Americans give their lives to bring about victory, then the priorities of U.S. military operations—and in turn, defense investment strategies designed to maintain technological superiority—will change.

But whatever the case, the issue of the necessary pace of conventional modernization has been placed in an entirely different context by the decline of the cold war. Budgetary pressures and the emergence of more diffuse military threats will necessitate that the pace of modernization be slowed; conversely, military incentives to buy the best weapons available and to conduct wars with minimal losses will require continued progress in such areas as aerial and space reconnaissance, stealth, target acquisition, theater ballistic missile defenses, and precision weapons. In the end the proper answer lies somewhere between the two: continued development of high-technology systems, but not in as many areas and not as quickly as would have been the case in the cold war. One logical possibility for savings doubtless will be found in the synergistic effect of a mix of high and low technologies; as demonstrated in the war, if 50 stealthy aircraft can suppress enemy defenses and clear the way for 500 unstealthy aircraft to operate with minor loss, there is no need to purchase 550 stealthy aircraft. In early 1992, the Bush administration's initial—and highly controversial—approach to this procurement issue became clear: It would continue research on the application of new technologies, officials said, but not actually put them into full-scale production. It remains to be seen if this "research but don't produce" policy will survive congressional vetting.

Related to the question of modernization is the subject of defense industrial preparedness. In the cold war, the robustness of the big acquisition programs of the Reagan defense buildup provided an important reservoir of production capability. If deterrence failed, a war with the Soviet Union was to be fought by well-equipped U.S. standing forces and any additional material that could be produced in short order. This "come as you are" strategy was designed to meet that specific threat. Any items that might be needed in greater quantity on short notice were to be produced from the built-in slack in the U.S. cold war defense industry.

But Desert Shield and Desert Storm revealed the fragility of the defense industrial base, and that weakness—if severely tested in a conflict longer or more costly than the Gulf War—could become a war-stopper. Needed computers and other electronic components had to be coaxed from Japanese producers who did not share the same sense of urgency about the crisis. Delivery systems for selected ammunition were brought up to maximum speed; even after this surge, at the end of the war the supply of a number of munitions was within days of being exhausted—including 25mm ammunition and some precision-guided weapons. The military food industry at first had difficulties in supplying enough rations. The sole producer of atropine, the agent used to combat nerve gas, never produced enough to supply the needed two doses per soldier.

From these examples as well as substantial analysis done by the Department of Defense after the Gulf War,[11] it is clear that a strategy of regional contingencies will require more explicit attention to critical defense technological and industrial sectors. An important priority may become maintaining at least minimal production and surge capacities for certain military items almost regardless of current demand.

War and Politics

Besides the military and strategic difficulties of the contingencies strategy, there are political challenges as well. War, as every armchair general has been quick to point out since Carl von Clausewitz made the phrase famous, is an extension of politics. Much of this study deals with relatively narrow military issues—the performance of specific weapons systems, the value of military strategy, the conduct of the war. At base, however, this war, like all others, was a political phenomenon. And as such, it offers a number of lessons on the interplay between war and politics, lessons that have not received much public attention. These lessons have particular application to the new U.S. contingencies strategy.

In the aftermath of a highly successful—and popular—war, it is easy to forget that one of the biggest challenges confronting President George Bush in August 1990 was an apparent lack of public support for military action. Polls showed little public enthusiasm for a war to oust Saddam Hussein from Kuwait. Worse, the Congress, particularly its Democratic leadership, was balking at the idea of actually declaring war or in some other way authorizing President Bush to initiate a major conflict.

In the end, of course, these public and congressional doubts were overcome (though not by much).[12] In part this was a result of the robust international consensus: Americans were apparently much more willing to accept the use of force if it was clear the world community did also and stood side by side with U.S. forces in the war. One well-known lesson was relearned in the Gulf—namely, involving friends and allies in any major U.S. military effort certainly contributes to, and may even be a precondition for, acquiring domestic public support for that effort.

Somewhat surprisingly, President Bush's decision to call up major elements of the National Guard and reserves also had a galvanizing effect on public opinion. Public support for the U.S. military deployment in the Gulf rose noticeably once the reserve call-ups were under way. In this sense the Defense Department's total force policy served its primary goal completely: After Vietnam, it was determined that in any future war, the whole American public would have to be involved, and thus the military services (and particularly the army) placed major support and combat elements into the National Guard and reserves, creating a "total force."

One of the clear lessons of the Gulf War therefore relates to the means by which national leaders can create support for a U.S. military intervention. Such support will result from a sense of shared purpose and a perception of a common goal, perceived not only among the American people but the world community as well. In this war, U.S. leaders were fortunate in that early in the buildup, the goal was clear—the expulsion of Iraq from Kuwait. In and of itself, however, that goal was apparently not persuasive to the American people at the moment Hussein's brutal armies crossed the Kuwaiti border on August 2. It only became persuasive with the emergence of a broad sense of international, and subsequently national, commitment to it.

A corollary of this experience is that prewar public opinion surveys may tell very little about how the American people will react once a conflict is under way. Current polls, for example, show only about half of the respondents as favoring U.S. military support to South Korea if it is attacked by the North. If, however, such an attack occurred, and if the American people were flooded with media images of South Korean people fleeing from northern aggression, and if the United Nations quickly and unanimously condemned the invasion and began assembling a military response, and if U.S. National Guard and reserve troops were called up and declared their pride in preparing to defend an ally—in short, if developments paralleled what went on in the Gulf—then there is little question that a vast majority of Americans would come to support U.S. intervention on the South's behalf.

Much will depend, of course, on the conduct of the war and on how quickly it is over. If it is defined by a specific, powerful moment—the Japanese attack on Pearl Harbor, President Harry Truman's decision to defend South Korea, President Bush's pledge that Iraq's aggression would "not stand"—the outset of a war will often serve to galvanize public opinion behind the U.S. military effort. The risks inherent in war can create a unique expression of shared fate and common purpose. It may only be when the war is extended and the casualty lists are burgeoning that the citizenry is confronted with the brutal reality of war and begins to rethink its wisdom. This is certainly what occurred in Vietnam.

The Bush administration never faced this problem, because miraculously only a few U.S. personnel died in the Gulf War, which was over very rapidly. But future U.S. leaders, if they confront more difficult regional contingencies offering a prospect of longer wars and higher casualties, may run up against more serious public opposition. In the contingencies strategy—dealing as it does with regional and not global threats and dealing only with vital, or less than vital, interests overseas rather than direct threats to the U.S. homeland—no set of national interests will be terribly compelling in the public eye. The challenge of the contingencies strategy is, as the name implies, a contingent response in defense of important U.S. global interests, but interests far short of national survival. If such interventions or wars are to be politically feasible, they will have to be of short duration with minimal casualties.

Partly because of this complexity, it is difficult to determine if the recent war invalidates the so-called Vietnam syndrome. After the U.S. debacle in Indochina, the American people were said to be utterly unwilling to support any foreign adventures. The U.S. ability to project power in the world was said to be fatally undermined, and some have portrayed the resurgence of Soviet foreign policy in the 1970s, culminating with the invasion of Afghanistan, as a calculated response to this U.S. paralysis. Some have argued that we defeated more than the Iraqi military in the Gulf War, that U.S. military forces smashed the Vietnam syndrome—already tottering after the U.S. interventions in Grenada (1983) and Panama (1989)—as well.

Yet it is important to keep in mind that the wars in Indochina and the Gulf are separated by more than time; they were completely different kinds of military campaigns. The Vietnam conflict was a counterinsurgency war, largely fought not against standing armies in the field but against shadowy guerrillas, pervasive infiltrators, child terrorists—almost a whole people, but one that was seldom seen in the media until after a battle. In the Gulf, by contrast, the targets of U.S. military power were very explicit and could be seen daily in the worldwide media—Iraqi tanks, trucks, air defense sites, military headquarters, bases, supporting civilian infrastructure, and the like. The stark difference between the two wars is perhaps best seen in the U.S. military's attitude to measures of success: In Vietnam enemy casualties were assiduously counted—and overcounted. In the Gulf, the victory having been won, the U.S. military refused to do more than speculate about the possible numbers of Iraqi dead and wounded. Interest groups had to file Freedom of Information Act requests to pry out even the most general estimates. U.S. military and political leaders wanted the focus on the political objective—evicting Iraqi forces from Kuwait.

Much of the Vietnam syndrome may therefore be alive and well. In the jungles of Indochina, the American people—and, we must remember, their military as well—learned a sharp distaste for fighting guerrilla wars, not necessarily for any kind of war. This distaste likely remains, even after the Gulf victory. Comparisons to Vietnam could still be conjured up recently in opposition to a U.S. drug interdiction intervention into Colombia, for instance. And in many ways this is as it should be, because military intervention alone will seldom solve the social and economic problems that underlie most insurgencies. As we learned in Vietnam, other instruments of power are absolutely necessary, and even then they may be insufficient.

The issues of public opinion and public diplomacy are further complicated by the pervasiveness of information technologies in today's world. During the

Gulf War, the Cable News Network (CNN) often broadcast stories in the United States before they were reported through military channels. Every U.S. network covered the war in excruciating detail, abandoning virtually all other programming for the war's first few days. The requirements for effective public diplomacy are more demanding than ever; the Department of Defense will face a media that is at times better informed about the battlefield situation than it is. If public support is to be maintained, U.S. interventions must be swiftly decisive; and during such operations the government's ability to report accurately and correctly must be the equal of the world's media.

No public will long support a military operation that appears poorly organized or incompetently conducted. A revolution in international communications has paralleled, and in some cases outstripped, the revolution in military technologies on display in the Gulf War. Regional hegemons in the future will attempt to manipulate U.S. and world media for their own ends either before or, as in the Gulf, during conflicts. At the same time, the decision-making process of free societies is becoming increasingly transparent. The challenge to U.S. leaders hoping to create and nurture public consensus is clear; and because of the unique nature of the Gulf War, this challenge has not yet been fully met, nor its fulfillment tested.

Limited Versus Total War

Another dilemma in the new military strategy is found in the confusion it promotes between the notions of limited and total war. Regional conflicts will threaten only limited U.S. interests and demand only a limited military effort, but the damage done to the target country will often approach that characteristic of a more total war. This problem is especially evident in two areas: the fragility of modernizing, developing economies and the challenge of war termination.

The fragility of the physical infrastructure of modern economies, especially in developing states (perhaps even in advanced economies as well), will complicate calculations of limited ends and means in regional wars. Iraqi infrastructure proved vulnerable to a surprising degree. An air campaign directed primarily at Iraqi military forces crippled Iraqi communications, transportation, and civil services such as the provision of health care, water, and electricity. The full ramifications of this destruction, in the form of malnutrition, starvation, or disease, only later became fully evident. This result is particularly ironic, because precision weapons supposedly had created the option of conducting wars with far less civilian damage than was common in the past. But although collateral damage was minimized in some cases, the destructiveness of precision weapons was such that more damage was done to certain targets than anticipated. Combined with a continuing embargo on trade, as in the case of Iraq, modern weapons are easily capable of inflicting permanent damage, damage simply beyond repair by indigenous means.

This war may therefore have demonstrated a paradox about U.S. contingency operations. U.S. military forces will use precision weapons and firepower restraint in an effort to reduce civilian deaths and suffering, but the inherent brittleness of developing economies may prevent them from achieving this goal. Morally and politically we are urged to avoid more lasting damage than necessary to accomplish the military objectives, but the fragility of the indigenous economy may confound our ability to do that.

Armchair strategists and military leaders who do not wish to see U.S. military actions restrained for humanitarian reasons are concerned about these issues. They are so concerned, in fact, that various offices in the Pentagon are battling for control of a dramatic new initiative for nonlethal warfare. By using blinding lasers and chemical immobilizers to stun foot soldiers and munitions with "entanglement" warheads to stop armored vehicles on land or ships at sea, it is hoped by some that the United States could some day fight a war that did not involve death, or at least few deaths.[13] The future of this initiative is unclear, but the motives are clear.

The second aspect of the limited–total war issue relates to war termination and what was learned about it in the Gulf War. The new security environment, with its focus on regional contingencies, lends itself to great confusion about political and military objectives. The inherent tension is between a contingency response normally thought to be restricted in scope and the nature of war, which oftentimes must be total and unrestricted in intensity even if the objectives are finite. National security policies focused on regional contingencies, including the military strategy designed to address such events, might encourage an overreliance on the short-term use of military power to solve issues that are at base political, economic, or social in nature. Constant media coverage and its effects on domestic attitudes also bias policy toward rapid, decisive action.

Once a war has begun, however, the opposite presumption—of limited rather than total ends—might emerge, in the minds of both leaders and their publics, to block war termination. In the case of Iraq, the Bush administration from the outset denied that it sought the removal of Saddam Hussein from power; at the time, these statements seemed appropriate to a war of limited ends. As it turned out, however, U.S. and coalition interests would have been better served by a more ambitious set of military and political goals *if* public consensus had been possible. Ruling out total victory also complicated war termination: When the key postwar U.S. goal was "getting out quickly," other goals—such as encouraging a transition to a democratic Iraq under different rule—fell by the wayside.

Once the basic objective of the war, evicting Iraqi troops from Kuwait, was accomplished, there was no clear path for the coalition to follow. Some advocated a tough policy, arguing that the coalition should finish its job and force Hussein from power; others warned of the dangers that a fragmented Iraq would produce and urged restraint. The apex of controversy was the Bush administration's decision to end the fighting before the Iraqi Republican Guard in the Kuwaiti theater of operations was completely destroyed.

It is once again clear from this war that military objectives and national objectives will not always coincide. The latter are preeminent and are established by political leaders looking at the whole array of U.S. military, political, and economic interests. As we are often reminded, war is an extension of politics, and as wars draw to a close, political considerations will often emerge predominant to dictate the nature of the outcome. It is not at all obvious that the coalition military effort should have gone on even an hour longer than it did; by the end of the war, coalition air and ground forces were merely slaughtering Iraqis for no pressing military purpose at the time. But the coalition's strategy for the transition from war to peace upon retaking Kuwait had not been decided, and this impeded winning victories in peacetime as great as those that had been won in war.

The U.S. failure to establish clear policies for war termination should actually have come as little surprise. U.S. leaders, perhaps because war is so distasteful to democracies in the first place, have been notoriously bad at war termination for decades, if not since 1776. During World War II, Franklin Roosevelt gave what many considered to be insufficient attention to the shape of the postwar world; most of the thinking he did do was aimed at the idea of forming a partnership with the Soviet Union, which proved impossible. The United States was drawn into the Korean War just a few years after the Joint Chiefs had decided to withdraw from the peninsula; having not foreseen its involvement, Washington was unprepared to establish clear conditions for victory. The failure to define goals in Vietnam is generally agreed.

War termination is an enormously complex business, particularly in a multilateral context. Nonetheless, precisely because they will hold the ultimate responsibility for bringing the war to a favorable conclusion, political leaders must think the endgame through more carefully and explicitly than was done in this case. All of this will be increasingly challenging in the years ahead. The cold war taught us to see a sharp delineation between war and peace; there was no mistaking which condition Washington and Moscow were in. Beginning in Korea, however, it became apparent that even in the cold war, war and peace were not black-and-white issues, that there were many shades of gray. This fact was confirmed in Vietnam, and unfortunately we came to believe the quagmire to avoid was in Vietnam rather than in the centers of decision in Washington. In future regional conflicts, the United States will be acting on a new stage where the definition of when a war is over and when normalcy is at hand will defy simple tests. In such cases, war termination must comprise more than simply fulfilling a pledge to return troops rapidly home.

Indeed, the "victory" in the Gulf has not yet been won; only a lasting peace can be considered true victory. Anthony Cordesman and Abraham Wagner, after one of the most rigorous examinations yet done of the lessons of modern war, note the inefficacy of military triumphs won in a political vacuum. In their study of the Arab-Israeli wars they note,

> Israel won a major victory on the battlefield [in each of the Arab-Israeli wars] which it could translate into a temporary gain in security, but not the kind of victory that decisively altered the politics of the region. While war often served as an extension of politics by other means, even the most dramatic victories simply laid the groundwork for another arms race and future combat.[14]

After an examination of the Iran-Iraq war, they concluded similarly: "One clear lesson that emerges out of both the Iran-Iraq War and the recent trends in the region is that everything possible must be done to contain the violence in the area and to fight the proliferation of weapons of mass destruction. Tomorrow's wars may be infinitely more dangerous to the West and infinitely more tragic for the peoples of the region."[15]

Deterrence

A final political-military difficulty of the new military strategy has to do with the changing nature, and declining relevance, of deterrence. Traditional deterrence theory, so reliable during the cold war, may not be up to the challenge of a more complex and multipolar post–cold war security environment; this was of course the major theme of Chapters 2 through 4.

The new U.S. military strategy has evolved in response to dramatic changes in international relations. All the familiar guideposts have evaporated: Moscow has abandoned adventurism (at least for now), and the domino theory has been thrown into reverse—in Nicaragua, Angola, Ethiopia, and Eastern Europe. This much is well known. What is not so widely appreciated is the impact the single-minded doctrine of containment had on the practice of U.S. defense policy. Faced with Soviet intransigence and expansionism, unable to match Soviet numbers in Europe or Soviet foreign military deliveries and ideological appeal elsewhere, the United States turned to a deceptively simple (and, in the eyes of some, efficient) tactic: deterrence. U.S. officials pledged dire consequences should Soviet or Soviet-inspired aggression strike at key U.S. allies or interests. U.S. troops, bases, tactical nuclear weapons, and political commitments were placed strategically around the globe, tripwires for a U.S. involvement that could escalate to nuclear war.

So pervasive was the theory of deterrence during the cold war that it virtually hijacked U.S. foreign policy. Raymond Garthoff has written that deterrence "became a strategy for containment with coercive overtones," and, "in time, a concept for crisis management and even management of foreign policy—the basis for alliances, and then for alliance strategy." In the process, deterrence "supplanted foreign policy," causing U.S. officials "to give priority to military basing and alliance relationships over other policy objectives: support of democracy, protection of human rights, nuclear nonproliferation, and others."[16]

Deterrence was foreign policy by implied threat. It was not based on negotiation, compromise, or a coherent global strategy other than containment. It was a punitive doctrine designed to protect U.S. allies and interests from Communist aggression. Hence the immediate U.S. reaction on learning of Saddam Hussein's threats against Kuwait was a search for a suitable deterrent signal or threat packaged so as not to provoke the very aggression the Bush administration hoped to avoid. Always, though, the strategy of deterrence suffered from a number of flaws, some of which were exposed again in the Gulf crisis and war of 1990–1991.

These flaws were examined at great length in Chapters 2 through 4. Effective deterrence depends on clear strategic warning, which will not always be forthcoming. Barriers often arise to enunciating a clear deterrent signal, and even if a signal is sent, deterrent threats often fail. Even more fundamental, deterrence promoted a studied ignorance of the underlying causes of instability. U.S. foreign policy in Vietnam, El Salvador, and a dozen other places ignored the local socioeconomic conditions that gave rise to rebellions. Relying on deterrence rather than negotiation prevented U.S. leaders from addressing the fundamental causes of threats to U.S. interests. Deterrence was a bandage, not a cure, an especially crippling handicap in an era of regional contingencies that often issue from instability and not premeditated aggression. Nations and their militaries cannot deter instability; it must be addressed through a more subtle combination of economic, political, and social remedies, with deterrence and other military sanctions present, if at all, in the background.

For precisely this reason, deterrence is less relevent for the foreign and defense policies of the post–cold war era because their focus has changed from containing a threat to preventing the rise of new threats. The former task made use of, even demanded, deterrence; the latter has little place for it. Settling civil wars, dampening regional hostilities, addressing such conflict-producing problems as drugs and environmental damage—these require a subtle combination of diplomatic and economic responses and only seldom require the threat of overt military intervention. As noted in the opening chapter, threats to U.S. and global security are now largely nonmilitary in nature.

Moreover, to the extent that deterrent strategies form part of the response to today's threats and challenges, they will increasingly be implemented *multilaterally* and *economically*. The United Nations, not the United States, will threaten a response against a North Korean threat south or an Iranian attack on Saudi Arabia (though there is much room left for unilateral U.S. statements, especially on issues on which the security council is divided). And when threats are made, they may have less of a military flavor, at least at first, than an economic one. The United Nations probably would not threaten an armed intervention to keep India and Pakistan from going to war, but it could threaten international economic sanctions. Again, this trend will not be without exception; the Gulf War provides a perfect example of a time when circumstances made reliance on economic sanctions alone unacceptable to U.S. political leaders.

U.S. leaders must therefore shift some emphasis from deterrence to inducement or reassurance.[17] As was suggested in Chapter 3, deterrence still has a place in U.S. strategy—keeping Iraq from invading Saudi Arabia, for example. Deterrence will remain valuable simply because the stick cannot be far behind the carrot. But the focus of U.S. foreign policy must change from threats to talk. To prevent aggression against U.S. interests, Washington must create alternatives to the use of force, making it clear that if aggressors moderate their policies and accept the rule of law, they will be rewarded.

Arms Control

In the aftermath of the Gulf War, calls immediately went up for a regional arms-control framework to help restrain the growth of military power in the world's most volatile area. In testimony after the war, Secretary of State Baker argued that "the time has come to try to change the destructive pattern of military competition and proliferation in this region and to reduce arms flow into an area that is already over-militarized." Yet the dilemmas involved in arms control quickly became apparent as the United States appeared to ignore its arms-control rhetoric in proposing a new $1.6 billion arms deal for Egypt and an $18 billion arms sale to other Arab states that participated in coalition operations.[18]

From the perspective of U.S. military planners, the key question is, what type of arms control best supports the U.S. contingencies strategy? The challenge to arms control today is to create *stability* at lower levels of weapons in a region just ravaged by war. Once again U.S. policymakers face something of a dilemma: Security assistance, as noted in Chapter 4, can be useful in preventing war, but this principle can also be taken to a destabilizing, and therefore illogical, extreme. Any attempts to restrain the flow of conventional arms into the Middle East, moreover, will run afoul of both Israeli and Arab claims that their support for U.S. policy in the recent war entitles them to new weapons.

Attempts to restrain the supplies of conventional arms are loaded with political and economic controversy. In two other areas, however, important progress can be made that would support U.S. interests. First, existing efforts to restrain the deployment of weapons of mass destruction should be doubled. The growth of nuclear, chemical, or biological arsenals in the Middle East would aggravate existing instabilities, nourish the ambitions of regional hegemons, and, could produce horrendous civilian casualties if used. The United States can significantly reduce the threat to its own forces posed by these unconventional weapons by a vigorous, international nonproliferation policy and by continued investments in protective measures, antimissile systems, and overall technological superiority. A multilateral diplomatic strategy to reduce or eliminate such unconventional arsenals is in the U.S. national interest, especially because of uncertainties associated with deterrence and compellence with such weapons in regional contingencies.

Second, in the area of conventional forces, the United States might wish to reduce its initial emphasis on supplier cartels and numerical constraints and look more closely at confidence-building measures, which are often necessary precursors to agreements on numerical parity. There is a wealth of experience on this issue from the European context, and several observers have already begun outlining possible transparency and confidence schemes for the Middle East.

Guiding Principles for
Future U.S. Defense Policy

Our analysis of the lessons of the Gulf War is complete. It remains, however, to draw their implications for U.S. defense policy. The goal of this book has been to examine the lessons of the Gulf War from a high-level, strategic defense perspective. Specific policy recommendations have generally been avoided. The lessons outlined in the preceding chapters, however, do translate readily into policy prescriptions: The notion that the quality of military personnel is as important as technological sophistication would, for example, caution against unbalanced cuts in operational readiness and training. Given that many data are still being gathered on the war, that numerous other lessons are being learned, and that studies are underway within the government, we hesitate to outline a list of policy recommendations. Defense policymakers in the Pentagon and on Capitol Hill undoubtedly recognize many of the problems we do and are developing their own lists of solutions.

Nonetheless, a volume on the lessons of a military conflict would be incomplete without some suggestions regarding current decisions on defense policy and defense investments. This focus cannot go beyond some broadly stated principles so soon after the war; still, these are principles based directly on lessons learned—or relearned—in the recent war in the Gulf. We believe the application of these principles will best position the U.S. military for future contingencies:

1. Place the greatest emphasis on the quality of military personnel and the effectiveness and readiness of deployed forces. Despite all the media coverage of technology, we firmly believe ready forces, quality personnel, and leadership won this war. The military readiness and personnel policies designed and implemented by both Congress and the administration will be the *single largest determinant of future U.S. military capability* during the coming decade.

2. *Logistics wins wars.* This war clearly demonstrated that an adequate logistical effort is indispensable to victory. The challenges in this area are clear: As noted in Chapter 1, U.S. forces enjoyed incredible advantages in the Gulf War in terms of time available to deploy and the facilities available at the receiving end; moreover, in all future wars the United States will depend to a great degree on its allies for logistical support. This principle counsels further efforts in two areas: acquiring a higher degree of strategic mobility to be able to respond to regional contingencies in far-flung locations; and working diligently to maintain existing logistical arrangements, both bilateral and multilateral, as well as to develop new ones. As the U.S. forward-deployed presence diminishes over the coming years, these precontingency logistical arrangements may again be the linchpin of successful military operations.

3. *Given U.S. political, logistical, industrial, and economic dependencies, forming international coalitions will be necessary for victory in any major contingency operation.* This fact demands continued security assistance programs, military-to-military interaction, and continued emphasis on peacetime exercises and planning among major allies. Simply stated, the end of the cold war means increased—not decreased—emphasis on closer contacts and interoperability with allied nations.

4. *Tactical ballistic missiles will continue to pose an increasingly significant threat to U.S. interests and military forces.* This points to the need for new antitactical ballistic missile systems (ATBMS), successors to the Patriot, as well as energetic, multilateral approaches to halt the proliferation of such capabilities.

5. *Emphasize improvements in carrier-based aircraft.* Aircraft carriers played a major role in the Gulf War and, more broadly, will continue to play such a role in the U.S. strategy of response to regional contingencies. But the U.S. Navy must reexamine its investment strategy, in particular focusing on improving the ability of carrier-based aviation to support regional land campaigns.

6. *Emphasize improvements in naval mine countermeasure forces.* Existing U.S. abilities to deal with even primitive mines are inadequate for the new military strategy.

7. *Maintain amphibious assault capabilities and sufficient expeditionary forces.* As the Gulf War demonstrated, amphibious forces can be enormously useful even when they are not actually landed. In other contingencies—when the logistical infrastructure of the host country is not as extensive as that of Saudi Arabia—sea-based assault forces may be indispensable.

8. *Command, control, and communications systems, integrated into a battle-management architecture, interoperable throughout the theater, will be among the key military systems of the future.* Advanced C3I systems serve as a force

multiplier, particularly in mobile warfare. They demonstrated their worth again in the Gulf, where coalition air, ground, and sea operations worked as a tightly coordinated whole.

9. The participation of U.S. Army National Guard and reserve combat units in contingency operations must be reexamined. As noted in Chapter 6, large combined-arms combat units of brigade size and above are probably too complex to be maintained at a level of readiness that would allow guard and reserve forces to be deployed within days, as many contingency operations might demand. Alternatively, the army could include in contingency forces reserve units built around single weapon systems or single operational functions.

10. The ability to employ military space capabilities in support of theater and tactical operations proved vital in. the Gulf War. Coalition forces relied on space assets for a host of functions, from communications to reconnaissance. U.S. forces will continue to depend on space technology; this dependency both demands continued development of space systems and creates an increasing vulnerability to antisatellite weapons in the hands of an adversary.

In sum, this list points more than anything else to the need for a *balanced defense investment strategy*. Concentrating defense resources in a few weapons systems or operational functions will produce a military organization that is ill-suited for the uncertain demands of future contingencies. For logistical and industrial as well as political reasons, U.S. military forces in many cases will not be able to function properly without Allied support. Most individual technologies cannot perform their missions adequately unless supported by other, complementary equipment. No military will fight effectively without well-trained personnel, professional leadership, and sound strategy. The devastation of the massive Iraqi army proved beyond doubt that military power is a complex, multifaceted entity and simply cannot be bought only in the form of advanced weapons systems.

In this period of budgetary frugality, U.S. defense policymakers, in Congress as well as the Pentagon, must not forget the principles enumerated here. An effective armed force is not made up of its weapons alone. It is the people who operate those weapons, the supporting technologies that control them, the logistics that sustain them, and a dozen other elements that make the difference between victory and defeat in wartime. Each of those elements requires significant resources. A balanced defense investment strategy would recognize this and put as much emphasis on people, concepts, battle management, and intelligence as on high-profile weapons. Because, like the Gulf War, the next war will be won by men and women—integrated, cohesive human organizations—not machines.

Notes

Chapter 1

1. Vignette of the 48th TFS comes from media pool report from Ed Offley, Calvin Collie, and Peter Copeland, January 17, 1991; Scripps Howard pool report No. 10.

2. Anthony H. Cordesman and Abraham R. Wagner, *The Lessons of Modern War, Volume I: The Arab-Israeli Conflicts, 1973–1989* (Boulder, CO: Westview Press, 1990), p. 349.

3. Don Oberdorfer, "Bush's Talk of a 'New World Order': Foreign Policy Tool or Mere Slogan?" *Washington Post,* May 26, 1991, p. A31.

4. Henry Kissinger, *American Foreign Policy: Three Essays* (New York: W. W. Norton, 1969), pp. 79, 91, 97.

5. Alexander George and Richard Smoke, *Deterrence in American Foreign Policy: Theory and Practice* (New York: Columbia University Press, 1974), p. 613.

6. For an emphasis on Washington's enduring interests, see Samuel Huntington, "America's Changing Strategic Interests," *Survival* 33 (January-February 1991).

7. See Eliot Cohen, "The Future of Force and American Strategy," *The National Interest* no. 21 (Fall 1990).

8. See Robert Johnson, "Exaggerating America's Stakes in Third World Conflicts," *International Security* 10 (Winter 1985–1986), and Stephen Van Evera, "Why Europe Matters, Why the Third World Doesn't: American Grand Strategy After the Cold War," *Journal of Strategic Studies* 13 (June 1990).

9. Paul Kennedy, "The (Relative) Decline of America," *Atlantic Monthly* (August 1987), p. 29. See also Kennedy, *The Rise and Fall of the Great Powers* (New York: Random House, 1987), especially the introduction and Chapter 8.

10. Alan Tonelson, "The Real National Interest," *Foreign Policy* no. 61 (Winter 1985–1986).

11. Eliot Cohen, "When Policy Outstrips Power," *The Public Interest* no. 75 (Spring 1984): 9–10, 16.

12. Zbigniew Brzezinski, "Selective Global Commitment," *Foreign Affairs* 70, no. 4 (Fall 1991): 19–20.

13. Paul H. Nitze, "America: An Honest Broker," *Foreign Affairs* 69, no. 4 (Fall 1990): 11, 14.

14. For an analysis of the U.S. balancing role in Southeast Asia, see Sheldon W. Simon, "U.S. Interests in Southeast Asia: The Future Military Presence," *Asian Survey* 31, no. 7 (July 1991).

15. Richard Haas, "The Use (and Mainly Misuse) of History," *Orbis* 32 (Summer 1988): 414.

16. Joseph Nye, "Understating U.S. Strength," *Foreign Policy* no. 72 (Fall 1988). See also Nye, *Bound to Lead: The Changing Nature of American Power* (New York: Basic Books, 1990).

17. For examples of a Middle East strategy constructed along such lines, see Richard Herrmann, "The Middle East and the New World Order: Rethinking U.S. Strategy After the Gulf War," *International Security* 16 (Fall 1991); and Martin Indyk, "Beyond the Balance of Power: America's Choice in the Middle East," *The National Interest* no. 26 (Winter 1991–1992).

18. See Andrew Fenton Cooper, Richard A. Higgott, and Kim Richard Nossal, "Bound to Follow? Leadership and Followership in the Gulf Conflict," *Political Science Quarterly* 106, no. 3 (1991).

Chapter 2

1. Leslie H. Gelb, "Mr. Bush's Fateful Blunder," *New York Times,* July 17, 1991, p. A21.

2. Boren quoted from the "McNeil/Lehrer News Hour," July 23, 1991.

3. For an argument that we could not have deterred Saddam, see Paul K. Davis and John Arquilla, "Deterring or Coercing Opponents in Crises: Lessons from the War with Saddam Hussein" (Santa Monica, CA: The RAND Corporation, 1991), pp. 67–72.

4. *Webster's New World Dictionary,* Concise Edition (Cleveland: World Publishing Company, 1960), p. 206.

5. In their seminal Bancroft-winning critique of deterrence theory, Alexander George and Richard Smoke make this distinction explicitly and criticize only deterrence theory's application to extended commitments. See George and Smoke, *Deterrence in American Foreign Policy: Theory and Practice* (New York: Columbia University Press, 1974), pp. 38–55.

6. Janice Gross Stein, "Calculation, Miscalculation, and Conventional Deterrence I: The View from Cairo," in Robert Jervis, Richard Ned Lebow, and Stein, eds., *Psychology and Deterrence* (Baltimore: Johns Hopkins University Press, 1985), p. 35.

7. George and Smoke, *Deterrence in American Foreign Policy,* pp. 59–60; emphasis in original.

8. Thomas Schelling, *Arms and Influence* (New Haven: Yale University Press, 1966), p. 35.

9. Ibid., p. 43.

10. These various strategies can be found in ibid., pp. 35–50; other related subjects appear in the rest of the chapter, pp. 50–91.

11. Paul Gigot, "A Great American Screw-Up: The U.S. and Iraq, 1980–1990," *The National Interest* (Winter 1990–1991): 4.

12. Elaine Sciolino, *The Outlaw State: Saddam Hussein's Quest for Power and the Gulf Crisis* (New York: John Wiley, 1991), pp. 139–158, 163ff.

13. Gigot, "A Great American Screw-Up," pp. 5–6. This is the source for the information on the Teicher-Fuller and Khalilzad memoranda.

14. John K. Cooley, "Pre-War Gulf Diplomacy," *Survival* 33 (March-April 1991): 126.

15. Sciolino, *Outlaw State,* p. 188.

16. Ibid., p. 173.

17. Gigot, "A Great American Screw-Up," pp. 8–9.

18. Pierre Salinger and Eric Laurent, *Secret Dossier: The Hidden Agenda Behind the Gulf War* (New York: Penguin Books, 1991), p. 5.

19. Foreign Broadcast Information Service, Near East–South Asia segment, February 27, 1990, pp. 2, 4.

20. Accounts and quotations in the following two paragraphs come from Salinger and Laurent, *Secret Dossier*, pp. 7–9.

21. Salinger and Laurent, *Secret Dossier*, p. xx.

22. Salinger and Laurent, *Secret Dossier*, pp. 10–11.

23. Foreign Broadcast Information Service, Near East–South Asia segment, April 3, 1990, pp. 32, 35.

24. "Iraq's New Threat," *Washington Post*, April 4, 1990, p. A26.

25. Cited in Bob Woodward, *The Commanders* (New York: Simon and Schuster, 1991), p. 201.

26. Cooley, "Pre-War Gulf Diplomacy," pp. 126–127; Salinger and Laurent, *Secret Dossier*, pp. 20–23; Sciolino, *Outlaw State*, p. 176.

27. This account is drawn from Woodward, *The Commanders*, pp. 199–204.

28. Robert H. Kupperman, "President Bush's Options on Iraq," *Christian Science Monitor*, April 24, 1990.

29. Richard Ned Lebow, "Miscalculation in the South Atlantic," in Robert Jervis, Lebow, and Janice Gross Stein, eds., *Psychology and Deterrence* (Baltimore: Johns Hopkins University Press, 1985), p. 101.

30. See John E. Reilly, ed., *American Public Opinion and U.S. Foreign Policy 1991* (Chicago: Chicago Council on Foreign Relations, 1991).

31. George and Smoke, *Deterrence in American Foreign Policy*, pp. 507–508.

32. Robert Jervis, "Perceiving and Coping With Threat," in Jervis, Lebow, and Stein, eds., *Psychology and Deterrence*, p. 21.

33. Lebow, "Miscalculation in the South Atlantic," p. 101.

34. Sciolino, *Outlaw State*, p. 207.

35. Ibid., p. 208.

36. See Robert Jervis, *Perception and Misperception in International Relations* (Princeton, NJ: Princeton University Press, 1976), pp. 100–113.

37. Ernest R. May, "The Nature of Foreign Policy: The Calculated vs. the Axiomatic," *Daedalus* 91 (Fall 1962): 661–662.

38. Jervis, *Perception and Misperception*, p. 56.

39. Ibid., p. 57.

40. Salinger and Laurent, *Secret Dossier*, p. 28.

41. Jackson Diehl, "U.S. Maligns Him, Iraqi Tells Senators," *Washington Post*, April 13, 1990.

42. Gigot, "A Great American Screw-Up," p. 8; Salinger and Laurent, *Secret Dossier*, pp. 23–25.

43. The following account is from Woodward, *The Commanders*, pp. 203–204.

44. Salinger and Laurent, *Secret Dossier*, pp. 26–27.

45. Ibid., pp. 29–31.

46. Barry Rubin, "Reshaping the Middle East," *Foreign Affairs* 69 (Summer 1990): 142–145.

47. Cooley, "Pre-War Gulf Diplomacy," p. 127.

48. Quoted in Salinger and Laurent, *Secret Dossier*, p. 40.

49. The following account is from Woodward, *The Commanders,* pp. 205–207. The timing here is not exact. Bob Woodward's book has the DIA seeing the Iraqi tanks "early in the week of July 16"—probably the sixteenth, because the narrative appears to place the nineteenth three days after the initial discovery. Previous press reports had not relayed confirmed reports that the Republican Guard was on the border until the twenty-first.

50. Gigot, "A Great American Screw-Up," p. 10.

51. Interview with RAND Corporation senior scholar, Washington, D.C., May 22, 1991.

52. Woodward, *The Commanders,* p. 210.

53. Sciolino, *Outlaw State,* p. 207; Salinger and Laurent, *Secret Dossier,* p. 45.

54. The classic work on this case is Roberta Wohlstetter, *Pearl Harbor: Warning and Decision* (Stanford: Stanford University Press, 1962).

55. For an excellent and detailed explication of this argument, see Jervis, *Perception and Misperception,* pp. 174–181.

56. For an analysis of the latter point, including statements of experts at the time, see Lebow, "Miscalculation in the South Atlantic," pp. 93, 110–112.

57. George and Smoke, *Deterrence and American Foreign Policy,* p. 575.

58. Jervis, *Perception and Misperception,* p. 172.

59. Lebow, "Miscalculation in the South Atlantic," pp. 90–93, 103, 107.

60. George and Smoke, *Deterrence and American Foreign Policy,* p. 575.

61. For a history of this process, see Gigot, "A Great American Screw-Up"; and Lionel Barber and Alan Friedman, "A Fatal Attraction," *Financial Times,* May 3, 1991, p. 2.

62. Don Oberdorfer, "Glaspie Says Saddam Is Guilty of Deception," *Washington Post,* March 21, 1991, p. A24; Thomas Friedman, "Envoy to Iraq, Faulted in Crisis, Says She Warned Hussein Sternly," *New York Times,* March 21, 1991, p. A15; Woodward, *The Commanders,* p. 21. For an extended version of the transcript, see James Ridgeway, ed., *The March to War* (New York: Four Walls Eight Windows Publishers, 1991), pp. 50–54; and Salinger and Laurent, *Secret Dossier,* pp. 45ff.

63. These quotes, and those of the following two paragraphs, come from David Hoffman, "U.S. Envoy Conciliatory to Saddam," *Washington Post,* July 12, 1991, pp. A1, A26.

64. Sciolino, *Outlaw State,* p. 181.

65. The following account is from Woodward, *The Commanders,* pp. 213–216.

66. Hoffman, "U.S. Envoy," p. A1, reports a mention in secret State Department cables of a July 28 message from George Bush to Hussein advising against "threats involving military force or conflict" against Kuwait but calling at the same time for improved U.S.-Iraqi relations. As Hoffman notes, such a combination of warning and promise was at best a "mixed message."

67. Shireen T. Hunter, "Iraq Is Not the Lesser of Two Evils," *Los Angeles Times,* July 29, 1990.

68. Caryle Murphy, "Iraq Expands Force Near Kuwaiti Border," *Washington Post,* July 31, 1990.

69. Woodward, *The Commanders,* pp. 216–217.

70. Subcommittee on Europe and the Middle East, Committee on Foreign Affairs, U.S. House, "Developments in the Middle East, July 1990," 101st Congress,

2nd Session, July 31, 1990 (Washington, DC: Government Printing Office, 1991), pp. 1–2.

71. Gigot, "A Great American Screw-Up," p. 10.

72. See David Jablonsky, *Strategic Rationality Is Not Enough: Hitler and the Concept of Crazy States* (Carlisle Barracks, PA: Strategic Studies Institute, U.S. Army War College, August 1991).

73. See Richard Ned Lebow, "The Deterrence Deadlock: Is There a Way Out?" in Lebow, Jervis, and Stein, eds., *Psychology and Deterrence,* pp. 180–182.

74. See Richard Ned Lebow, "Conclusions," in Lebow, Jervis, and Stein, eds., *Psychology and Deterrence,* pp. 231–232.

75. Jervis, "Perceiving and Coping with Threat," p. 32.

76. The account of the Arab conference comes from Cooley, "Pre-War Gulf Diplomacy," pp. 128–129.

77. Cooley, "Pre-War Gulf Diplomacy," p. 128; Salinger and Laurent, *Secret Dossier,* p. 76.

Chapter 3

1. Bob Woodward, *The Commanders* (New York: Simon and Schuster, 1991), p. 212.

2. Ibid., pp. 220–221.

3. Paul Gigot, "A Great American Screw-Up: The U.S. and Iraq, 1980–1990," *The National Interest* (Winter 1990- 1991): 10.

4. International Institute for Strategic Studies (IISS), *Strategic Survey, 1990–91* (London: IISS, 1991), p. 15.

5. U.S. Department of Defense, *Conduct of the Persian Gulf War,* Final Report to Congress, Washington, DC: DoD (April 1992), p. 1.

6. Elaine Sciolino, *Outlaw State: Saddam Hussein's Quest for Power and the Gulf Crisis* (New York: John Wiley, 1991), p. 182.

7. Fouad Ajami, "The Summer of Arab Discontent," *Foreign Affairs* 69 (Winter 1990–1991): 14.

8. Paul K. Huth, *Extended Deterrence and the Prevention of War* (New Haven, CT: Yale University Press, 1988), p. 201.

9. This information is drawn from the after-action report of the 24th Mechanized Division.

10. Early-arriving army units faced a problem of personnel accountability. Army TACCS computers were supposed to have been brought by all units; only about half the units brought them, and of those only about half had their information loaded. The army goal was to set up a reliable personnel accountability system in-theater by January 16. It was not met. In this case, the shortfall was never too much of a problem because casualties were kept low, but the army might need to rethink this sytem for future contingencies.

11. IISS, *Strategic Survey 1990–91,* p. 16.

12. Foreign Broadcast Information Service, Middle East, September 21, 1991.

13. The following account is from Woodward, *The Commanders,* pp. 304–307.

14. Ibid., pp. 318–320.

15. Pierre Salinger and Eric Laurent, *Secret Dossier: The Hidden Agenda Behind the Gulf War* (New York: Penguin Books, 1991), p. 188.

16. Michael Gordon, "Bush Sends New Units to Gulf," *New York Times,* November 9, 1990, p. 1.

17. The following information and statistics were supplied to CSIS by the Logistics Management Institute, which has carefully tracked and summed up U.S. logistical operations in the Gulf.

18. Cited in David Bond, "Troop and Material Deployment Missions Central Elements in Desert Storm Success," *Aviation Week and Space Technology,* April 22, 1991, p. 94.

19. CDR Tom Delery, "Away, the Boarding Party," *Proceedings* Naval Review 1991, pp. 65ff.

20. The account of the *Amuriyah* incident is taken from ibid., p. 71.

21. Hussein quotes in Foreign Broadcast Information Service, Near East–South Asia edition, November 30, 1990, pp. 18, 20.

Chapter 4

1. Cited in *Newsweek,* November 19, 1990, p. 27.

2. The Brzezinski, Schlesinger, and Crowe testimony is all drawn from a CSIS reprint of xeroxed, written testimony, "CSIS Scholars: U.S. Policy in the Persian Gulf," January 1991.

3. Committee on Armed Services, U.S. House, "Crisis in the Persian Gulf: Sanctions, Diplomacy, and War," 101st Congress, 2nd Session, December 1990 (Washington, DC: Government Printing Office, 1991), pp. 31, 35.

4. Ibid., p. 313.

5. Ibid., p. 710.

6. Henry Kissinger, "A Dangerous Mirage," *Washington Post,* November 11, 1990.

7. Henry Kissinger, "Beware Timidity in the Endgame," *Los Angeles Times,* September 23, 1990.

8. Bob Woodward, *The Commanders* (New York: Simon and Schuster, 1991), pp. 352–353.

9. Ibid., pp. 345, 350–351.

10. All the following quotations are drawn from reprint of the Amnesty International report, "Iraq/Occupied Kuwait Human Rights Violations Since August 2," reprinted in the *Congressional Record,* January 11, 1991, pp. S197ff. This quotation comes from p. S197.

11. Ibid., p. S211.

12. The account of the NIE is drawn from Woodward, *The Commanders,* p. 351.

13. Thomas Schelling, *Arms and Influence* (New Haven: Yale University Press, 1966), p. 69ff.

14. Raphael Patai, *The Arab Mind* (New York: Charles Scribner's, 1983), pp. 228–229.

15. Robert Jervis, "Perceiving and Coping with Threat," in Jervis, Richard Ned Lebow, and Janice Gross Stein, eds., *Psychology and Deterrence* (Baltimore: Johns Hopkins University Press, 1985), p. 20.

16. Janice Gross Stein, "Calculation, Miscalculation, and Conventional Deterrence I: The View from Cairo," in Jervis, Lebow, and Stein, eds., *Psychology and Deterrence,* p. 44.

17. Foreign Broadcast Information Service, Near East–South Asia segment, February 27, 1990, p. 5.

18. Quoted in Pierre Salinger and Eric Laurent, *Secret Dossier: The Hidden Agenda Behind the Gulf War* (New York: Penguin Books, 1991), p. 52.

19. *Washington Post,* January 17, 1991.

20. Woodward, *The Commanders,* pp. 355–360.

21. Richard Nixon, "A Bad Peace Is Worse than War," *St. Louis Post-Dispatch,* January 8, 1991; reprinted in the *Congressional Record,* January 11, 1991, p. E119–E120.

22. Aziz quotes in Foreign Broadcast Information Service, Near East–South Asia edition, January 9, 1991, p. 19; hereinafter cited as FBIS NES.

23. Elaine Sciolino, *Outlaw State: Saddam Hussein's Quest for Power and the Gulf Crisis* (New York: John Wiley, 1991), p. 241.

24. Tildner report from FBIS NES, January 9, 1991, p. 23.

25. Aziz remarks cited in FBIS NES, January 10, 1991, p. 27.

26. Sciolino, *Outlaw State,* p. 242.

27. Baker and Aziz cited in FBIS NES, January 10, 1991, pp. 26–27.

28. Hussein quoted in FBIS NES, January 10, 1991, p. 31.

29. See FBIS NES, January 11, 1991, pp. 20–23.

30. Rep. Edwards cited in *The Congressional Record,* January 11, 1991, p. H199.

31. See Sam Nunn's remarks, *The Congressional Record,* January 11, 1991, pp. S189–191.

32. Rep. Collins cited in *The Congressional Record,* January 11, 1991, p. H203.

33. Rep. Boxer cited in *The Congressional Record,* January 11, 1991, p. H218.

34. Rep. Lagomarsino cited in *The Congressional Record,* January 11, 1991, p. H207.

35. Senator Johnston cited in *The Congressional Record,* January 11, 1991, p. S189.

36. Rep. Hunter cited in *The Congressional Record,* January 11, 1991, p. H203.

37. Sen. Kerry cited in *The Congressional Record,* January 11, 1991, pp. S250–251.

38. The facts in this section are drawn from the several stories in FBIS NES, January 14, 1991, pp. 35–36.

39. A.J.P. Taylor, *Origins of the Second World War* (London: Hamish Hamilton, 1983), p. 96.

40. Taylor, *Origins,* pp. 96–97.

41. Albert Speer, *Inside the Third Reich* (New York: Avon Books, 1970), pp. 112–113.

42. Michael Howard, "Gulf: No Time for Sanctions to Bite," *Times* (London), January 2, 1991, p. 10.

43. The account of the 53rd TFS comes from a media pool report by Edith M. Lederer, Associated Press, and David Evans, *Chicago Tribune,* January 16, 1991.

44. Iraqi media quoted in FBIS NES, January 16, 1991, p. 17.

45. Israeli report from FBIS NES, January 10, 1991, p. 41.

46. Saddam's letter is drawn from FBIS NES, January 17, 1991, pp. 17–19.

Chapter 5

1. The quote and the account of the command center come from "The Secret History of the War," *Newsweek,* March 18, 1991, p. 30, and CSIS interviews and briefings with top air force officers.
2. Miller quotes are from media pool report by Edith Lederer, Associated Press, and David Evans, *Chicago Tribune;* filed February 8, 1991.
3. CSIS interviews with air force officers; other details of this paragraph and following sections from *Conduct of the Persian Gulf Conflict: An Interim Report to Congress.* Washington, DC: U.S. Department of Defense, July 1991, p. 4–2.
4. Stealth strike percentages are from General Merrill McPeak, "The Air Campaign: Part of the Combined Arms Operation," official air force briefing on the history and lessons of Desert Storm, 1991.
5. Tony Capaccio, "Iraqis Used Hawk Radars, but Not Missiles, on Allied Pilots," *Defense Week,* April 15, 1991, p. 3.
6. Whitley account based on media pool report by Frank Gruni of the *Detroit Free Press,* January 18, 1991.
7. Peter Hayes, ed. "Chronology 1990." *Foreign Affairs* 70, no. 1 (1991): 226.
8. Otto Friedrich, ed. *Desert Storm: The War in the Persian Gulf* (Boston: Little, Brown, 1991), p. 157.
9. Hayes, "Chronology 1990," p. 231.
10. Friedrich, *Desert Storm,* p. 161.
11. Ibid.
12. Ibid., p. 165.
13. Most sources give 81 as the total number of Scuds fired. The number of Scuds fired at particular targets is a matter of some dispute, but Israel and Saudi Arabia appear to have been roughly equally targeted. Author's numbers are taken from a compilation of sources, including R. A. Mason, "The Air War in the Gulf." *Survival* 33, no. 3 (May-June 1991), pp. 211–229; Department of the Navy, "The United States Navy in 'Desert Shield' 'Desert Storm.'" Office of the CNO, May 15, 1991; and McPeak, "The Air Campaign: Part of the Combined Arms Operation."
14. "F-16As Proved Usefulness," *Aviation Week and Space Technology,* April 22, 1991, p. 62.
15. "F-111 Was Key to Killing Tanks," *Defense Week,* March 4, 1991, p. 11.
16. F-18 air combat story from media pool report by Neil MacFarquhar of the Associated Press, Combat Pool 3, January 19, 1991.
17. See McPeak, "The Air Campaign."
18. R. A. Mason, "The Air War in the Gulf," p. 218.
19. Indeed, when first counterattacked by the then-superior Iranian air force in 1980, the Iraqis dispersed their aircraft to friendly Arab countries to prevent their destruction. For a discussion of the Iraqi air force's performance in the Iran-Iraq war, see Anthony H. Cordesman and Abraham Wagner, *The Lessons of Modern War, Volume II: The Iran-Iraq War* (Boulder, CO: Westview Press, 1990).
20. See McPeak, "The Air Campaign."

21. Tate quotes are from media pool report by David Alexander, pool 14, filed February 3, 1991.

22. Mason, "The Air War in the Gulf," p. 219.

23. Department of the Navy. "The United States Navy in 'Desert Shield' 'Desert Storm.'" Washington, DC: Office of the Chief of Naval Operations, May 15, 1991, pp. A-20–A-21.

24. Allen B. Thomas, F. Clifton Berry, and Norman Polmar, *War in the Gulf* (Atlanta: Turner, 1991), p. 147.

25. Department of the Navy, *The United States Navy,* p. A-23.

26. Statistical summary of the preceding several paragraphs taken from ibid., p. A-24.

27. David Gergen, "Bringing Home the 'Storm': What the Victorious American Military Could Teach the Rest oif Us," *Washington Post,* April 28, 1991, p. C2.

28. Department of the Navy, *The United States Navy,* p. A-27.

29. Ibid.

30. Rick Atkinson, "600 Iraqi Tanks Ruined, Allies Say." *Washington Post,* February 9, 1991, p. A1.

31. Guy Gugliotta and George C. Wilson, "Land Probes May Be Bait to Goad Iraqis Into Open." *Washington Post,* February 9, 1991, p. A1.

32. Edward Cody and Barton Gellman, "Cheney Says Iraq Still Strong, Sees 'Limit' to Air War." *Washington Post,* February 10, 1991, p. A1.

33. Thomas, Berry, Polmar, *War in the Gulf,* p. 140.

34. *Washington Post,* February 14, 1991.

35. The story of the GBU-28 penetrating bomb was taken from David A. Fulghum, "USAF Nears Completion of 30 GBU-28s, Plans Advanced Penetrating Bomb." *Aviation Week and Space Technology* 135, no. 10: 22–23.

36. USS *America* joined USS *Midway, Theodore Roosevelt,* and *Ranger* in the Arabian Gulf. USS *Saratoga* and *John F. Kennedy* remained in the northern Red Sea. *America* and *Roosevelt* began the war in the Red Sea.

37. Statistics on the air war come from White Paper, "Air Force Performance in Desert Storm," April 1991.

Chapter 6

1. Huddleston quotes from media pool report by Patrick Bishop of the *London Daily Telegraph* and Jim Michaels of the *San Diego Tribune* with Marine Pool 2 (two different reports), January 30, 1991.

2. The story of the trapped marines is from a media pool report by Jim Michaels of the *San Diego Tribune,* Marine Pool 2, February 1, 1991.

3. After-action report, 24th Mechanized Division.

4. "Anatomy of a Cakewalk," *Newsweek* 117, no. 10, March 11, 1991, p. 48.

5. U.S. Department of Defense. *Conduct of the Persian Gulf Conflict: An Interim Report to Congress.* Washington, DC: DoD, July 1991.

6. Jack Kelley, "Life in the Iraqi Bunkers a Nightmare," *USA Today,* July 30, 1991, p. 1.

7. Logistics information from the DoD *Interim Report,* p. 4-X.

8. Steve Vogel, "A Swift Kick: The 2nd ACR's Taming of the Guard," *Army Times,* August 5, 1991; and British after action report, supplement to the *London Gazette.*

9. Ibid., p. 18.

10. DoD, *Interim Report,* pp. 4–7.

11. Sean D. Naylor, "Flight of Eagles: 101st Airborne Division's Raids into Iraq." *Army Times,* July 22, 1991, p. 14.

12. Ibid., p. 14.

13. DoD, *Interim Report,* pp. 4–8.

14. Ibid.

15. "From Germany to Kuwait: VII Corps in Action During Desert Storm." After-action summary report obtained from VII Corps, May 1991.

16. Vogel, "A Swift Kick," p. 18.

17. Ibid.

18. Ibid., p. 28.

19. Ibid., p. 18.

20. Ibid.

21. Ibid.

22. John Barry, and Evan Thomas, "A Textbook Victory." *Newsweek* 117, no. 10, March 11, 1991, p. 39. Postwar marine discovery of a bunker containing chemical artillery shells on March 1, 1991, reported in Department of the Navy. *The United States Navy in "Desert Shield" "Desert Storm."* Washington, DC: Office of the Chief of Naval Operations, May 15, 1991.

23. DoD, *Interim Report,* pp. 4–8.

24. The 101st Airborne Division is composed of three infantry brigades and one aviation brigade. Each infantry brigade is composed of three infantry battalions. So, when 3rd Brigade air-assaulted into Landing Zone "Sand" with about 1,000 soldiers, they had one-third of the 101st's total infantry.

25. Naylor, "Flight of Eagles," p. 14.

26. British after-action report (supplement to the *London Gazette*).

27. See "From Germany to Kuwait: VII Corps in Action During Desert Storm."

28. DoD, *Interim Report,* pp. 4–8.

29. "Retreat down Highway of Doom," *Washington Post,* Mar. 2, 1991, p. A1.

30. Ibid., p. A10.

31. Ibid.

32. Ibid.

33. William Taylor and James Blackwell, "The Ground War in the Gulf." *Survival* 33, no. 3 (May/June 1991): 230–245.

34. See "From Germany to Kuwait: VII Corps in Action During Desert Storm."

35. DoD, *Interim Report,* pp. 4–9.

36. "Move Forward and Shoot the Things." *Newsweek* 117, no. 10, March 11, 1991, p. 45.

37. J. Paul Scicchitano, "Eye of the Tiger: Stalking Iraqi Prey with the Tiger Brigade." *Army Times,* June 10, 1991, pp. 18, 61.

38. DoD, *Interim Report,* pp. 4–9.

39. Ibid.

40. See "From Germany to Kuwait: VII Corps in Action During Desert Storm."

41. DoD, *Interim Report,* pp. 4–9.

42. After-action report, 24th Mechanized Infantry Division.

43. British after-action report (supplement to the *London Gazette*).

44. Barton Gellman, "Gulf War's Friendly Fire Tally Triples." *Washington Post,* August 14, 1991, p. A1.

45. Peter Cary, "The Fight to Change How America Fights." *U.S. News and World Report* 20, no. 10, May 6, 1991, pp. 30–31.

46. DoD, *Interim Report,* pp. 4–9.

47. Vogel, "A Swift Kick," p. 61.

48. Ibid.

49. See "From Germany to Kuwait: VII Corps in Action During Desert Storm."

50. "Truce Halts Tanks on Brink of Battle." *Washington Post,* March 2, 1991, p. A1.

51. See "From Germany to Kuwait: VII Corps in Action During Desert Storm."

52. Barry and Thomas, "A Textbook Victory," p. 42.

53. *Washington Post,* March 2, 1991, A10.

54. "The Rout of the Republican Guard." *Washington Post,* March 2, 1991, p. A10.

55. Jim Tice, "Coming Through: The Big Red Raid." *Army Times,* August 26, 1991, p. 20.

56. "1st Armored Division in Combat 21–28 February 1991." After-action report of the U.S. 1st Armored Division.

57. "Truce Halts Tanks on Brink of Battle," p. A12.

58. "Bush to 'Move Fast' on Mideast Peace." *Washington Post,* March 2, 1991, p. A1.

59. After-action report, 24th Mechanized Infantry Division.

Chapter 7

1. Quoted in Steve Coll, "Talks Remind Iraqis Who Won," *Washington Post,* March 4, 1991, p. A1.

2. Department of Defense, *Conduct of the Persian Gulf Conflict: An Interim Report to Congress* (Washington, DC: DoD, July 1991), pp. 4–10.

3. David Hoffman, "Middle East: Unstable as Ever," *Washington Post,* March 1, 1991, p. A29.

4. At this writing (March 1992), the basic official document of U.S. strategy is Colin Powell, *National Military Strategy of the United States* (Washington, DC: Government Printing Office, January 1992).

5. See Don Oberdorfer, "Strategy for a Solo Superpower: Pentagon Looks to 'Regional Contingencies,'" *Washington Post,* May 19, 1991, p. A1.

6. Final Report of the CSIS Conventional Arms Control Project, *A New Military Strategy for the 1990s: Implications for Capabilities and Acquisition* (Washington, DC: Center for Strategic and International Studies, January 1991), p. 29.

7. Center for Strategic and International Studies Panel on Defense Economics, *Defense Economics for the 1990s: Resources, Strategies, and Options* (Washington, DC: CSIS, April 1989).

8. For some eighteenth- and nineteenth-century examples of this process, see Edward M. Coffman, *The Old Army: A Portrait of the American Army in Peacetime, 1784–1898* (New York: Oxford University Press, 1986).

9. See Charles E. Heller and William A. Stofft, eds., *America's First Battles: 1776–1965* (Lawrence: University Press of Kansas, 1986).

10. The Base Force, as of early 1992 the administration's preferred force structure option, consists (in active-duty forces) of some 12 army divisions, 12 navy carrier battle groups, and 16 air force tactical fighter wings.

11. See DoD, *Interim Report.*

12. The vote in the Senate only supported the president by a margin of 52–47. In the House, the margin was slightly larger—250–183, with eighty-six Democrats voting in the majority. U.S. News and World Report Staff, *Triumph Without Victory: The Unreported History of the Persian Gulf War* (New York: Times Books, 1992), p. 207. By most accounts, the congressional debate was a detailed and important discussion of the use of force and a president's powers in that area.

13. Barbara Opall, "Pentagon Units Jostle over Non-Lethal Initiative," *Defense News*, March 2, 1992, p. 6.

14. Anthony Cordesman and Abraham Wagner, *The Lessons of Modern War, Volume I: The Arab-Israeli Conflict, 1973–1989* (Boulder, CO: Westview Press, 1990), pp. 350–351.

15. Anthony Cordesman and Abraham Wagner, *The Lessons of Modern War, Volume II: The Iran-Iraq War* (Boulder, CO: Westview Press, 1990), p. 600.

16. Raymond L. Garthoff, *Deterrence and the Revolution in Soviet Military Doctrine* (Washington, DC: Brookings Institution, 1990), pp. 10–11.

17. See Janice Gross Stein, "Reassurance in International Conflict Management," *Political Science Quarterly* 106, no. 3 (1991).

18. Don Oberdorfer and R. Jeffrey Smith, "U.S. Faces Contradiction on Mideast Arms Control," *Washington Post*, March 7, 1991, pp. A31, 33.

About the Book and Authors

From Saddam Hussein's first bold threats in 1990 to the stunning ground phase of Desert Storm in early 1991, the crisis in the Gulf captured the world's attention. This high-tech, low-cost war was televised nightly from beginning to end, accompanied by on-the-spot interpretations of strategy and its implications. But what did we learn from this crisis? Did the United States bungle its attempts at discouraging Saddam's aggressive actions, or is deterrence simply not a reliable foreign policy tool? Are chemical weapons truly the "poor man's atom bomb"? Does the war represent a good model for future crises, or did circumstances make this war more of an anomaly than a precedent? How did the all-volunteer U.S. force perform? By combining exciting, detailed vignettes of the crisis with insightful discussions of its consequences, this book opens up an informed debate concerning the true military and geopolitical lessons of the conflict.

Representing a distillation of the best thinking on defense and foreign policy in Washington, *Desert Storm* also incorporates the testimony of the inside players during the crisis—the people who actually planned and fought the war. Combining academic rigor and in-depth military expertise, the authors challenge the complacency of the emerging conventional wisdom regarding the conflict, taking us beyond mere chronicling and instant analysis to a riveting reenactment of the war and the serious consideration of its long-term implications.

Michael J. Mazarr is a senior fellow in international studies at the Center for Strategic and International Studies (CSIS). He is the author of several books on U.S. defense and foreign policy, including *Light Forces and the Future of U.S. Military Strategy* (1990), and is adjunct professor at the Georgetown University National Security Studies program. **Don M. Snider** is associate director of political-military affairs at CSIS. A career military officer, Snider has served as army theater planner for Europe, as director of defense policy studies on the National Security Council, and as a top staff officer with the Joint Chiefs of Staff. **James A. Blackwell, Jr.,** is director of political-military affairs at CSIS. He was CNN's chief military analyst during the Gulf War and is the author of *Thunder in the Desert* (1991).

Index